The Flourishing SOUL

SCOTT —
MAY GOD BLESS YOU
AND CONTINUE TO
USE YOU FOR HIS
HONOR & GLORY!
KEVIN
PS. 63

The Flourishing SOUL

POSSESSING A RICH SOUL BY DEVELOPING A REMARKABLE SOUL:
Living our Christian life
BASED ON THE PALM TREE

KEVIN GEPHART

XULON PRESS ELITE

Xulon Press Elite
2301 Lucien Way #415
Maitland, FL 32751
407.339.4217
www.xulonpress.com

Printed in the United States of America.

ISBN-13: 978-1-5456-7897-8

ACKNOWLEDGMENTS

This book is dedicated to my loving wife, Cindy.
Your love and support throughout the years of serving
the Lord together has been the joy of my life!
Thank you for all that you mean to me,
your love for our Savior, your
love for our family, and your love for me!

I want to take the time to acknowledge some people who helped shape and mold me into the person I am today. My pastor in my youth was M. Donald Curry. Pastor Curry and his family came to our church right after we joined it back in 1966. I can still recall his teaching on God's Word with the tenderest of hearts, as tears flowed down his cheecks. As a teenager would often do, I sat in the back and goofed off during many church services. But his love for God and His Word began to take affect in my heart and life. I soon moved to the front of the auditorium and began to take notes on his sermons. It was under his minsitry that God moved in my heart to serve Him vocationally. What a great role model of loving and adoring the Bible. I pray that I'll take that same love to my grave. "Well done good and faithful servant."

Shortly thereafter, our church called a new youth pastor. Frank Workman and his young family came to serve the Lord and us at our church. Here was another man that I soon fell in love with.

His passionate concern for "his kids" was extremely obvious to all who cared to listen and observe. Many times he would call me into his office to "have a chat" with me over something I did, right or wrong. His loving and caring, but sometimes direct words rang true to me. I will never forget those many talks we had, howbeit short, through those few years we had him as our teen pastor. It wasn under his ministry that God continued His work of sanctification in my heart and life. "Well done good and faithful servant."

One of my great teachers in Bible college was Dr. Warren Jacobs. The first day of class he would call the roll, ask some personal questions about ourselves, call out our names several times and seemingly lock that information away in his mind and heart. In the next class, when calling upon us to answer a question, he used our first names! The 80 or so in that class just sat in disbelief that he knew who we all were. But the greatest thing I remembr about Dr. Jacobs was after we made some "idotic" statement about a passage of Scripture. He would just smile, raise his Bible, and ask the same question, "Please give me chapter and verse." This taught all of us who sat under his teaching never to base our doctrine on our thoughts or opinions, but to always look to the infallible Word of God. "Well done good and faithful servant."

Then I would like to thank Karen Patton. Karen was my high school English teacher in my school in Michigan. She poured over my original manuscript and made many corrections. If I was to receive a grade for that first draft, I think I would land in the "B" range. Her many hours of editing and suggesting different words or phrases is greatly appreciated. While working with her many years ago, I could always depend on Karen to pull through another situation in which I needed advice in making a major decision concerning our school. Her love for "our kids" at school was an amazing and key factor in shaping my ministry for future ministries. I'm sure the Lord will tell Karen one day, "Well done good and faithful servant."

CONTENTS

FOREWORD

$\mathcal{G}$od's greatest of intentions is for our lives to become vibrant and flourishing, ever living in and through His awesome resources that will cause in us His amazing refreshment. If we encounter setbacks to this exciting way of living, then we have no one to blame but ourselves. Scripture is full of expressions of these "greatest of intentions" from our Lord God, Who is the Almighty and Creator of heaven and earth. Psalm 92:12-15 is one such passage of promise: "The righteous flourish like the palm tree and grow like a cedar in Lebanon. They are planted in the house of the Lord: they flourish in the courts of our God. They still bear fruit in old age; they are ever full of sap and green, to declare that the Lord is upright; He is my rock, and there is no unrighteousness in Him."

The very words themselves give us the idea that an exceptional Christian life can be lived, and even more so, promises us that such a life is within everyone's reach. All my life, I've wanted to make significant contributions to the work and Kingdom of Christ. It's been my heart's desire for the Lord to allow me to have a part in producing phenomenal disciples to and for His glory. My prayer has been to see lasting differences in the lives of others that my Lord has allowed me to serve and minister to. In so doing, I've wanted to point out what a pleasing Christian life looks like and is explained or defined in God's Holy Word. In other words, what really pleases the Lord and how can a person arrive at such a destination?

We all know how difficult the Christian walk can be. We all realize the roller coaster we often find ourselves endeavoring to "flesh out" and live a flourishing and cedar of Lebanon kind of Christian life. Every day we're met with challenges and choices, trials and temptations, duties and decisions. For all of life's turns, we need and must cry out for His direction, guidance and wisdom. But what can and does help us in this journey, is a vital, amazing, outstanding and astonishing relationship where I tell the Lord, "I love You," and He responds, "I know, I love you, too!" To some, this kind of relationship with the Lord of Heaven may seem unimaginable, unthinkable or maybe even unbelievable. However, the wondrous truth is that "the righteous flourish like the palm tree and grow like a cedar in Lebanon!" Pay attention to the wording of The Amplified Bible regarding these verses: "The (uncompromisingly) righteous shall flourish like the palm tree (be long-lived, stately, upright, useful, and fruitful); they shall grow like a cedar in Lebanon (majestic, stable, durable, and incorruptible). Planted in the house of the Lord, they shall flourish in the courts of our God. (Growing in grace) they shall still bring forth fruit in old age: they shall be full of sap (of spiritual vitality) and (rich in the) verdure (of trust, love, and contentment). (They are living memorials) to show that the Lord is upright and faithful to His promises; He is my Rock, and there is no unrighteousness in Him." That description of the Christian experience in this world is spectacular and breathtaking to say the least! The awe-inspiring and Holy Spirit inspired words found in this portion of God's Holy Word ought to serve for us all as the benchmark and standard to view our daily walk and relationship with Jesus, as well as the work in which He has called on us to do for His pleasure and glory.

In this book, it's my intention to not only describe in great detail what God's Word instructs us about living such a Christian life, but to also provoke some serious desire on your part to move from your present condition that you may find yourself in regarding your Christian life and walk with the Lord. Wherever you find yourself in your personal relationship with Jesus Christ, may you move that relationship to a walk that's incredible, uncommon and fabulous! May you begin to experience, perhaps for the very first time, living your Christian life in flourishing fashion! Or maybe, for you, it's a return and renewal to that Christian life that's fantastic and flourishing. As you travel through the pages of this book, it's my prayer and desire for you to be full of the "sap" of our God, to live the "ever green" life found in Him, and to be planted in His house, flourishing and growing in grace like never before! As Eugene Peterson puts it in "The Message:" "My ears are filled with the sounds of promise: 'Good people will prosper like palm trees, Grow tall like Lebanon cedars; transplanted to God's courtyard, They'll grow tall in the presence of God, lithe and green virile still in old age.' Such witnesses to upright God! My Mountain, my huge, holy Mountain!"

May our **Awesome God** do His work of grace in your life and fill you with all His **Amazing Grace**! Here's to your fabulous journey to our Mountain that is Our God, Who brings with Him all that will result in our souls to flourish like the palm tree!

1

A RIGHTEOUS SEED

"The **RIGHTEOUS** flourish like the palm tree…" Psalm 92:12a

*I*n thinking about this word "righteous" with regards to God's Holy Word, the idea that's always conveyed is simply this – righteousness is meant in every aspect of thought and action as judged by the highest standard of all – God Himself. The very thought of "rightness" or "justice" must begin and end somewhere, and that somewhere is Jehovah God – our heavenly Father. This righteousness comes to us via His character and is quickly summarized in Exodus 20, which contains the very foundation of all life and societies – God's 10 Commandments. All of life can be summed up in the words found on those two tablets, written with "the finger of God." Exodus 31:18 Every other human virtue or national law flows from those original 10 commandments. Down through the ages, empires, kingdoms, nations and world leaders have all come and gone based upon their relationship with God's supreme, sublime and sovereign law. When a person or nation fails to recognize the "rightness" and "justice" found in those supreme mandates, then that person or nation will find themselves in peril of losing their moral compass for the remainder of life or history.

If we, as humans, can learn anything from history, it's this very fact. Follow a person's life that ends in tragedy. At some point during their life, they missed the mark of God's righteousness, went their own way, and found the circumstances of that way extremely painful and hurtful, to not only them, but to others, as well, and in some cases, many others. From the notorious to the "never even heard of them" people, you can rest assured that at some point, they turned their back on the truth of God's Word of righteousness, made their list of commandments to run and rule their life, and suffered the consequences for doing so.

God's Word is extremely clear on the point of man's condition before a holy God. Romans 3:23 states this truth clearly and plainly: "For all have sinned and fall short of the glory of God." Let's unfold this verse a little further. "For all" means that every person who has ever lived on earth is a sinner in the eyes of God. There is no one – I mean no one – that has escaped this personal characterization, save one – the Lord Jesus Christ. He was the Perfect Son of God, Who was tempted in every point like us, but yet without sin (Heb. 4:15). The thought behind "sinned" means "at one point in the past." In other words, one lie told by me when I was seven made me a liar, thus making me a sinner. It only takes one sin in a person's past that makes that person a sinner. However, when Paul uses the phrase, "and fall short," we're being told that we are forever coming up short of the main goal of any person's life – "the glory of God." So, if I can put it this way, "For everyone has become a sinner because of one bad choice at some point in my past, and I will forever keep coming up short of attaining to the glory that is found in heaven's, holy and righteous God." The tenses in the Greek have changed with these two statements. The first is in what's known as the aorist tense. A one-time action in the past has made the present what it is. But, the second statement is in the present perfect tense which tells us that it's true now, in 5 minutes, in 5 months, in 5 years, always. Wow! When we read

Romans 3:23 that way, we notice immediately that we have a real problem on our hands, don't we? And to make things worse, Isa. 64:6,7 tells us these truths, "We have all become like one who is unclean, and all our righteous deeds are like a polluted garment. We all fade like a leaf, and our iniquities, like the wind, take us away. There is no one who calls upon your name, who rouses himself to take hold of you..." Not only do we perform acts in our lives that are regarded as sin in God's eyes, but the "good" things we think are making a difference when it comes to our reputation with a holy God are nothing more to Him as "polluted garments." Ouch, that one really hurts! What Isaiah was referring to as a "polluted garment" were rags that lepers would wrap their putrid sores, discarding them when they would become soaked with the disease as they walked along some roadway. God says that the good things I do to get in good with Him are like those diseased-filled rags. That really brings it home, does it not?

Well, Romans 3:10-18 provides us with some more insight here: "As it is written: 'None is righteous, no, not one; no one understands; no one seeks for God. All have turned aside; together they have become worthless; no one does good, not even one. Their throat is an open grave; they use their tongues to deceive. The venom of asps is under their lips. Their mouth is full of curses and bitterness. Their feet are swift to shed blood; in their paths are ruin and misery, and the way of peace they have not known. There is no fear of God before their eyes.'" What a description of man's spiritual condition before an Almighty, holy, just and righteous God. This description leaves no room for discussion or argument. The playing field is level with God. Everyone finds themselves in this sinful and awful condition. There are no exceptions. The laboring person getting very dirty on a daily basis to the minister who dresses in a suit and rarely finds himself getting his hands dirty – the CEO or CFO to the custodian of any large corporation – the addict on the street looking for their next hit to the attractive model

3

living in a mansion or penthouse – the person who makes minimum wage to the person whose income far surpasses that – ALL are in the same condition before the Almighty God – ALL are in need of a Savior – ALL must come to that Savior the exact same way! ALL must come to the end of themselves, recognize their personal need to obtain this help from that Savior. Jesus is THAT Savior. He didn't come to just show us how to live a selfless or sacrificial life, although He did. He didn't come to just perform signs and miracles and help some people out while He walked the dusty roads of Israel, although He did that, too. No, He came to take care of our main problem – sin. His death on the cross provided the way for us to find a loving and righteous God. His death was for our life. He died so we don't have to. I'm not speaking of a physical death, but of a spiritual death. The most often quoted and used verse in all of Scripture is John 3:16, 17. Eugene Peterson in *The Message* lays it out so we all can really grasp these amazing words and truths: "This is how much God loved the world: He gave His Son, His one and only Son. This is why: so that no one need be destroyed; by believing in Him, anyone can have a whole and lasting life. God didn't go to all the trouble of sending His Son merely to point an accusing finger, telling the world how bad it was. He came to help, to put the world right again."[1] "To put the world right again" – "to put me right again." He continues in John 3 – "Anyone who trusts in Him is acquitted; anyone who refuses to trust Him has long since been under the death sentence without knowing it. And why? Because of that person's failure to believe in the one-of-a-kind Son of God when introduced to Him."[2]

We're all in the same boat with the same fatal condition. Every one of us is a sinner, making us unrighteous in the eyes of God. But He loved us so much that He sent us His One and Only, Beloved Son – Jesus Christ. Jesus came to become the sacrifice to pay for our sin. Jesus was the only One who could've done this, for He was perfect – without sin or blemish. Romans 5:8 says, "But God shows

His love for us in that while we were still sinners, Christ died for us." Death is the price of sin. "For the wages of sin is death, but the free gift of God is eternal life in Christ Jesus our Lord." (Romans 6:23) Sin came about because of Adam's fall in the garden. His nature infected the rest of us and when we had the choice to do wrong and sin, we did. Remember, one sin in our past makes us a sinner and creates the problem of having a relationship with a holy and righteous God. But listen to Romans 5:17, "For if, because of one man's trespass (Adam), death reigned through that one man, much more will those who receive the abundance of grace and the free gift of righteousness reign in life through the one man, Jesus Christ." Did you notice that huge offer of a "free gift?" My friends, that "free gift" is righteousness! Paul said it a little differently in Phil. 3:9, "Being found in Him, not having a righteousness of my own that comes from the law, but that which comes through faith in Christ, the righteousness from God that depends on faith."

We have no righteousness of our own for we "have all sinned" and will continue to "fall short of God's righteous, just and holy glory." However, there is One who has a righteousness that we need and that Someone is Jesus Christ. This is the way that it's always been. We're told in Gen. 15:6 about Abraham's acceptance of this righteousness "And he believed (exercised his faith) the Lord, and He counted it to him as righteousness." This is verified in Romans 4:1-3, "What then shall we say was gained by Abraham, our forefather according to the flesh? For if Abraham was justified by works (which are as leprous, filthy rags in the sight of God), he has something to boast about, but not before God. For what does the Scripture say? 'Abraham believed God, and it was counted to him as righteousness.'" Romans 10:9,10 tells us how to make this truth personal: "That if thou shalt confess with thy mouth the Lord Jesus, and shalt believe in thine heart that God hath raised him from the dead, thou shalt be saved. For with the heart man belie-veth unto righteousness; and with the mouth confession is made unto salvation."[3] (KJV) The King James Version was used in this case because it uses the word "righteousness." In the *New Living Translation*, we read verse 10 this way, "For it is by believing in your heart that you are made right with God, and it is by confessing with your mouth that you are saved."[4] The *New International Version* puts it this way, "For it is with your heart that you believe and are justified, and it is with your mouth that you confess and are saved."[5] "Righteousness" – "Right with God" – "Justified" – When we place our faith in Christ by believing in Him and confessing Him, He gives us His righteousness, thus making us right with God, justifying us in the Father's sight. The theological word "justification" means that to God, we have been made righteous like Christ in the area of our sins. It has made us flawless in God's eyes, just as if I've never committed one sin! My sins are gone forever, washed in the blood of Christ, buried in the depths of the deepest ocean (Micah 7:19) and as far as the east is from the west. (Psalm 103:12)

Right now, as you have read these words, let me simply ask you this question: "Do you know that you have been made right before God?" "Are you certain that you have dealt with the sin question before a holy and righteous God?" Before we proceed any further, let me ask you to ask Jesus Christ to come into your life and save you, confessing your sins to Him, believing that He has risen from the dead. Romans 10:13 tells us simply to do this, "For anyone who calls on the name of the Lord will be saved." We call on the Lord in prayer. Will you call, pray, on Him right now? Please allow me to give you a sample prayer. You may use it or say similar words. But do it today and don't delay a moment longer. When you do, He will come into your life and create a new person, giving you the gift of salvation and making you right before Him.

"Dear Jesus, I realize that You love me and that You gave Your life for me. I know that I'm a sinner before You. I realize that you died for me in my place. I now invite You into my heart and life. Please save me and make me right in your sight. I'm trusting only in Jesus' righteousness as my own. I turn my life over to You right now. Thank You for saving me. In Jesus name, Amen."

I hope and pray that you made that decision today by taking Christ as your Savior. I've never met a single person who has regretted doing so. This is the very first event in any person's life in restoring the relationship between us and the God of Heaven.

In our beginning text, we read these words: "The righteous shall flourish as the palm tree..." This imparting of righteousness in justification by faith in us makes us right in God's eyes, mind and heart. And remember, it's not by anything that we have done ourselves, except placing our trust and faith in the finished work of Christ on the cross. II Corinthians 5:21 states this truth in dramatic terms, "For God made Christ, who never sinned, to be the offering for our sin, so that we could be made right with God through Christ." This is all known as "positional righteousness." Christ met the demands of the law of God and the law of sin – "the wages of sin is death." (Romans 6:23) Everyone who has placed their faith in the person and blood atonement of Christ have been placed in this position, forever secured based on the promises and person of God. Since it is impossible for God to lie (Titus 1:2), we have this confidence for time and eternity.

To fully help us understand, as much as we can about this tremendous truth, let's turn our attention to an awesome passage of Scripture – Romans 8:1-4 – "Therefore, there is now no condemnation (judgment) for those who are in Christ Jesus, because through Christ Jesus the law of the Spirit of life set me free from the law of sin and death. (Pause right here - let those words totally grab hold and sink in) For what the law was powerless to do in that it was weakened by the sinful nature, God did by sending His own Son in the likeness of sinful man to be a sin offering. And so He condemned sin in sinful man, in order that the righteous requirements of the law might be fully met in us, who do not live according to the sinful nature but according to the Spirit." This chapter continues to explain that victory over the events explained and described by the Apostle Paul in Romans 6 & 7 can be won through God's Spirit. Peterson, in *The Message*, explains some of these difficult thoughts in the simplest of terms, "The law always ended up being used as a band-aide on sin instead of a deep healing of it. And now what the law code asked for but we couldn't deliver is accomplished as we, instead of redoubling our own efforts, simply embrace what the Spirit is doing in us."[6] As a Christ-follower, I have total confidence that the sin question has been answered in Christ. With the sin question past me, I now rest in the very fact and promise that there isn't any sin, past, present or future, is standing between me and God, thus making me totally righteous in the sight of God. Jesus was that perfect and holy and righteous sin offering IN MY PLACE! His righteousness was imputed (to attribute something to a person or reckoning something to the account of another) or given to me. That was forensically done for me through justification – me placing my faith in the finished work of Christ on the cross. Since the day of my salvation, I've been considered as having no condemnation or judgment against me or my sin, for that payment was paid in full by Jesus Christ.

But now attention must be placed on our "day after salvation" event. Because of my justification, what now? Our text says that "the righteous will flourish as the palm tree…" With my positional righteousness taken care of, what about my practical righteousness?

In King David's song of deliverance from Saul, who sought to kill him, we're given some insightful truths, "The Lord dealt with me according to my righteousness; according to the cleanness of my hands He rewarded me. For I have kept the ways of the Lord and have not wickedly departed from my God. For all His rules were before me, and from His statutes I did not turn aside. I was blameless before Him, and I kept myself from guilt. And the Lord has rewarded me according to my righteousness, according to my cleanness in His sight." (II Samuel 22:21-25) David is letting us know that God rewarded him regarding his actions pertaining to his relationship with Saul. He strove to honor the Lord through those actions of restraint by taking matters into his own hands. This testimony certainly goes deeper than just this, as we know that God's testimony of David is "a man after" His heart "who will do all my will." (Acts 13:22) God acted toward David in direct accordance with all that was part of the fabric of David's heart and life. Now I fully realize that David was not perfect or sinless, not by a longshot. He had the affair with a married woman and subsequently had her husband left alone on the battlefield so he would die. All of this was done in order to cover up his sin. But God sent His prophet, Nathan, to get him back on the right road. It took David a whole year to sort through this mess, but he came out on the other side as a person who walked through godly confession. We can't help but read through Psalm 32 and 51, especially 51, which was written as a direct result of those two terrible sins (all sin is terrible), and feel the heart of a broken man, but a man who fully recognized the price of his sin. All of us have been down this road, not once or twice, but many, many times. It may not be as terrible, in human terms, as sexual sin or murder, but it's sin, nonetheless, and grieves the Spirit of God, hurting Him and causing Him to cry. We're commanded in Ephesians 4:30, "And do not grieve the Holy Spirit of God, by whom you were sealed for the day of redemption." That word "grieve" is used as a verb, meaning: "to cause to feel grief or sorrow." So, we're not to cause grief in the Holy Spirit of God because of our life's choices. If I choose the wrong path or make an unwise decision which results in sin, then I've grieved the Spirit. When I choose unrighteous acts or have unrighteous attitudes, then I grieve God's Holy Spirit.

In David's great song of deliverance from Saul, II Samuel 22, we see some amazing insights for helping us avoid unrighteous choices.

9

- "For you are my lamp, O Lord, and my God lightens my darkness." (v. 29) Light is the great divider. When the Lord created this universe, He gave us the sun, moon and stars. This was to provide our world light and warmth. But we're also told that He did so to "separate the day and night." He put a distinction between light and darkness, and so it is with righteousness and unrighteousness. Psalm 119:105 is huge for us on this point, "Your word is a lamp to my feet and a light to my path." Lamps in the East were kept burning all night. They are still regarded as one of the most refined comforts the Orientals can enjoy, and for which they would make any sacrifice. The origin of the custom of allowing their lights to flicker all night, may have been to preserve themselves from serpents and other noxious reptiles. The old serpent, the Devil, Satan, is walking around our world looking for those people he can absolutely bring down to destruction. The putting out of lights is a figure of great danger, as the light is the symbol of safety and security, which is the foundation of success and prosperity. Understanding that our righteous position is all dependent on God and we have nothing to do with it except believe and accept it, then we also need to understand that the practical side of righteousness is also completely Him. Psalm 18:28 opens this truth up to us perfectly, "For it is you who light my lamp; the Lord my God lightens my darkness." Positional righteousness and holiness are provided to us through the finished work of Christ on the cross. But our practical righteousness and holiness is also produced in us through God's great messenger – His Holy Spirit – and His great message – His Holy Scriptures. The Holy Spirit provides the power behind the holy principles and promises of His Word. God lights our lamp at salvation and has brought light into my dark life. He also lights the lamp of my life with His Scriptures which continually teach me right from wrong – and gives me the what's, why's and how's of living a righteous and godly life while walking this earth. Listen to David continue in Psalm 18 (by the way, this is another song of victory of David after the Lord's rescue of him form the hand of all of his enemies, especially Saul – it should be read alongside II Samuel for detailed clarification concerning this vital part of our walk with the Lord) "For by you I can run against a troop, and by my God I can leap over a wall." (v. 29) I call to mind the great novel, "A Christmas Carol," by Charles Dickens. When Ebenezer Scrooge woke from his long night of ghostly visitations, he wanted to know what day it was. "Why, it's Christmas,"[7] the boy responded from the street. He started running around his house like a mad man. He said that Scrooge said, "I'm as light as a feather, I am so happy as an angel, and I am as merry as a schoolboy."[8] He described his feelings as being so very happy, even while undeserved. I love the part when he wanted to stand on his head on the chair while his chambermaid watched, who quickly ran screaming out of the room! He ran after her telling her that "I haven't lost my senses, I've come to them" and promptly gave her a large raise in salary. This was David's explanation of how he felt! He told us that he could attack many enemy soldiers by himself and jump over a wall – with God's assistance and help, though. I so remember the times of refreshing I've had after recognizing God's presence and light in my life. This may have come after confession of sin or a time of fresh commitment to His purposed sanctification in my life. And I'm sure you've experienced the exact same thing. Then David continues, "This God – His way is perfect; the word of the Lord proves true; He is a shield for all those who take refuge in Him." (v. 30) I know God's Word is true

– I believe that. But you know what? I also know His Word is true because "I've tasted" of it and know the benefits of His Word working in my day-to-day events and inter-actions with others. (Psalm 19) What a major blessing to understand that we hold in our hands the eternal, infallible and inspired Word of the Living God, Creator of heaven and earth. The Bible "proves true" over and over, without exception or error. Many times as I've read through my Bible, the Spirit will highlight something that I've read, and low and behold, some days later it's exactly what I need for that day and is "proving" Itself to me all over again. God's way is "perfect" or "blameless" because He is altogether and completely righteous – without sin, mischief, or guilt. Therefore, He is our "shield" as we take refuge in His pres-ence, experiencing rejoicing in His promises, and renewal in His principles. All of this leads us to living a life of righ-teousness or "right living" on a daily basis, resting in Him, relying on His principles as we "work out our salvation."

• "For who is God, but the Lord? And who is a rock, except our God? – the God who equipped me with strength and made my way blameless." (vv. 31, 32) There's a debate about which God is right or what we should call him in our world today. There's some question as to His name and identity. What do we call Him? Is His name "Jehovah" or "Buddha" or "Allah?" The Word of God makes this point very clear – His name is Jehovah. Let's examine what the Lord tells us about this vital truth from the book of Isaiah: "I am the Lord; that is my name; my glory I give to no other, nor my praise to carved idols." 42:8 "For I am the Lord your God, the Holy One of Israel, your Savior." 43:3 "…Before me no god was formed, nor shall there be any after me. I, I am the Lord and besides me there is no savior." 10, 11 "Thus says the Lord, the King of Israel and his Redeemer, the Lord of hosts: 'I am the Lord, your Holy One, the Creator of Israel, your King." 43:15 "I am the first and I am the last; besides me there is no god. Who is like me? Let him proclaim it. Let him declare and set it before me, since I appointed an ancient people. Let them declare what is to come, and what will happen. Fear not, nor be afraid; have I not told you from of old and declared it? And you are my witnesses! Is there a God besides me? There is no Rock; I know not any.'" (44:6-8) The only power or person in all of the universe who has created it all – the only power or person in all of the universe who controls it all – the only power or person in all of the universe who contains it all – the only power or person in all of the universe who commands it all – has one name – The Lord – The Lord Almighty – The Lord God – Jehovah – Yahweh! There is only One God and His name is Jehovah – Lord God – Jesus Christ! It is this God who enables us and equips with daily strength to face our daily trials and tests, struggles and strivings, as well as all our normal activities of any normal day. But now notice that it's also our God Who "made my way blameless." As we go about our daily routines, the Lord sets out to protect us from the evils of that day. As we submit and surrender ourselves to His Spirit, He helps direct our steps. Galatians 5:16-18 clears this up for us so well: "So I say, live by the Spirit, and you will not gratify the desires of the sinful nature. For the sinful nature desires what is contrary to the Spirit, and the Spirit what is contrary to the sinful nature. They are in conflict one with the other, so that you do not do what you want. But if you are led by the Spirit, you are not under law." Being "led by the Spirit" of God is where we all need to be in our Christian walk. We must allow Him to guide, lead, direct and plan our daily walk. As we do, He will make our way blameless as we "walk in the Spirit and not in the flesh." I Peter 3:12 tells us this memorable truth, "For the eyes of the Lord are on the righteous and His ears are attentive to their prayer, but the face of the Lord is against those who do evil." As we submit to God's Spirit daily, and as we walk according to His Spirit not fulfilling the cravings of our sinful flesh, we'll stay under the watchful eye of our God as His eyes are focused on the righteous. Psalm 1:6 states that "the Lord watches over the path of the godly" or righteous. We're told that Noah found "favor in the eyes of the Lord." (Genesis 6:8) When we read something like this in Scripture, we find out the why or the how that took place in a person's life. "Noah was a righteous man, blameless among the people of his time, and he walked with God." In v. 22 of Genesis 6, we are given another key element to Noah's "blameless" life: "Noah did everything just as God commanded him." Noah performed two dynamic elements in his life to gain God's favor: Noah walked in God's presence, and Noah walked with God's purpose. The first is him establishing a personal relationship with the God of heaven through daily fellowship; the second is him engaged in practical reverence for the God of heaven through dutiful faithfulness. When we make it our daily focus to have a relevant, vital and daily relationship with the Lord, it'll be our joy and natural outcome to do what He wants us to do. In doing this, we will begin to live righteous lives, thus bringing us into the arena of flourishing like the palm tree. Psalm 30:7 supplies us with one more element to build upon here: "By your favor, O Lord, you made my mountain stand strong…" Through the favor of the Almighty is the only way for our lives to remain flourishing and strong as we make our journey through life's adventures, both the ups and down, highs and lows.

- "You gave a wide place for my steps under me, and my feet did not slip." (v. 37) Psalm 18, the parallel chapter to II Samuel 22, also speaks of God making our steps sure and steadfast. We read these words in v. 19, "He brought me out into a broad place; He rescued me, because He delighted in me." And then we read these words in v. 36, "You gave a wide place for my steps under me, and my feet did not slip." As we travel through these strategic truths for our lives, God makes our paths sure and steadfast. He sets our feet on the high ground – overlooking all other ground that will be below our present course of travel. He not only sets out feet on the high ground, this ground under our feet will be solid, with no quicksand in sight for possible ruin or destruction. A long and meditative look at Psalm 37 would be appropriate at this point. Verse 23 tells us, "The steps of a man are established by the Lord, when he delights in his way." Simply put, our exact steps in life will be a measured success IF we bring ourselves to delight in God's way. The thought is taken to another level in the next verse, "though he fall, he shall not be cast headlong, for the Lord upholds his hand." Even if we get sideways because of a wrong decision, God will be quick to come to our assistance because we have taken the course of delighting in our God's Word, way and will! Now here's the key to longevity in the Christian life: "The law of his God in in his heart; his steps do not slip." (v. 31) It's Noah building a personal relationship with the Lord through his daily walk with Him. It's Enoch who "walked with God" and learned about the Lord's coming and of coming judgment on the earth. It's David who established himself as "a man after God's own heart" by hiding "His Word in his heart that he might sin against God." It's Daniel who confessed his sins and the sins of his countrymen as God sent detailed directions

15

about our world's history and the end of time. How do we arrive at these awesome destinations? All of the following thoughts are found in Psalm 37: "Fret not yourself because of evildoers" – v. 1 - "Trust in the Lord and do good" – v. 3 – Delight yourself in the Lord" – v. 4 – "Commit you way to the Lord" – v. 5 – "Be still before the Lord and wait patiently for Him" – v. 7. And the benefits of such living? – "they will soon fade like the grass" – "He will give you the desires of your heart" – "He will act" – "He will bring forth YOUR RIGHTEOUSNESS AS THE LIGHT, AND YOUR JUSTICE AS THE NOONDAY" – "those who wait for the Lord shall inherit the land." What a future we have, but what blessings God has extended to us in this present life, as well!

The righteousness of God can be defined as "an absolute quality of moral standards." Righteousness of man is limited or of a relative quality, corresponding directly to a standard of our rightness or obligations to God. In putting these two truths together, let's read Psalm 89:14-16, "Righteousness and justice are the foundation of your throne; steadfast love and faithfulness go before you. Blessed are the people who know the festal shout, who walk, O Lord, in the light of your face, who exult in your name all the day and in your righteousness are exalted." The Almighty God of heaven, the One and Only, the Creator of heaven and earth, is characterized by many attributes, but the foundation of His being is righteousness (absolute immaculate greatness) and justice (absolute incorruptible rightness). Because of these two pillars of absoluteness, He's majestic in His faithfulness and famous for His matchless love. When a person who understands these marvelous truths concerning the One, True God, and walks in His presence, the light of heaven's righteousness, which is Jesus Christ, comes to live and reign in that person's heart and life, and they live out God's righteousness and justice, faithfully serving Him and loving Him with all of their being. No wonder Psalm 146:8 says, "The Lord sets the prisoners free; the Lord opens the eyes of the blind. The Lord lifts up those who are bowed down; the Lord loves the righteous." Amen and Amen!

Psalm 111:2 and 3 provides the necessary depth to how the premise of "The righteous shall flourish as the palm tree..." – "Great are the works of the Lord, studied by all who delight in them. Full of splendor and majesty is His work, and His righteousness endures forever." The splendor and majesty of our God, evidenced in His splendid creation and sacrificial cross, speaks of His enduring righteousness and holiness. Therefore, the living truth of that amazing and awesome righteousness can be transferred to us, His children, making the way possible through our positional righteousness in Him, and living out a practical righteousness throughout our earthly journey. Because of Him, we can most assuredly flourish as the palm tree! "But seek first His kingdom and His righteousness, and all these things will be given to you as well." (Matthew 6:33)

So what's next for the righteous, child of God? It will only get better as we grow and grow, flourishing in our Lord God, experiencing all that our God has promised us in His Word!

2

A REMARKABLE STATURE

"The righteous FLOURISH like the palm tree..."
Psalm 92:12

I've always wanted to be taller. When I was in the sixth grade, I measured a whopping 5'4". I also could've used some weight management training, but that's none of your business. As the saying goes, "I wasn't over-weight, I was under tall." However, that summer I went through a growth spurt. I couldn't believe what was happening right before my very eyes! I shot up four and half inches and lost some of my extra weight! However, what was happening was that extra weight became a little more evenly distributed over my new, long, lengthy and taller body. Many of my friends, the ones I didn't hang with over that summer's vacation, couldn't believe it when we got back in school. I was the talk of the school for the first – 2 hours or so. But, really, I thought I was on my way. I kept thinking that I would keep growing and growing so I could be a taller version of myself for the rest of my life. I went from a stumpy, little kid, to being one of the tallest in my class in the seventh grade. As such, I played center on our seventh-grade basketball team. I learned all the post moves, and could kind have jump, too. It was totally different than what I was used to playing.

I loved it, that is, until we played a team from Madison Heights who had a 6'5" center. I then felt small again. My memory is a little sketchy at this point, not sure if we won or lost that game, but I digress. Let's get back to me being tall – or – taller. I grew a little bit more that year, finishing that timely growth spurt at 5'9". Wow! I was on top of the world! Surely this would continue, right? Not so much. It stopped abruptly. To this very day I have no idea what happened. My family genes took over, for, you see, my mother was only 5'2" and her father was only a few inches taller than that. I began to look over my family tree on her side and no one was tall. My dad was of normal height, and no one on his side of "the fam" was tall, either. I began rooting for those recessive genes to kick in eventually. But to no avail. It was over. My dreams of being a tall person were taken away in just a few years, never again to surface. Consequently, I played forward on the basketball team that next winter. While many of my basketball buddies kept growing, I slowly creeped up to 5'9" and a half my freshman year in high school and was destined to play guard the rest of my high school playing days. Yep, that's where it ended. No more height gained, only weight gain, but again, that's none of your business.

I wanted to be tall. I wanted to keep growing physically so I could, or so I thought, be more valuable to my basketball team. But the desire to be tall didn't meet up to the reality of it all. While I thought about my physical stature as a young man for athletic purposes, God had other intentions for my life. I loved basketball. Being born in Indiana, you MUST love basketball. If you don't, they kick you out of the state – nearly. But I REALLY LOVED FOOTBALL! While the height issue didn't come to help me in b-ball, my stature was more suitable for the gridiron. I worked hard at my physical conditioning on a consistent basis. I trained in the weight room and ran my fool head off. I studied running backs in the college and pro game to better my own game while a high school stud, I mean player. I began to be recognized around my small hometown when I would walk down the street or into stores. I loved the attention and glamor of it all. Although, as a team, we weren't very good my freshman year as we finished with a record of 0 wins and 9 loses. But we all worked that much harder in the off season and saw that record change to 7 wins and 2 loses the next year. We were all looking forward to having another flourishing year football wise, which would've been my junior year.

While all of this was taking place regarding the physical conditioning of my body, God was working on the spiritual conditioning in my heart. This is where my life would take a dramatic turn. While going through summer football drills in the heat of the "dog days" of a summer in Michigan, God finally grabbed my full attention. He was calling me into His workout room. I felt the need and call to prepare my life for His work. I didn't know what that all meant then. I didn't know the exact details of what, when, where and how, but I knew that He was wanting me to take that next step. I made the huge decision to leave a large public school and started attending a small Christian school located in Pontiac, Michigan. I explained all of this to my parents and then told (and tried to explain to) my coaches. The head coach talked to me for an hour and half, trying to convince me to change my mind. He showed me letters from some colleges asking about me and my football talents. Colleges can't contact a high school athlete until their junior year, my coach was setting up meetings with those college coaching staffs, supplying them with our game schedule so they could come and scout me. My backs coach approached this step in my life completely different. He just told me that I needed to follow my heart's desire and to do what was best for me. I still don't know if Coach Orchard was a Christ-follower, but he sure talked like it. My mom got in the act and just asked if I was sure about my decision. She was my biggest fan. Whatever the weather and wherever the game, she was in the stands cheering me on. I think she was caught up in all of the "fan" fare and excitement of my small-town notoriety, such as it was. She told me she was looking forward to watching me play the next few years and then on into my college career – if there was going to be one. I really think that my parents were looking for that athletic scholarship – that never came, to help them pay for my college education. God had a whole new ball game for me, and He was getting ready to show me His game plan.

Many palm trees can grow to heights of 80 feet. Most palm trees range in the area between 30 to 70 feet. They grow tall and they grow straight. However, palm trees really aren't trees at all. They're more of a grass and are considered so by botanists. They're called "Monocots" and belong to a distinctive family of plants known as the "Arecaceae." There are more than 2,600 species in this family. Most of them follow the classic palm shape of a single tall trunk with a cluster of large, spreading leaves at the top; but there are many exceptions, too. This family of plants includes shrubs, vines and trees, ranging in size from small bushes to the Quindio Wax Palm, which grows to 200 feet. According to the experts, they've been around for a long, long time. They don't have "growth rings" like regular trees do within their trunks that tell us how old they are. Instead, they're trunks are made up of compressed leaves. This composite makes them extremely flexible so that they can stand up to fierce winds that often happen in the climates where palm trees live. The palm tree has many varieties just like all other trees. Each variety carries a different thickness to its trunk. The thicker palm varieties have more mass to them, which presses down during storms and points to the ultimate strength – the base of the tree. Most palm trees weigh more than telephone poles. They're thick and dense in mass but are extremely flexible. The root system of the palm digs itself three feet below the surface. Palms have a large root ball, though, which is to be planted deep in the soil. The hole that is to be dug for the root ball should be at least twice the size of that root ball. However, their root system grows quickly and is spread out over a larger area than other trees, making their base even stronger because of the space that's utilized under the ground's surface. They have numerous roots, howbeit short in length.

Palm tree growth rates are as wildly diverse as their size and uses. The "Rainforest" species, which are about two-thirds of all palms, are in a lifelong race for energy. A slower growing palm will be crowded out by these huge trees in no time because the first ones rise above the fray that's taking place near the ground will become the winners of seeking the sunshine, which they so desperately need for their growth, energy and sustainability. Their leaves, or fronds, are competing with one another for sunlight, which is the key to their growth. The more sun a palm gets the faster it will gain height. Rich soil or the right nutrients or fertilizer added to the soil will also make a big difference. There are palms that grow a few inches a year, while others climb at many times that speed. Depending on the variety of the palm, its growth could be slow, moderate or fast. As was mentioned, some grow only a few inches per year, while others can grow as much as six feet. Their height will vary, again depending on the variety. Most palms grow to 40 to 50 feet while others grow only to 10, 12, 25 or 30 feet. Others can grow to 70 or 100 feet, while the Wax Palm towers above them all at 200 feet. Their leaves or fronds will also vary in size, mostly measuring 12 to 20 feet. Again, some smaller, some larger.

Physical growth is expected. When we see people who are supposed to be a certain height or weight and isn't, we often take a second look and wonder if they have some sort of disease. It's the natural order of our life to grow from infancy through childhood and into adulthood. The same is true in nature. Trees, flowers, grass and the farmer's crops all are supposed to grow. If not, then something is certainly wrong.

So why wouldn't we expect the same thing in our spiritual lives? We come to Christ in "child-like" faith. Jesus said, "Unless we come to Him as a little child" then we can't be saved. Think about a baby's and child's faith. They trust their parents that the food they're feeding them is healthy and good for them, free from toxins or poisons. They don't give it a second thought. When Mom or Dad make the airplane full of food dive into the hanger, the baby willingly opens the door to the hanger and the food-laden plane makes a safe landing inside! That's faith. Then think about the act of faith when we turn on/off a light switch – or turn the key or push a button to start our cars – or lower ourselves into a chair – all of these are simple acts of faith – motions that we often take for granted, but have faith in performing them. When we place our faith in Christ, we do so simply, willingly and lovingly, not giving another thought about whether the Lord will keep His Word and promise that He would save us.

Where do we go from that point? Well, just as babies grow into children and children grow to be teens and teens turn into adults, a baby Christian will also experience growth. I Peter 2:1, 2 lays this out for us in these terms, "So put away all malice and all deceit. Like newborn infants, long for the pure spiritual milk, that by it you may grow up into salvation – if indeed you have tasted that the Lord is good." Spiritual growth is a process of denying some things and desiring other things. Just as Paul says in I Corinthians 13:11, "When I was a child, I spoke like a child, I thought like a child, I reasoned like a child. When I became a man, I gave up childish ways." This is another natural way of life. We GROW UP! Our lives change. We put away those elements that accompany childhood. Life becomes much more complex and oftentimes confusing, filled with successes and setbacks, thrills and spills. I remember watching a TV show called "The Wide World of Sports." Their tag line was appropriate, for not only sports, but life, as well. It said, "The thrill of victory – and the agony of defeat." That pretty much sums up many lives in our churches today. In the realm of Christianity, though, the Lord expects us to change in order to experience the "thrill of victory" most of the time, if not all the time. We have become children of God, leaving behind the actions and attitudes of this world. In I Peter 2, we see that we are to "put away" some common issues that pertain to our world – Malice – "badness in quality; vicious character; wickedness" – Deceit – "guile; a bait or snare" – Hypocrisy – This is in its plural form, implying many and various areas – "a reply, an answer as in play acting; making a pretense" – Envy – The same as the word "hypocrisy" in that it's in its plural form, as well – "the feeling of displeasure produced by witnessing or hearing of the advantage or prosperity of others" – Evil Speaking – Also in its plural form – "backbiting." Man, do we all have some work to do in all these areas, am I right? Peter is telling us in one short, simple verse what needs to be removed from our lives. But then, after we put away evil practices, we're to pursue the Almighty's edifying Principles! "Like newborn infants, long for the pure spiritual milk, that by it you may grow up into salvation..." Growth, spiritual growth, should be the outcome of becoming a child of God. We're to move from one plain or level to the next, to the next and so on. As much as I was excited, yes, ecstatic, about my physical growth between my sixth and seventh grade years, I'm to be even more so about my spiritual growth and progress.

Which brings me to our main text – "The righteous FLOURISH like the palm tree..." (Psalm 92:12) The word "flourish" as used here means "to sprout, blossom; to be vigorous and strong."[1] This word, in its tense, as used in the Hebrew language, is used just three other times in the Old Testament. We find it in Psalm 72:7, "In his days may the righteous flourish, and peace abound, till the moon be no more!" This is speaking directly of King Solomon but is prophetic of the Lord Jesus Christ. It's written by King David about his son, praying for the people of the kingdom to flourish as they live righteous lives. This word is used again in Proverbs 11:28, "Whoever trusts in his riches will fall, but the righteous will flourish like a green leaf." The flourishing that God provides isn't necessarily about having riches in this present world. The key word, however, found in this verse is the word "trusts." The righteous person realizes that he cannot put his trust in the uncertain and fleeting riches of this world, for it sorrow of heart and many other evils. We read in I Timothy 6:10 these words concerning money, "For the love of money is a root of all kinds of evil. Some people, eager for money, have wandered from the faith and pierced themselves with many griefs." When we read this verse correctly, money isn't the problem. The "love" or "eagerness" to obtain it is the difficulty. If we're not careful, we can allow the affections and cares of our world to usurp the Lordship of Christ over our lives, permitting money and the things it can purchase to replace the real, true and lasting joy of our lives – Jesus Himself. Therefore, we have this insightful warning – some have left the faith, while others have lit the flame of failures. Finally, this word is seen one more time in Isaiah 66:14, "You shall see, and your heart shall rejoice; your bones shall flourish like the grass; and the hand of the Lord shall be known to His servants, and He shall show His indignation against His enemies." Again, we see these two words, "righteous" and "flourish" used together. Do you think the Lord is trying to get a message across to us by doing so? I sure think He is.

The word "flourish" appears elsewhere in different tenses. Look at its use in Proverbs 14:11, "The house of the wicked will be destroyed, but the tent of the upright will flourish." The "wicked" have a house, but because of their lifestyle it will eventually be destroyed. The "upright," or righteous, only have a tent to live in. If we ask any person on the street this question, "Which would you rather live in, a house or a tent?" I would venture a guess that the overwhelming answer by most would certainly be a house, me included. I know we have many who are campers, but still, living in a tent all the time? I don't think most would ever want that. But notice – those living in that tent, who are upright or righteous, will experience a flourishing life! In the beautiful love letter that is The Song of Solomon, we read in 6:10, 11 these marvelous words, "Who is she that looks like the dawn, fair as the moon, bright as the sun, majestic as the stars in procession? I went down to the grove of nut trees, to see whether the vine flourished, and the pomegranates budded." The groom was looking to see if his work had paid off by producing magnificent fruit, or, not so much. He wanted so much to see his vineyard flourishing and blooming, producing wonderful fruit. Our Lord wants that for us. As Solomon pictures the Father and Jesus Christ, while the bride or beloved pictures Israel and now the church, this love story is to become OUR love story between the Lord and us. His desire over us is to experience and enjoy flourishing fruit to His honor and for His glory!

One more use of this word "flourish" is found using another tense. This time, it's found in Ezekiel 17:24, "All the trees of the field will know that I the Lord bring down the tall tree and make the low tree grow tall. I dry up the green tree and make the dry tree flourish." We often want to take credit for the blessings on our life. We often think that it was our idea or genius that came up with some brilliant plan that brought to us some level of prosperity or success. We like to pat ourselves on the back for a "job well done." We can find ourselves like the rich man who didn't know what to do with all his extra goods, so he just wanted to build more or bigger barns to store all his possessions. The only problem is that the Lord told him that he would have to give those things up because God was requiring his soul that night, and he would have to leave all his earthly goods to another. Ezekiel is letting us in on the Lord bringing down judgment on His city, Jerusalem. He was reminding His own people that it was all about Him. Our God is responsible for the raising up of one and putting down of another. David wrote in Psalm 109:27, "Let them know that it is your hand, that you, O Lord, have done it." After my bypass surgery, I was told over and over, "I can't believe how well you're doing!" They were doctors and nurses – friends and family members – church members and co-workers – to which my response was always the same, "I give all the glory to my Lord and Savior, Jesus Christ! I have many people praying for me and it's because of their prayers that I have recovered so quickly." We read these words in Psalm 75: 6, 7, "No one from the east or the west or from the desert can exalt a man. But it is God who judges; He brings one down, He exalts another." When Israel exited Egypt via the Red Sea, God was extremely quick to give them some instructions. His man at the time was Moses, perhaps the greatest leader of all time. In Deuteronomy 8, Moses is using some very strong language to keep the people moving forward in loving their God. The Lord in His matchless grace and marvelous wisdom laid down some strong warnings of what to expect when the nation arrived in the Promised Land. Moses, through the Lord, didn't mince any words - "be careful to follow every command" and "observe the commands of the Lord your God, walking in His ways and revering Him." They both knew how fickle man's heart can be when it comes to loving the Lord and living for Him. He told them that when they have eaten and are satisfied with the great splendor of the land that He was bringing them into, not to forget Him, which would result of failure in observing His ways. He warned them about building awesome houses to live in, only to forget their God. He talked to them about their crops being mightily blessed, only to forget their God. He said that their livestock would increase greatly, but not to forget their God. Then this, "He gave you manna to eat in the desert, something your fathers had never known, to humble and to test you so that in the end it might go well with you. You may say to yourself, 'My power and the strength of my hands have produced this wealth for me.' But remember the Lord your God, for it is He who gives you the ability to produce wealth, and so confirms His covenant, which He swore to your forefathers, as it is today." This was Ezekiel's message in chapter 17. "All" people will know that it is the Lord God Almighty that exalts one and lowers another; or causes the person who is low to grow or the dry person to flourish! The trees mentioned in 17:24 refer to people and these other verses bear out the fact that the Lord is responsible for causing us to FLOURISH in our Christian lives.

God's thesis statement found in Psalm 92:12 is as true today as the first day it was written: "The RIGHTEOUS FLOURISH like the palm tree." Our positional righteousness we have in Christ has enabled us to live out practical righteousness for His glory. Ephesians 2:8, 9 covers the first aspect of our Christian life, "For it is by grace you have been saved, through faith – and this not from yourselves (or of ourselves) – it is the gift of God – not by works so that no one can boast." Everyone comes to the cross of Christ on a level field. No one is better than another. But then we read v. 10, "For we are God's workmanship, created in Christ Jesus to do good works, which God prepared in advance for us to do." The word "workmanship" is the Greek word "poeme`'" and is where we get our English word, "poem." God has written our lives as a poem, creating good works for us to perform for Him even before we were alive on this earth. God does it all! He has saved us, and He is sanctifying us. God works to bring about change in our hearts and lives. He accomplishes this spiritual and monumental task by convicting us through His Holy Scriptures and by conforming us to His Son, coordinating it all through His Holy Spirit's indwelling, instruction and intercession.

Peter ends his second epistle with these powerful words, "But grow in the grace and knowledge of our Lord and Savior Jesus Christ. To Him be the glory both now and to the day of eternity. Amen." In *The Amplified Bible,* we take this away with us by reading these words, "But grow in grace (undeserved, favor, spiritual strength) and recognition and knowledge and understanding of our Lord and Savior Jesus Christ (the Messiah). To Him (be) glory

29

(honor, majesty, and splendor) both now and to the day of eternity. Amen (so be it)!"[2]

I went through a "growth transformation" between sixth and seventh grades. Besides my periods of growth as an infant, which I don't recall, that was my only "major" growth spurt. The scientific family in which the palm tree resides has over 2,600 species, all of which grow at different speeds and different heights, possessing different looking fronds or leaves. Some palms grow slowly, while others have a more moderate growth rate, and still others grow quickly. As is the case, conditions need to be right in order that physical plants to experience their natural growth periods. They must be planted in the optimum soil, watered correctly, and have the needed and prescribed sunlight. As far as my physical growth, I've already told you that I have no words or explanation for that magnificent, three-month time period of marvelous, wonderful growth!

So I stopped my physical growth "back in the day." It did not continue. I didn't experience what many other people thought would happen to me for the next "growing" years of during my teens. This brings me to the word "grow" that's used in II Peter 3:18. This word "grow" is in the present, active imperative tense in the Greek. Therefore, because of the tense that the Holy Spirit used, we can read the first part of this verse as follows, "But keep on growing." Unlike my physical growth, and I would venture a guess here that you also stopped growing at some point, our spiritual growth is to be an ongoing process. Tomorrow ought and should be better than today. My spiritual life should experience a continual climb, not to be saved, but because I am saved. This is in direct contrast to the previous verse, v. 17, "You therefore, beloved, knowing this beforehand, take care that you are not carried away with the same error of lawless people and lose your own stability." We see here that we are to guard our profession, while in v. 18, we're to guard our progress. Our profession is our salvation – our progress is our sanctification. Our profession is positional righteousness we have through the death of Christ – our progression is our practical righteousness we have through our desire for Christ. We secure salvation as a gift from the Lord – we stimulate sanctification as we grow in the Lord. The great pastor and Bible teacher at Moody Church in Chicago, Harry Ironside, wrote the following: "The final admonition is found in the last verse: 'Grow in grace, and in the knowledge of our Lord and Savior Jesus Christ.' This is the unfailing panacea for all spiritual ills. As we go on to know Christ better and become increasingly like Him, and as we feed upon His Word, and it has its sway over our hearts, our progress will be consistent and continuous."[3] This agrees with the original intent of the word "grow." As we "keep on growing in a continuous fashion," we will see the result of living a consistent and consecrated life.

As palm trees experience their natural growth according to their variety, Christians will also grow because of their "variety" of the Christian life. As the Christian person submits himself to the Word and will of God, his growth will be continuous, resulting in a consistent Christian lifestyle. If this isn't the case, then that Christian person will be the exact opposite, living through a daily experience resembling a roller coaster ride – up and down, down and up. The Lord is quick in telling us to maintain a humble, submissive spirit toward His person, principles, passion and purpose.

C.S. Lewis wrote, "Relying on God has to start all over every day, as if nothing had yet been done."[4] Spiritual growth is never finished in our earthly existence. We will never cross the finish line of being all that God wants or desires us to be while living in this world. There are no "perfect" Christians anywhere. Each and every day, we must begin our pursuit of the person Who exhibits Majesty and Might, Who is the epitome of Light and Love, and Who exemplifies Perfection and Purpose. The goal of Matthew 5:48 has never altered or been changed by the Lord. It's the same today as it was when Jesus uttered the words found there: "You therefore must be perfect, as your heavenly Father is perfect." Maturity. Christian maturity. Christian adulthood. Becoming like our heavenly Father, the Lord God Almighty! That's the desired end for us. "And we know that for those who love God, all things work together for good, for those who are called according to His purpose. For those whom He foreknew He also predestined to be conformed to the image of His Son..." (Romans 8:28, 29) The Lord uses all of our life's experiences as ingredients in His grand plan for us, all for the purpose of conforming us to the spitting image of Jesus. Paul goes on to say in Philippians 1:6, "And I am sure of this, that He who began a good work in you will bring it to completion at the day of Jesus Christ." Chuck Swindoll said, "We are all faced with a great series of opportunities brilliantly disguised as impossible situations."[5] What happens when you're faced with the impossible situation of a family member dying – the doctor telling you those dreaded words, "I'm sorry, its cancer" – the loss of your job – your spouse leaving the family? Denial? Unpleasantness? Depression? Quitting on God? This is where our Christian growth is greatly affected – for the good or for the bad. This is the reason we must take daily refresher courses in the grace of God. God's amazing grace will grow in our hearts by leaps and bounds as we take time to be with Him during these "dark" hours. When we handle these impossible situations, living and walking in the grace of our God, hiding ourselves in its great workings, we will then grow in our personal knowledge of our Lord and Savior, Jesus Christ. Once again, Paul gives us some insights into this great truth, "that I may know Him and the power of His resurrection, and may share His sufferings, becoming like Him in His death.' (Philippians 3:10) Knowing Him is followed by knowing the power of His resurrection. The growth step between those two statements is one huge step! Getting to know Him on a level like that of Abraham, a friend, is gigantic. The great personalities of the Bible took this step. Every person who wanted to become a disciple of the Lord went from just being saved to a true follower. In the vine chapter of John 15, Jesus takes His guys on a journey to the center of His heart. Jesus begins to wrap His conversation up by saying, "You are my friends if you do what I command you. No longer do I call you servants, for the servant does not know what his master is doing: but I have called you friends." (John 15:14, 15) They just turned a corner in their relationship. The disciples learned about growth as they listened to The Master Teacher telling them that they were His friends if they became obedient to Him. From that moment, Jesus told them that the house servants didn't know the inner desires of the master of the house, but his friends did, because he told them! In the next few chapters, Jesus would embark on what the coming days were going to look like – for Him and them. Obedience leads to openness – openness led to oneness. If we want to know the power of His resurrection, then we must gain a heart of passionate pursuit after our Beloved!

Peter once denied knowing the Lord Jesus Christ. Peter was ashamed and expressed it when the Lord looked at him while He stood before Pilate. He wept and went out, leaving Jesus. When the sublime story of salvation was all finished, we find Jesus restoring him after another night of a failed fishing trip. Jesus lovingly brought him back from the edge. Jesus simply asked him if he loved Him. This question was posed to him not once or twice, but three times, the same number of times he had denied Him. Peter was getting back on track. His denying past would soon become his dedicated future.

Peter leaves us with some extremely edifying insights for not going through the same experience that he had gone through. These three principles will enable us to flourish like the palm – growing in our stability, steadfastness and sanctification.

- Guard Yourself from Spiritual Error – Peter began to get off track when he walked among the evil men who put

Christ on trial. He then sat down with them and warmed himself by the fire. When he was approached by the little girl about knowing Jesus, he said that he didn't. He broke all the principles of Psalm 1; and in so doing, he was "uprooted" from beside the rivers instead of being planted. Jesus warned him. Jesus told him, "When you have turned again, strengthen your brothers." Peter, who had been so unstable, was changed by God's grace into the "rock" of steadfastness.

- Grow Yourself in Grace and Knowledge of the Lord – Growth depends on life. Growth is an absolute necessity. Just like palm trees, growth is gradual and will be up to the individual Christian. Growth will be difficult. Because of where palm trees are planted and live, they experience horrific storms from time to time. We will also go through some horrific times during our lives. Therefore, we MUST grow in His GRACE! We're saved by His grace, Ephesians 2:8; and we're sustained by the same grace, II Corinthians 12:9. C.H. Spurgeon, the pastor of Metropolitan Tabernacle in London, in his devotion, "A Psalm for the New Year," explained grace using the following words: "'Grow in grace.' What is this? It must be in the outset implied that we have been quickened by grace. Dead things cannot grow. Growth shall prove your life. Grow in that root-grace, faith. Seek to believe more truth; let it increase in firmness, getting a tighter grip of every truth; let it increase in constancy, not being feeble or wavering, nor always tossed about with every wind; let your faith daily increase in simplicity, resting more fully and more completely upon the finished work of our Lord Jesus Christ."[6] D. Martin Lloyd-Jones added these thoughts on this topic: "Personally I can be certain I am growing in grace if I have an increasing sense of my own sinfulness and my own unworthiness; if I see more and more the blackness of my own heart."[7] Then there's growth in the knowledge of Christ. This will be our safeguard against heresy and apostasy. The study of "The Truth," Who is Christ, will keep us from all error found in every doctrine that is found outside of His Holy Word – The Bible! As we learn "facts" about our lovely Savior as revealed in Holy Scripture, our faith in our lovely Savior will be renewed and refreshed over and over through His Holy Spirit.

- Glorify Jesus Christ as Lord – "To Him be the glory, both now and to the day or eternity, Amen." The deity of Jesus is presented to us in those few words. Jesus is God! The Lord shares His glory with no one, so Jesus must be God in human flesh. The theme of our Christian experience, here on earth and one day in heaven, is nothing less than living to and the giving of glory to the God of the universe! John the Baptist's testimony was simply this, "He must increase, but I must decrease." (John 3:30)

Palm trees grow to different heights and at different rates. Palm trees, according to their varieties, have different looking leaves or fronds. Christians are no different. We grow at different rates, display different fruit, and grow to varying heights. But here are the keys to all their growth experiences – they're planted – their roots have a broad base – they grow according to their individual variety – they all have the inner being or fabric. The basis for us to "flourish as the palm tree," we must also be planted. Planted in good, rich soil, fertilizing that soil with the Spirit of God working the Scriptures of God into the fabric of our being. While we may be different "heights" in our individual growth process, we all have the same Father working His Word in our lives and looking to work

His will out of our lives. Our spiritual roots must go down deep and create a broad base for our lives beneath the public surface that we display to the world. For when the storms of life come, and they will to us all, we'll be strong because our roots in our God will be deep and wide, creating a stable and steadfast base to withstand any storm that will come our way.

May we all guard ourselves from spiritual error, grow in the grace and knowledge of Him, and live to glorify His wonderful name, in order that we, the righteous ones, will live a flourishing life, just the palm tree!

3

ROOTED IN
GOD'S SANCTUARY

"They shall be PLANTED in the house of the Lord…"
Psalm 92:13

The palm tree, like other trees, has a root ball. When planting a palm, the hole needs to be two to three times the size of the root ball. Before setting it in place, the roots need to be spread out from the ball, allowing them freedom to grow and expand. Palms have a large root system. Most roots are short in length, but then others can be rather lengthy. Since most palms have a root ball, it already has a tree or shrub that is growing out of the ball.

The seeds of most palms are held on branching fluorescence and vary in appearance depending on the species. Some are small and red, like berries, while others, such as the coconut palm, are more instantly recognizable. The fresher the seeds, the quicker they'll sprout. The test here is this – drop the seeds in a bowl of warm, tepid water. Seeds that float aren't any good because they lack the internal organs called "endosperms" that are necessary for reproduction. If the seed sink to the bottom of the bowl, you have viable seeds, ready for planting. The only exception to this test would be the coconut. It can sprout after floating for some time in the bowl of warm water.

To begin the seed-sprouting process, plant the seed in a small pot with an extremely thin layer of soil on top. In fact, the seed could be half-buried in the soil, and it'll be just fine. Palm seeds don't readily sprout if they are buried too deep in the soil. It doesn't take much dirt to make them happy enough to begin their growth into a remarkable, flourishing palm tree. God has designed them to have their seeds scattered by the wind and animals, and they are rarely buried before they are expected to sprout. From the very beginning, palm trees love the sunlight. For most species, the more they experience the sun, the quicker they begin their growth process.

Once this process has begun, move the pot or container to a very warm, very humid place. They need the warm atmosphere to get them kicked into gear. The hotter, the better. Take them into the bathroom so they can soak up that steamy air from your hot shower. A little green house can be made to store them in as they begin their germinating process within their confines of the seed, soil and pot.

Their time spent in this warm, cozy climate is just what the doctor ordered. (The Doctor in this case is the Lord Almighty!) They need warmth. They need the conditions to be just right in for germination to take place. The time to germinate varies among palm species, but it's probably longer than you'd expect. Some palm trees will sprout in 70 or so days; others such as the coconut, can take as long as six months to sprout. Don't be concerned if the seed appears to be ragged and rough. Be patient while you're waiting to get it planted. It's not out of the question or uncommon for palm seeds to shrivel and wrinkle, looking as if they have no life in them at all. Don't alarm yourself. Something is happening on the inside of that little seed that will result in a tall, straight, thriving and flourishing palm tree!

The righteous will flourish in their souls just as the palm trees flourish in their warm, humid climates. They experience this flourishing because "they are planted in the house of the Lord; they flourish in the courts of our God." (Psalm 92:13) The righteous have made a conscious decision where they desire to be planted – in God's sanctuary. This is their **foundation**. Their strength isn't found in themselves. Their stability isn't found in their abilities or talents. Their steadfastness is not the result of their own hands. No, their foundation is being "planted in the house of the Lord." Their **root** is firmly planted so the result is for them to have a desired consequence. They haven't left anything up to chance. They haven't lived life without purpose or focus. The righteous person has made a conscious decision to plant himself in God's house. Therefore, he flourishes and enjoys the **fruit** of his decision because he finds himself in the courts of the Lord. The "planting" is the **foundation** or **root**, stemming from a conscious decision made during some event or experience. The "flourish" aspect of all of this is the **fruit** or **results**, which becomes the desired consequence of being planted in the Lord's sanctuary. For many Christians who have just begun their Christian adventure and walk with the Lord, their "freshness" will be exciting for them and for all who see their growth. "Like newborn infants, long for the pure spiritual milk, that by it you may grow up into salvation" is what I Peter 2:2 tells us. There's nothing like watching a new, baby Christians lapping up the milk of God's Word! It's like a treasure hunt. They can't wait to share all their newly discovered truths found in the treasured Word of our God. But patience is the watch word in their cases. Transformation will be carried out through God's Scriptures by the means of God's Spirit. Allow them to "germinate" and grow in their Christian life. And as babies fall, cry and pick themselves up, so too will our young Christian friends. Our responsibility becomes producing the environment that remains conducive for their continued growth and maturity.

Life is all about making conscious decisions. Sometimes we make wise choices. At other times, we become complete and total idiots. We can be almost as wise as Solomon, while other times we can come off as silly fools. We know that "the fear of the Lord is the beginning of wisdom," Proverbs 1:7. This is elementary level spiritual stuff here. We aren't out of the 5th grade on this one. In order to get things in their proper perspective, we need to possess a healthy approach to a revering of God. "The fool says in his heart, 'there is no God.'" The rest of Psalm 53:1 tells us why people have this approach to God, "...They are corrupt, doing abominable iniquity; there is none who does good." The exact expression, "there is no God," literally means, "There is no God for me." They have made a life's choice to attempt living life without a God in or over their lives. So, because this has become their choice, they find themselves with no "fear of God before their eyes," opening themselves up to live in, experience and perform all sorts of evils our world has to offer. They have rooted themselves – they have planted themselves – outside of God's soil of righteousness, holiness and justice. They will now begin to see the results of living such a life. Romans 1 explains that as the world keeps making foolish decisions, not based on fearing God, that He will eventually turn them over to a mind that is totally opposed to Himself, doing and acting in ways that will bring upon them the fruit or results of a just reward. Go ahead, read Romans 1 again and watch man's depravity getting worse and worse as God gives mankind over to reprobation! Is it any wonder we see on the news all the horrific incidents around our world? Incredible evil is sweeping across the globe like a tidal wave, getting worse and worse every week, and will continue to be so until the Prince of Peace returns to this world to set up His earthly reign.

So back to our palm seeds. They need warmth and moisture or humidity to germinate. They flourish in moist heat. The Lord's sanctuary or courts is our moist heat. Proverbs 2:6-8 states, "For the Lord gives wisdom; from His mouth comes knowledge and understanding. He stores up sound wisdom for the upright; He is a shield to those who walk in integrity, guarding the paths of justice and watching over the way of His saints." If we are to grow in grace and knowledge of our Lord, we need to get ourselves to the warm climate found in His sanctuary. The message we receive from spending time with Him, either privately or publicly, is wisdom and knowledge and understanding. As a person would carefully watch over and care for their palm seeds, we read that He is "watching over the way of His saints." The "seed" of the Word begins to germinate in our hearts. His wisdom begins to root within our being. Life begins to make sense because He gives us understanding – His understanding. We soon realize that His ways aren't our ways, and His thoughts aren't our thoughts. But soon, very soon, like the palm seed sprouting in 70 days, our lives begin to see the renewal of real, true and vibrant life! Wisdom is stored away for the upright and righteous, so it can be used when needed. His wisdom becomes our shield of defense as we journey through life, enabling us to walk in integrity. He's our guide and guard, carefully taking us from viable seeds to vibrant lives. The righteous seed that was planted in our hearts and souls will germinate, growing into flourishing, sanctified lives, living to glorify the God of glory, ever in need of more and more Son light to bring us to His desired end.

Our "inner being" is the most important part of our spiritual and emotional being. We are mind, body and spirit. We often think that we are a body that possesses a soul. Not true. We are a soul housed in a body. With our bodies, we move and have our being, going about our daily tasks. We carry ourselves from point A to point B and back again. With our souls (heart, will and emotion), we relate to others as humans. But with our spirits, we relate to a holy God. An unsaved person cannot have a relationship with God because his spirit is dead. When a person gets saved or born again, that spirit is made alive again and can walk with the Lord

– we then can relate to a holy God. As the palm seed must have life within itself in order to sprout and grow, so do we, as people, possess life within our inner being in order to grow a spiritual being. Let's follow Paul's thinking processes as the Spirit reveals these truths to him in Ephesians 3:14-19, "...according to the riches of His glory, He may grant you to be strengthened with power through His Spirit in your *inner being*, so that Christ may *dwell in your hearts* through faith – that you, being *rooted and grounded* in love, may have strength to comprehend with all the saints what is the breadth and length and height and depth, and to know the love of Christ that surpasses knowledge, that you may be *filled with the fullness of God.*" (Italics mine) Your inner person or being needs to be "rooted and grounded" in Him, in order that He may "dwell in your hearts." When you and I make that conscious decision to be "rooted and grounded in love," we will experience the desired consequence of being "filled with the fullness of God." **The foundation and root are all about planting ourselves in His sanctuary. In turn, this will bear fruit and become the result we so greatly want, desire and need!**

Perhaps the greatest passage in Scripture that conveys this truth of being rooted, grounded and planted is found in Psalm 1. Verse 1 speaks of the blessed person who understands the negative aspect of the Christian walk – "Blessed is the man who walks not in the counsel of the wicked, nor stands in the way of sinners, nor sits in the seat of the scornful." The digression of a downward testimony is on full display in this powerful verse. This "blessed" person DOES NOT "walk," then "stand," and finally "sit" in any aspect of life that involves evil people. The Bible defines this person as "wicked," "sinners," and "scornful," describing another indication of a downward trek that will certainly lead to mischief, error and sin. We're to avoid these practices in our lives at all costs. When we do a careful reading of Peter's denial on the night before Christ's crucifixion, we see Peter journeying down this horrible path as he finds himself walking into the courtyard of those ready to indict and kill Christ. It's a cold night so he warms himself by the fire, standing and listening to the scorners gathered there. He has surrounded himself with the wicked, sinners and scornful. The only natural outcome to this dark time in Peter's life was to deny his Lord. He did. Three times.

Then, we read in v. 2 these amazing truths, "But his delight is in the Law of the Lord, and on His Law he meditates day and night." Denial of certain evils comes first; then we can delight in His edifications as found in His Living Word! The delighting in God's Word will lead us into our delaying or meditating for periods of time with God and His Word. Meditation is the Christian's key to success according to Daniel 1:8. Delighting ourselves in God's Word – Delaying ourselves in God's Word; Always Delight/Good Times and Bad Times – Abundantly Delay/Day and Night. A life fully committed leads us down the path to a life fully consumed in, of and by the Lord.

After this, we read about the God-given results of living such a life: "He is like a tree planted by streams of water that yields its fruit in its season, and its leaf does not wither. In all that he does, he prospers." (Psalm 1:3) This verse is full of God's hope for a bright, prosperous future for the "blessed" person, putting into motion the Delighting in God's Word and Delaying with that Word! His life is pictured as a tree, which is planted besides multiple "streams," bearing its fruit in due season, experiencing success and prosperity in every area of his life. As we follow this progression of spiritual thought: listening to evil advice leads to evil actions. On the other hand, loving God's advice and principles leads to abundant prosperity. Planted – Rooted – Grounded – by the streams of God's richest and vibrant blessings.

However, the opposite is true of those who practice evil and sin. "But," and thus, with that one word, we have the total opposite of the "blessed." "But this is not true of the wicked. They are like worthless chaff, scattered by the wind. They will be condemned at the time of judgment. Sinners will have no place among the godly." (Psalm 1:4, 5) The contrast between the "blessed" and "wicked" is drastic, stark and measured. Instead of being "planted by the streams," they are "scattered by the wind." Instead of bearing much needed fruit, they experience a life of "worthless chaff." Instead of prosperity in all areas of life, they will face only condemnation, judgment and will "have no place among the godly." This will be the result of all those who refuse to delight themselves in God's Word and delay themselves with God's Word. This action will cause and create a planting that leads to a flourishing life filled with satisfying fruit. The wicked and sinner will journey through a life of chewing on worthless chaff.

"For the Lord watches over the path of the godly, but the path of the wicked leads to destruction." (Psalm 1:6) The pathway of the godly or blessed person will enjoy God's presence, experience God's preservation, and exist in God's protection. "But" the pathway of the ungodly will be filled with peril and perplexity, resulting in perdition. To the wise of heart, they will observe the outcome of these two contrasted lives and make the obvious choice to choose to delight and delay in the Word of God. Then, as the natural outcome takes place, find themselves planted by God's waters of fresh life, bearing fruit in each season of life, never having to experience the turning of their leaves from green to a fall color!

Every Christ-follower must decide in his heart to have a private, planting time in the presence of his Lord daily. Time to Delight and Delay in and with the precious Word of God. Time to refresh himself from the heat of the day. Time to recapture the sweetness of a loving, heavenly Father. Time to unload this, that and the other. Time to "find rest for our souls" as said to us by Jesus in Matthew 11:28-30. Time to "be still and know that He is God" as commanded in Psalm 46:10, in order that we may once again rest on the promise of Psalm 46:11, "The Lord of hosts is with us; the

God of Jacob is our fortress." Yep. A, daily planting of ourselves in the courts of our God.

At this point, I can't help thinking about the many who have cast off the regular meeting together as a corporate, unified body of believers. Yes, I'm talking about the simple practice of going to church. Take a moment to delay in Hebrews 10:22-25: "Let us draw near with a true heart in full assurance of faith, with our hearts sprinkled clean from an evil conscience and our bodies washed with pure water. Let us hold fast the confession of our hope without wavering, for He who promised is faithful. And let us consider how to stir up one another to love and good works, not neglecting to meet together, as is the habit of some, but encouraging one another, and all the more as you see the Day drawing near."

Because the "Day" is drawing near, the day of the Lord's return, we all must take seriously our Christian walk or planting. The elements of the Christian endeavor we've just read must become the fabric of our being. The "drawing near" is at the root of it all. This is us making up our minds to live a life of consistent closeness to our Lord. The "holding fast" is when we decide to take that next step of living a life of committed consecration. Then we can "stir up" others to do the same as we live in community with others, becoming companions of people of like-mindedness. The author, through God's Spirit and inspiration, lays out for us exactly how we can get this done. He makes it extremely clear in this fantastic passage of Scripture. Let us follow the "let us" in these verses:

- **Let Us Pursue God With Assurance** – Permission Granted Because of our Forgiveness – v. 22 – The veil has been torn down, allowing us to enter the Holy of Holies, enjoying God's presence and edifying ourselves by God's Principles.

- **Let Us Perform Our Affirmation** – Participation Gained Because of Christ's Faithfulness – v. 23 – Following the example of Christ's faithfulness allows us to move through the wilderness and into the promised land of His blessings, looking for that blessed hope of His return.

- **Let Us Provoke Others to Action** – Practiced Grace Becomes Fortification for Others – v. 24 – One of the key aspects of the Christian life is to provoke or incite others to live out their Christian experience through love and good works.

For each Christ-follower, the foundation of it all is found in heeding the command in Hebrews 10:25, "not neglecting to meet together..." Being rooted in God's sanctuary is all about every believer establishing a daily, meaningful and vital relationship with the Lord. Privately, I am to follow the admonition of Micah 6:8, "He has told you, O man, what is good; and what does the Lord require of you but to do justice, and to love kindness, and to walk humbly with your God?" Publicly, I am to follow the admonition of meeting together with other Christ-followers. Even back then, we're told that some were breaking this habit. The lack of corporately meeting together is becoming more and more prevalent in our day and age, as well. When we see others join us for church, we become encouraged. And the warning comes to us that we must continue this "habit" as we the "Day" of Christ approaching.

I was taught to be present at church. I grew up in a church that had regular church services Sunday mornings and Sunday nights. We also had church on Wednesday nights and special meetings throughout the year, such as revival meetings or missionary conference. Along with all of these, I was also expected to attend our youth group meeting held each week. That was a lot, I know. Well, one Wednesday night I came home from school and practice and didn't want to go to church that night. I faked some sort of illness and my parents bought it! I really couldn't believe it! I thought, "Man, am I smart. I'm going to have a blast tonight while all those other people are going to have to suffer through another boring church service." Oh, brother, was I wrong. The time got closer for church to start. 7:05. 7:09. 7:13. 7:15. The minutes were dragging on so s-l-o-w-l-y. Finally, I couldn't take it any longer. I grabbed my Bible and headed out to Tienken Road. No, I didn't have my license. No, I didn't call anyone to come and pick me up. I had a better idea. I hitchhiked my way to church! I walked along Tienken down to Rochester Road. It wasn't very long when I got to Rochester Road that a VW Bug stopped to pick me up. To my utter surprise, the occupants were a hippie guy and a hippie girl! I climbed in the back of their smoke-filled Bug and made my way to church. The guilt began to subside. My inner torture was quickly turning to an inner triumph! I was so proud of myself. I was so glad to get this "monkey" off my back. I got to church just a few minutes late and didn't miss any of the teaching from Pastor Curry (one of the godliest men I've ever known and one of the greatest Bible teachers). It was awesome! I couldn't believe that I had won the battle over the devil that night!

As I was sitting there, I soon began to think of how I was going to explain this to my parents. My joy soon turned back into guilt. No, what I was feeling was fear and panic! Yes, it was true. I was in church. But I had lied my way out of church at the beginning of the night. I now had to make another decision – was I going to tell another lie and say that I felt better? Or, was I going to lay every-thing out in the open and be totally honest? I chose to be honest. All my mom said was, "I knew you weren't sick. I knew you were telling us a lie. But I also prayed that the Lord would convict you about what you had said. We're not happy with how you got here, but we are happy that the Lord answered our prayers and you felt shame and guilt." What a great lesson I learned that night all the way around. To this day, I recall that night vividly and thank my parents for teaching me to find myself rooted in God's sanctuary. Yep, you guessed it. They also grounded me for a week.

I don't know who said this, but it fits here perfectly:

> **"I never understood why going to church made you a hypocrite, because nobody goes to church because they are perfect. If you've got it all together, you don't need to go. You can go jogging with all the other perfect people on Sunday morning. Every time you go to church you are confessing again to yourself, to your family, to the people you pass on the way there, that you don't have it all together. And that you need their support, need their direction, you need some accountability, you need some help. ABOVE ALL YOU NEED A SAVIOR!"**

George Handel said, "What a wonderful thing it is to be sure of one's faith! How wonderful to be a member of the evangelical church, which preaches the free grace of God through Christ as the hope of sinners! If we were to rely solely on our works? My God! What would become of us?"[1]

D.L. Moody wrote, "Church attendance is as vital to a disciple as a transfusion of rich, healthy blood to a sick man."[2]

Then, John Calvin quipped, "Wherever we see the Word of God purely preached and heard, there a church of God exists, even if it swarms with many faults."[3]

Psalm 92:13 tells is like it is, "They are planted in the house of the Lord; they flourish in the courts of our God." We need God. We need God every day. Some of those days becomes obvious, while other days just blend into the year. Whichever is the case, we need the Lord every single moment of every day! We need to be planted in His house so we can flourish in His courts! Privately and publicly, we must delight and delay in the wonderful news that's found in His Treasure Chest – The Holy Bible! And in so doing, we will be rooted and grounded in God's sanctuary, experiencing Him to the fullest, because we're planted by His many streams that can satisfy every longing of our human heart!

4

REVELING IN
OUR SALVATION

"Nevertheless, do not rejoice in this, that the spirits are subject to you, but rejoice that your names are written in heaven." Luke 10:20

The *New Living Translation* describes Philippians 4:4 this way, "Always be full of joy in the Lord. I say it again – rejoice!"[1] There are many reasons why we as Christ followers can follow the principle that we've read or heard preached all our lives. Our future is signed and sealed but waiting to be delivered. We're told by Paul in Romans that those He justified He has also glorified. In other words, in God's eyes and mind we're already living in His very presence. The eternal security of the believer is a doctrine in Scripture that ought to bring all of us to the epitome of exuberant joy! Once a person has bowed his knee at the foot of the cross, repenting of his sin, asking for forgiveness from a loving, heavenly Father, and possessing His Spirit in his heart and lives, that person has been sealed with the Spirit of promise until the day of redemption. That in and of itself is mind-blowing. The future promise that a day on the near horizon is coming for all believers that will bring them to the feet of Jesus is almost unbelievable and unfathomable. But it is coming, and we are going to experience that very day.

However, in an ancient church known as the church of Thessalonica, the Christians were beginning to die. This cold, hard, fact was leaving many of those left behind full of questions and anxiety. So, they went to their living Bible source, the Apostle Paul, reaching out with the question of what was happening to their loved ones. At this time, followers of Christ believed that His coming back was going to be fulfilled within their lifetimes. At least that's how they understood them. They surely weren't expecting the sorrows that accompany the deaths of family members and friends. Then, the Lord inspires Paul to write his first letter to this church struggling with these feelings. We find references to the Lord's coming in each chapter of this letter, with one major treatment found in chapter 4 explaining the Lord's return in detail. Follow the progression of these thoughts as we travel through the book of I Thessalonians:

- **Personal Rescue** – "And they speak of how you are looking forward to the coming of God's Son from heaven – Jesus, whom God raised from the dead. He is the one who has rescued us from the terrors of the coming judgment." (1:10) The Lord's coming for His bride, the church, is going to be a rescue mission. His "coming" or "return" will be to remove His children from the coming terror that is fast approaching to the peoples of our world. Daniel's 70th week of judgment is yet to be fulfilled. This "week," or 7 years, will take place immediately after the "snatching away" of all believers from the earth. Revelation 3:10 tells us this truth, "Because you have kept my word about patient endurance, I will keep you from the hour of trial that is coming on the whole world to try those who dwell on the earth." The "earth dwellers," as this verse calls those who do not know

Jesus as their Savior and Lord, will experience this "hour of trial." But because there is "no condemnation (or judgment) for those who are in Christ Jesus," (Romans 8:1), we will be spared this judgment by being personally rescued by the Lord! The sins of those who have placed their trust and faith in Christ were judged when Jesus died and bled on the cross. The way I see things shaping up for us in this world, the Lord's coming will be a personal rescue mission for all Christians.

• **People Redeemed** – "After all, what gives us hope and joy, and what is our proud reward and crown? It is you! Yes, you will bring us much joy as we stand together before our Lord Jesus when he comes back again. For you are our pride and joy." (2:19, 20) Let's take a moment and think of people who will be in heaven because of our life's testimony and our lips' testimony. I know that we're going to be in heaven because of the love that God has for us, and that He demonstrated that love to us by sending to us His One and only Son, to die for us, taking our sins upon Himself, redeeming us back to the Father. However, all of us were told of God's love by another human being, whether in a church service or in our living rooms, at work or someplace else. We had to have heard the story of John 3:16 in some form or fashion. There are so many biblical examples that could be recited here, but let's just mention a few. The New Testament Ethiopian eunuch was returning to his country after worshiping the Lord in Jerusalem. He was led by the Spirit of God to read Isaiah 53, telling us the story of the suffering Lamb of God that would be led to slaughter. Philip, the evangelist, asked him if he understood what he was reading. The eunuch replied, "How can I, when there is no one to instruct me?" (Acts 8:31) So Philip climbed on board the man's chariot and told him about Jesus, the Savior of the world! The Ethiopian eunuch came to Christ that day, was baptized, and went on his way "rejoicing." On another occasion, Jesus was very busy ministering to the many people that came to Him to be healed of their physical woes or to hear His spiritual word. Luke tells us in his book, chapter 5 and verse 27, that "Later, as Jesus left the town, he saw a tax collector named Levi (Matthew) sitting at his tax collection booth, 'Come, be my disciple!'" He left it all behind and began following the Lord. That night, that very first night of following this new teacher, Matthew prepared a huge dinner party for all his friends – the "scum" of society – his many tax collector friends! He wanted to share with those he associated with all that he found that day in Jesus. Another time, Jesus and His guys were on a long, warm journey. Jesus sat down by a well, sending the disciple into town to buy some food for lunch. A woman, a Samaritan, came, at noon, to draw water. Several items of interest have already occurred. We're told in John 4:4 that "He (Jesus) had to go through Samaria on the way." His "had to" always meant that something was going to take place to bring glory to the Father. During this time in history, if a woman wanted to get water for her family, this task was done early in the morning. The time was now noon. Also, back in this day, men didn't talk to women on the streets. And finally, Jesus was a Jew – this woman was a half-breed – a Samaritan. These two peoples despised each other. All of this didn't matter to Christ. He came to tear down these types of barriers. He broke all of society's rules of that time. He strikes up this deep and moving conversation with this woman. The scene at the well wraps up with the woman coming to saving faith in Jesus Christ! But it doesn't stop there. She races back to town and begins to tell everyone about this amazing person she just met at the well! Then we read this in John 4:39-32, "Many Samaritans from the village believed in Jesus because the woman had said, 'He told me everything I ever did!' When they came out to see him, they begged him to stay at their village. He stayed for two days, long enough for many of them to hear his message and believe. Then they said to the woman, 'Now we believe because we have heard him ourselves, not just because of what you told us. He is indeed the Savior of the world.'" All three of these stories have some common threads: people came to a saving knowledge of Christ because another human being told them; the people who received Christ had a burning desire to obey the Lord in baptism, or get others to hear from the Lord Himself, or immediately told others of their new found faith because of what they experienced in the Lord. They were changed inwardly and then they were charged outwardly to express that inward change.

- **Purposed Result** – "And may the Lord make your love grow and overflow to each other and to everyone else, just as our love overflows toward you. As a result, Christ will make your hearts strong, blameless, and holy when you stand before God our Father on that day when our Lord Jesus comes with all those who belong to him." (3:12, 13) Physical growth, for the most part, happens naturally. We eat and exercise, causing our bodies to go through the biological functions of physical growth. Christian growth is also something that will take place within the inner being of those who have accepted Christ. It will be "the Lord to make your love grow and overflow to each other." The spiritual progression and walk of a Christ-follower is an onward and upward walk, and, at the same time, a nurturing walk that grows deeper and deeper as the years come and go. Let's follow the life of John. Christ meets him and his brother James in their boat, mending their nets after a night of fishing. As John grows in his discipleship and walk with Jesus, we see Jesus taking the "inner three" with Him to some pretty special events, i.e. the transfiguration, the last supper, with John leaning on Christ's chest, asking Him who it was that was to betray Him, and the Garden of Gethsemane as the group who went "a little further" with Christ as He prayed. We then see him at the foot of the cross, the only disciple mentioned as being present. Christ turns His attention, as He's saving mankind from their sins, to the care of His mother, leaving her in the hands of John. We then see John out run Peter to Christ's tomb after His crucifixion, waiting at the door of the tomb for Peter to arrive, and then entering it alongside Peter. Besides the Apostle Paul, John is honored by the Lord to have humanly authored more books of the Bible than anyone else – five – finishing with The Revelation of our Lord Jesus Christ. Upon further inspection of his writings, have you ever noticed how often John writes on the topic of love? It is, after all, John 3:16, and not Matthew, Mark or Luke 3:16. The next time you read through I, II and III John, make notes on the number of times he mentions loving the Lord or the love of God. "God is love" – I John 4:8. "Dear friends, let us continue to love one another, for love comes from God. Anyone who loves is born of God and knows God." (I John 4:7) "Dear children, let us stop just saying we love each other; let us really show it by our actions." (I John 3:18) "We know what real love is because Christ gave up his life for us. And so we also ought to give up our lives for our Christian brothers and sisters." (I John 3:16) "Perfect love expels all fear." – I John 5:18. "May grace, mercy, and peace, which come from God our Father and from Jesus Christ his Son, be with us who live in truth and love." – II John 3. The results of John's life are reflected in his love for his Lord, Master and King!

- **Persistent Refreshing** – We now come to one of the greatest descriptions of the order of events that will transpire when the Lord returns for His bride – the church. I Thessalonians 4:13-18 is the detailed account of what will happen to those Christians who have passed away and those Christians who will still be alive at that monumental event! I've used this passage over and over when conducting life celebrations of believers who have crossed the divide between mortality and immortality. At the very end of this passage, we read these words in v. 18, "So comfort and encourage each other with these words." The "words" preceding this verse are full of hope, expectation and peace, knowing that the loved ones who have left us bodily is enjoying complete joy in the presence of their Lord and Savior. The fact of knowing that the Lord is going to bring their spirits back with Him to resurrect their bodies in order to reunite their soul and body once again for all eternity ought to bring us, who are left behind, total peace and comfort. The only outcome of a per-spective on life and death that could result from knowing these facts has to be continual comfort and encouragement. The salvation that the Lord provides us takes us safely through this "ordeal" of life that we all must face at some point in our lives. "It is appointed for man once to die" we're told in Hebrews 9:27. Should the Lord not return in the next fifty-years, I would venture to say that most of us reading this book will have passed into eternity. This fact, coupled with the facts presented to us in I Thessalonians

4, should bring to us the Persistent Refreshing of abundant comfort and encouragement.

- **Plenteous Renewing** – The final chapter holds these truths for us, found in 5:10, 11, "He died for us so that we can live with him forever, whether we are dead or alive at the time of his return. So encourage each other and build each other up, just as you are already doing." Once again, we have the awesome word *encourage* commanded of us to give to others. The Lord has given His life for us, in order that we'll be able to live with Him for all eternity. This will happen to every child of God, to those who have placed their trust and faith in Christ, whether they're dead or alive. Paul lays all this out for us in II Corinthians 5. We read in v. 1, these truths, "For we know that when this earthly tent we live in is taken down – when we die and leave these bodies – we will have a home in heaven, an eternal body made for us by God himself and not by human hands." "For we know" – this is our assurance. God has told us, and He cannot lie. When we leave this world via our death, we will be living in heaven. Paul continues in vv. 6-8 as he gives us additional insight on this subject, "So we are always confident, even though we know that as long as we live in these bodies we are not at home with the Lord. That is why we live by believing and not by seeing. Yes, we are fully confident, and we would rather be away from these bodies, for then we will be at home with the Lord." Simply put, while we're alive on earth, we are not in the actual presence of the Lord. However, we're "confident" that when we lay our bodies down in death, we will immediately be in the actual presence of our loving Savior! Therefore, according to I Thessalonians 5:11, we are to "encourage" and "edify" other believers, and in so doing, provide plenty of renewing for their spiritual welfare.

Another look at all these verses provides us with some more insight. Every one of them speaks of the Lord's coming, thus, bringing with that coming the comfort that all of us so desperately want and crave. Remember all the stories involving the Lord when He walked the roads of Israel. "If you had been here my brother would not have died" was presented to Him by Martha and Mary. So many other people expressed the same sentiments as they either "touched the hem of His garment" or asked Him to come and heal a loved one that was near death's door. The Lord's **COMING** ALWAYS BRINGS WITH IT THE LORD'S **COMFORT!**

So, what does all of this have to do with palm trees? I'm glad you asked. Salvation comes in three stages:

- **Justification – Salvation from the Penalty of Sin – A one-time Event in Life**
- **Sanctification – Salvation from the Power of Sin – A continual Process throughout Life**
- **Glorification – Salvation from the Presence of Sin – A one-time Event in Life**

We use many symbols or activities to remember those special moments in life. We wear wedding rings to remind us of our marriage vows and to tell others, without saying a word, we belong to another. We have certificates hanging on our walls that say we've graduated from this or that school, or, have gained some-kind of accomplishment in life. We win trophies and medals or wear patches that express some athletic championship or accomplishment. We celebrate specific dates, places or seasons with those we love in our lives. We place grave markers on the graves of our family members who have passed away to mark their resting place on earth, giving a testimony of God's promise of returning for them one day. We read the plaques or markers on buildings or pieces of property that spell out the historical significance of that place. We remember. We want to recall to our minds what all these people or events meant to us in our past. God's salvation is no different.

The people in Thessalonica were concerned about their loved ones who had passed away. They asked Paul for clarification on this subject, and the Lord gave Paul the answers needed through the Spirit and inspiration. He tied in their redemption with His return, which resulted in their radical comfort. When we recall to our mind special events, circumstances and situations, as well as the many special individuals that make up the fabric of our being, we're also filled with radical comfort. The entirety of our salvation, which includes us being in the very presence of our Lord, is what comprises the doctrine of salvation. The Lord never views anything of His creative work without seeing it in its final state of completion. Therefore, we read that "those He justified He also glorified." We often view things in partial terms. The Lord does not.

Because of all this, the Lord uses physical or visible elements in our world to remind us of His spiritual truths of eternal consequence and completion. This brings me to the palm tree. In Leviticus 23:33-44, we read about the details of God's Feast of Tabernacles. This is also known as Feast of Booths or Feast of Shelters. This feast was to be held annually, five days after the Day of Atonement; and it was to last for seven days. On the first day and the eighth day of the festival the people were to take off from their daily work schedules. They were to bring offering to the Lord by fire, whole burnt offerings and grain offerings, sacrificial meals and drink offerings, each on their respective days during the festival. Let's pick up the details in reading verses 39-43, "Now on the first day of the Festival (Feast) of Shelters, after you have harvested all the produce of the land, you will begin to celebrate this seven-day festival to the Lord. Remember that the first day and closing eighth day of the festival will be days of total rest. On the first day, gather fruit from citrus trees, and collect **palm fronds and other leafy**

branches and willows that grow by the streams. (Bold type is mine) Then rejoice before the Lord your God for seven days. You must observe this seven-day festival to the Lord every year. This is a permanent law for you, and it must be kept by all future generations. During the seven festival days, all of you who are Israelites by birth must live in shelters. This will remind each new generation of Israelites that their ancestors had to live in shelters when I rescued them from the land of Egypt. I, the Lord am your God." This festival or feast was to be a festival of their rescue by the Lord's hand out of their 400 years of slavery in Egypt! It was to be a "rejoicing in their salvation." They were to pick ripe citrus fruit – cut down palm branches and other leafy branches from all the palm family – then they were to mightily rejoice before the Lord for seven days! Citrus fruit represents freshness and newness. Palm branches represent celebration and rejoicing. They were then told to live in some type of make-shift shelter for those seven days. The purpose of all this was to serve as a reminder for all the young people born after The Exodus of this momentous time in Israel's history – the time of Israel's **Salvation** and **Freedom** from living a life of slavery in Egypt!

In keeping with this idea of using physical and earthly elements to remind us of our salvation, the Lord instituted the Lord's Supper with His disciples at what is known as The Last Supper. We eat the bread and drink the juice exactly how the Lord instructed those twelve on that night. The purpose for all of this? "This is my body, which is given for you. Do this in remembrance of me..." "...This cup is the new covenant between God and you, sealed by the shedding of my blood. Do this in remembrance of me as often as you drink it." (I Corinthians 11:24, 25) This is our Feast of Tabernacles. This is our celebration in order to rejoice in our salvation when we remember how Jesus provided for our salvation. Like all the other reminders we have in life to reflect on life's joys of people, places and purposes, we pause, "as often as we drink it," to recall the wonderful day of our own salvation!

This was the idea behind Peter's plans to build the booths for Jesus, Moses and Elijah, on the Mount of Transfiguration. He was a Jewish boy who knew all about this annual festival. He simply wanted to celebrate the presence of those three magnificent personalities. But Jesus said, "No, it isn't time to do that just yet. We must go down off the mountain because my message has to go out into the many villages where so many live without truth." He also told them not to tell anyone what they had just witnessed. We read in Mark 9:9, 10, these words, "As they descended the mountainside, he told them not to tell anyone what they had just seen until he, the Son of Man, had risen from the dead. They kept it to themselves, but they often asked each other what he meant by 'rising from the dead.'"

Now we come to John's Gospel account of Christ's life on earth. We pick up the story in chapter 12, verses 12-19, "The next day, the news that Jesus was on the way to Jerusalem swept through the city. A huge crowd of Passover visitors took **palm branches and went down the road to meet him**. They shouted, 'Praise God! Bless the one who comes in the name of the Lord! Hail to the King of Israel!' Jesus found a young donkey and sat on it, fulfilling the prophecy that said: 'Don't be afraid, people of Israel. Look, your King is coming sitting on a donkey's colt.' (That was Zechariah 8:8) His disciples didn't realize at the time that this was a fulfillment of prophecy. But after Jesus entered his glory, **they remembered that these Scriptures had come true before their very eyes**. Those in the crowd who had seen Jesus call Lazarus back to life were telling others all about it. That was the main reason so many went out to meet him – because they had heard about this mighty miracle. Then the Pharisees said to each other, 'We've lost. Look, the whole world has gone after him!'" (John 12:19) The reason the Pharisees were so upset and distraught was because they knew exactly what this "triumphal entry" of Jesus all meant. When they saw the people lay down the palm branches in front of Christ and the donkey on which He was riding, they understood that the people were celebrating and rejoicing just as if it were the Festival of Tabernacles! John's testimony of Christ in chapter 1 and verse 14 was this, "So the Word became human and lived here on earth among us. He was full of unfailing love and faithfulness. And we have seen his glory, the glory of the only Son of the Father." The word "lived" or "dwelled" literally means "tabernacled." The Lord came to fulfill the Festival of Tabernacles in, by and through Himself! The main point of all the feasts, festivals and offerings was to highlight some aspect regarding the Messiah – the Lord Jesus Christ! On the first day of the Festival of Booths or Tabernacles, the people were commanded to cut down palm fronds or branches to use for their celebrations and rejoicing. The people were using these palm fronds to express their joy at the coming of the King, the Savior, the Lord and Master of Heaven; and these Pharisees knew it. Matthew 21, Mark 11 and Luke 19, all cover this event to be remembered in the life of Jesus. We're told there that these Pharisees told Jesus to tell His disciples to stop shouting that He was their King. Jesus turned and said, "If these were to be silent, the stones would cry out praise." Jesus was quoting Habakkuk 2:11, "The very stones in the walls of your houses cry out against you..." The pinnacle and reason of the coming of the Son of God to earth was now on full display. John mentions He came into Jerusalem as a fulfillment of prophecy. So many eyewitnesses to the raising of Lazarus were present and extremely ready to tell others all about that magnificent miracle. The people shouted, "Blessed is the King who comes in the name of the Lord! Peace in heaven and glory in the highest!" These words as said were almost identical to the words shouted by the heavenly host at Christ's birth, "Glory to God in the highest, and on earth peace among those with whom he is pleased!"

The feast days and festivals are all type or foreshadowing of the coming Messiah. The only way for the Lord to have people remember important events was to use these feasts and many physical items to do so. Citrus fruit was to be picked, speaking of refreshment. Palm fronds or branches were to be used when expressing joy of the people. The people were then told to live in booths, shelters or tabernacles, reminding them of the time of God's deliverance of Israel from the slavery in Egypt. It was to be a time of remembrance and reflection. It was to be a time of refreshment and rejoicing. Their ordeal of being slaves was over.

Our ordeal of slavery to sin and Satan is also over. Therefore, we celebrate the Lord's Supper "as often as you do this, in remembrance of me." Egypt in the Bible is a type of the world. We have been redeemed from sin and the world through the sacrificial death of Jesus Christ on the cross! Communion, or the Lord's Supper, is that time of remembrance and reflection on His death, but it's also to be a time of rejoicing and refreshment. Before we partake in the meal, we're to search our hearts and confess any known sin in our lives, making sure that there's isn't anything between us and our God.

Then comes Palm Sunday, the triumphal entry of Christ into Jerusalem. His fame and notoriety had spread throughout the countryside of Judea and Samaria, reaching into the center of towns and villages. Miracles like the resurrection of Lazarus had caused such a dramatic stir, that the Pharisees said "that the whole world has gone after Him! We've lost!" But when the people shouted what they shouted, and when they laid the palm branches on the road in front of Jesus, they were beside themselves with anger and envy. The picture was complete. The Festival of Tabernacles was brought into its ultimate meaning and fulfillment. The Word that was made flesh was indeed Jesus Christ, the Feast of Tabernacles as He "tabernacled" among us, living out every aspect from all the feasts and festivals the Jews celebrated. He brings with Him complete refreshment; and because of that, we can completely rejoice in the salvation that He provides.

Yes, we're told in Luke 10:20 this marvelous truth, "Nevertheless, do not rejoice in this, that the spirits are subject to you, but rejoice that your names are written in heaven." In A. T. Robertson's, "Word Pictures of the New Testament," he writes that the phrase, "are written," as meaning, "a state of completion, stand written, enrolled or engraved."[2] Upon receiving Christ as Savior, our names are sealed in the Lamb's Book of Life! This act is a final and complete process, sealed with the Spirit of God. Our names are on the rolls of heaven, never to be removed! That is what the Lord told His disciples to rejoice in, not in the fact that demons are subject to them when they use the name of Jesus Christ. In a devotional by D. A. Carson, he relays the time Martyn Lloyd-Jones was dying of cancer. "One of his friends and former associates asked him in effect, 'How are you managing to bear up? You have been accustomed to preaching several times a week. You have begun important Christian enterprises; your influence has extended through tapes and books to Christians on five continents. And now you have been put on the shelf. You are reduced to sitting quietly, sometimes managing a little editing. I am not so much asking therefore how you are coping with the disease itself. Rather, how are you coping with the stress of being out of the swim of things?' Lloyd-Jones responded in the words of Luke 10: 'Do not rejoice that the spirits submit to you, but rejoice that your names are written in heaven.'"[3] The old hymn that tells us, "When the roll is called up yonder, I'll be there" is a truth that every child of God can claim based upon the promises found in God's Word, and that's all we need to revel in His salvation He so richly gives to us!

5

HIS RAVISHING SPOUSE

"How beautiful and pleasant you are, O loved one, with all your delights! Your stature is like a palm tree..." Song of Solomon 7:6, 7

*T*he way Christ came into our world was not what most people expected. His coming was prophesied by many Old Testament prophets, with many precise details about that coming. One of the most interesting details we have about Jesus' birth was for Him to be born in the little, obscure place called Bethlehem. On top of that, His parents were also very obscure. So much so, that when the angel Gabriel announced Christ's coming to Mary, she couldn't believe that God had chosen her to deliver the Savior to the world! Then, to make it even more obscure, He was to be born in an animal stable! No one saw that coming, especially Israel's religious leadership during that time. His family moved up north to a city called Nazareth, another obscure, out-of-the-way place. Nazareth was not very well respected by other Israelites. For someone to be known as growing up and living there didn't exactly look good on one's resume as it relates to his personal data.

So here comes Jesus Christ with all His "history" hounding Him as He enters the public eye. When the time came for Him to declare His mission, He walked into a synagogue, asked for a copy *of Isaiah*, and proceeded to read these words, "The Spirit of the Lord is upon me, because he has anointed me to proclaim good news to the poor. He has sent me to proclaim liberty to the captives and recovering of sight to the blind, to set at liberty those who are oppressed, to proclaim the year of the Lord's favor." (Luke 4:18, 19) He then rolled up the scroll, gave it back to the person in charge, and sat down. Every eye was staring at Him after this public declaration. I can just imagine what they were all thinking, "Who does he think he is?" Then Jesus made this bold statement, "Today this Scripture has been fulfilled in your hearing." At first, the people marveled and praised Him to others. However, after they thought about all that had just transpired, some of them began to verbally question what they just heard. The natural response of many was simply voiced with this one question, "Is not this Joseph's son?" This was not meant to be a compliment. They were questioning Christ's learning and pedigree, as well as His right to say such things. Jesus continued His speech as He explained what was going to take place in the next three years. He told them that many would say to Him, "Physician, heal yourself...Truly, I say to you, no prophet is acceptable in his hometown..." Christ then spoke of the widow that Elijah had ministered to in Zarephath and the healing of Naaman, the captain of the Syrian army, who was dying from the dreaded disease of leprosy. Christ's point – there were many widows in Israel and there were many lepers – but only these two individuals were helped. The Lord's ministry was going to be selective. Everybody wouldn't embrace Him as Messiah, let alone Lord or King. At that point, the people were ready to get rid of Him right then and there. They grabbed hold of Him and led Him to the outskirts of town, near a cliff that was located at that exact spot. However, some how He got lost in the crowd and escaped their evil intentions. Guess where all this took place? Nazareth – His hometown! So much for Christ's first day in public ministry.

Here's my reason for providing all these details concerning the back story of Christ's life. I want to capture the significance of Peter's confession concerning Jesus. From these inauspicious beginnings, for the next three years, Christ "went about doing good." He taught many people the eternal and holy principles His Father had given Him. He healed many others of their physical, spiritual or emotional infirmities. Reading through Matthew, Mark, Luke and John, the human authors of the four gospels, we have only 53 days of recorded history of Christ's life! John, writing in his gospel account, tells us in 20:30, 31, these truths about Christ, "Now Jesus did many other signs in the presence of the disciples, which are not written in this book; but these are written so that you may believe that Jesus is the Christ, the Son of God, and that by believing you may have life in his name." **That statement gives us the purpose and expectation of the book of John in no uncertain terms**. Then, in 21:25, we read these words, "Now there are also many other things that Jesus did. Were every one of them to be written, I suppose that the world itself could not contain the books that would be written." **That statement provides the proportion and extent of Christ's life in no uncertain terms**. Our Savior and Lord rose from a birth in an obscure place, to growing up in another obscure place, to beginning His earthy ministry during an obscure provocation, to an obvious and open expression by Peter of Who Christ was and is. In Matthew 16:16, we read this outstanding description concerning Christ, which is something for us to embrace ourselves totally and expound to others! As Christ's message of hope was being preached and His ministry of healing was being practiced, people were brought to personal acceptance of Him. However, Jesus wanted to know who people thought He was on this day. Their answer was that some people were saying that Christ was John the Baptist, others threw out the names of Elijah or Jeremiah, or maybe one of the other prophets. He then asked them point blank, "Who do you think I am?" Peter, as was his custom and nature, immediately spoke up, "You are the Christ, the Son of the living God." Jesus Christ, as He made His way through those 33 years on earth, went from living a life of obscurity, to having one of His disciples make an obvious confession as to His identity!

The purpose for Christ coming to earth was to redeem a people back to Himself. He came to "give His life as a ransom for all," as I Timothy 2:6 tells us. The giving of His life on the cross began God's rescue mission of the pinnacle of His creation – us - humanity. Jesus Himself gave testimony to this fact in Luke 19:10, "For the Son of Man came to seek and to save the lost." When Adam transgressed God's Word and fell into sin in the Garden of Eden, God began His redemptive work for us. After being deceived by Satan, Eve gave Adam the forbidden fruit. He ate of that fruit and cast all of humanity headlong into sin. His nature, the Adamic nature, was passed on to us. We would've done the same thing had we been in Adam's place that day. We choose to sin, so our human nature is flawed from the very beginning. After their fall, they discovered some things about themselves; their eyes were open, and they realized they were naked – physically and spiritually. In order to cover their nakedness, they made themselves some clothes from fig leaves. When the Lord came to have His usual talk with them that day, they hid themselves because of their guilt. God began His recovery of them by asking some direct questions of them. He knew all along what they had done, for God sees and knows all. However, for the redemption process to begin, He had to get them to admit to their act of sin against Him. Then, in order to show His love and forgiveness, as well as making it clear that the shedding of blood was necessary for forgiveness from sin and its removal from us, He made them coats from animals. Of course, this implies the death of the animal, causing its blood to be shed, thus beginning the "blood line" in Scripture. All throughout the Bible, we see the wonderful results of when blood is applied to a repentant soul – cleansing, forgiveness and redemption!

One of the greatest comparisons in Scripture is between the physical marriage of husbands and wives and that of the church. We read these awesome words in Ephesians 5:25-27, "Husbands, love your wives, as Christ loved the church and gave himself up for her, that he might sanctify her, having cleansed her by the washing of water with the word, so that he might present the church to himself in splendor, without spot or wrinkle or any such thing, that she might be holy and without blemish." Jesus came to earth to call a people to Himself. This people, whom He is redeeming, is from every corner of our globe. The message of the Gospel is going to reach into every nation in order to win people of every tongue. This is His church – His Bride! We're told that "Christ loved the church," which is why He "gave himself up for her." Salvation's message will be heard in all four corners of our world. But His work also entails "that he might sanctify her, having cleansed her by the washing of water with the word, so that he might present the church to himself in splendor, without spot or wrinkle or any such thing, that she might be holy and without blemish." After Christ saves us from the penalty of sin, He turns His efforts and attention to our sanctification, which is the part of salvation that is delivering us from the power of sin.

This brings us to the marvelous story of Solomon, the shepherd, and a farm girl, the Shulamite. The conversation goes back and forth between the two of them, with others entering their intimate talk. That's the basic storyline. As we dig deeper into the meaning of this glorious poem, we understand that it also represents the love God has for His people, the nation of Israel. But upon further study and investigation, we also see many expressions that tell us that this is a "hallowed type, the Lord Jesus and His mystic bride, the church; and, therefore, by a warrantable appropriation, each Christian believer may claim a true individual application."[1] (J. Sidlow Baxter) Song of Solomon 2:10-13 is a clear reference to the Lord returning for His loved ones, "My beloved speaks and says to me: 'Arise, my love, my beautiful one, and come away, for behold, the winter is past; the rain is over and gone. The flowers appear on the earth, the time of singing has come, and the voice of the turtledove is heard in our land.'" Revelation 4:1 - 3 presents this picture to us, "After this I looked, and behold, a door standing open in heaven! And the first voice, which I had heard speaking to me like a trumpet, said, 'Come up here, and I will show you what must take place after this.' At once I was in the Spirit, and behold, a throne stood in heaven, with one seated on the throne. And he who sat there had the appearance of jasper and carnelian, and around the throne was a rainbow that had the appearance of an emerald." The voice that will sound like a trumpet is Jesus Christ. The Person speaking in verse 1 is Jesus Christ. I Thessalonians 4:16 says, "For the Lord himself will descend from heaven with a cry of command, with the voice of an archangel, and with the sound of the trumpet of God."

J. Sidlow Baxter continues his description of this wonderful book: "It is the mystic presence of Christ and the church in the Song of Songs which gives it its deepest wonder and inmost meaning. It is this which has made it unutterably precious to the inner circle of the Lord's lovers; and it is from this that there comes to us its central message, namely: Such is the union between Christ and His redeemed people, when realized in its deepest and tenderest meanings, that it can only be expressed to us under the figure of an ideal marriage union. This is true whether we think of this union as between Christ and His people collectively, as the Church, or between Christ and His people individually, as the redeemed and sanctified members of that Church."[2]

As we put the three Scripture passages together, Song of Solomon 2:10-13, Rev. 4:1-3, and I Thess. 4:16, we understand that the Lord is going to come back for us, asking us to "Come away with Him," beginning our eternal life with Him! When Jesus was present on earth, He began to tell His disciples that He would be going away. They were upset and afraid. They really didn't understand what He was talking about. As the Lord got closer to His sacrificial death on the cross, He began to speak plainly to them about these events. We pick up the narrative in John 14, verses 1-3, "Let not your hearts be troubled. Believe in God; believe also in me. In my Father's house are many rooms. If it were not so, would I have told you that I go to prepare a place for you? And if I go and prepare a place for you, I will come again and will take you to myself, that where I am you may be also." Jesus promised us that He would return to get us in order to be where He was! Breaking down v. 3 a little more, I see these fantastic truths:

"I" – The Person

"I will" – The Power

"I will come" – The Promise

"I will come again" – The Prospect

"I will come again and receive you" – The People

"I will come again and receive you that where I am" – The Place

"I will come again and receive you that where I am there you may be also" – The Purpose

But in the meantime, the Lord is working on our sanctification. The theological term "sanctification" simply means "to be set apart." The Lord's purpose for our lives after salvation is for our lives to be different to all those we know and meet. We read in Deuteronomy 1 that it was only an eleven days' trip from Egypt to the Promised Land. The Lord brought Israel out of Egypt (a type of the world) via the Red Sea, in one night. Our salvation is also a quick event that involves placing our faith in Christ. However, Israel was so full of the ways of Egypt that it took the Lord 40 years to get Egypt out of Israel! The same is true of us. The ways and wiles of worldly living is felt heavily ingrained in our hearts and lives. Jesus may save our souls, but our souls need to enter the Lord's process of sanctification or "setting apart" after we come to Him for salvation. The text we quoted at the beginning of this chapter finds the shepherd describing his beloved as having a "stature like a palm tree." Every travel brochure of any far away, exotic and warm destination has pictures of beautiful, picturesque palm trees lining the beaches! Their appearance and beauty screams to us, "Come and enjoy yourself in this magnificent place! You know you really, really want to!" I recall my many trips to Florida and seeing palm trees lining the streets and beaches. It was as if I had gone to a different world. Growing up in Michigan, we didn't have anything that resembled a beach scene with palm trees growing to majestic heights along awesome, sandy beaches. I remember my trips to California and walking its beaches and city streets, feeling as if I had jumped into one of those travel brochures. As we drove through Beverly Hills, I found myself in complete awe and amazement. I had no idea that any place like that even existed on planet earth. Besides the stores and homes, the beauty of the area was only enhanced that much more by the stature of the thousands of palm trees! It didn't matter what direction you looked or what city you visited, they were prevalent and awesome! It was a totally different world than I had ever experienced up to that point in my life. The man in the Song of Solomon gave us a description of the girl he loved. Her physical beauty must have been something else, but he said that her "stature was like a palm tree."

As I understand Scriptures, God's love for us is unconditional. He loves us no matter what. We can't do anything to make Him love us more, and we can't do anything to make Him love us less.

He loves us. However, He loves us too much to leave us the way He found us. His banner over us is love and He desires to bring us to His banquet. He is coming back to take us to be with Him one of these days. That is based on His own Word and promise. For all of eternity, wherever He will be, we will be, also. The plans He has for us is to live with Him forever. The next event on God's calendar is His coming. However, His plans for us all include for us to change. We are to be "conformed to the image of his Son." (Romans 8:29) This takes a lifetime. His sanctifying work is never finished this side of eternity. This process is accomplished as the Lord works Himself into the fabric of our being. He is putting His Word into our inner being as He is taking out the world from us.

There are many verses in God's Word that address this exact issue of sanctification. But because of time and space, I want to limit this aspect in this chapter to the passage found in II Peter 1:3-11. This section of Scripture holds some vital insights for our development as Christ-followers. We begin in verse 3, "As we know Jesus better, his divine power gives us everything we need for living a godly life. He has called us to receive his own glory and goodness!" As we grow in our own personal relationship with Jesus, He provides EVERYTHING we need to seize a godly life, as well as secure God's glory and goodness. This is transformation-God working in His Word and working out the world. He follows this with verse 4, "And by that same mighty power, he has given us all of his rich and wonderful promises. He has promised that you will escape the decadence all around you caused by evil desires and that you will share in his divine nature." He provides His principles for our learning, in order to transform our inner self to live out those principles. He then provides His promises upon which I can lean, in order to transform us into His likeness. Jesus said in the Sermon on the Mount that we "must be perfect, as your heavenly Father is perfect." (Matthew 5:48) We have prized principles in verse 3 to assist us living godly lives. We have precious promises in verse 4 to assure us as we live out those godly lives.

Then we move on to verses 5-7: "So make every effort to apply the benefits of these promises to your life. Then your faith will produce a life of moral excellence. A life of moral excellence leads to knowing God better. Knowing God leads to self-control. Self-control leads to patient endurance, and patient endurance leads to godliness. Godliness leads to love for other Christians, and finally you will grow to have genuine love for everyone." We make purposeful progress as we add these profound priorities to our life. We also must take note of the specific order in which God has placed these priorities. First, He begins by saying, "Make every effort to apply" this, that, and the other. In some versions, we read, "Giving all diligence, add to your faith." *The Amplified Bible* states it this way, "For this very reason, adding your diligence (to the divine promises), employ every effort in exercising your faith to develop..."[3] Peterson paraphrases this verse in *The Message* as, "So don't lose a minute in building on what you've been given, complementing your basic faith..."[4] Then notice God's precise order of adding these priorities into our inner being: Faith – Virtue – Knowledge – Self-control – Steadfastness – Godliness – Brotherly affection – Love. If anyone builds upon his faith any of these virtues out of order, then that person will get out of balance. Say he wants to add knowledge first. Then he will become intellectually corrupt. What about putting love first? I mean love is the greatest, right? We've all read that in I Corinthians 13. No, then that person will become too sentimental and not regard God's truth as the final say. Emotions will take over and that person will be ruined doctrinally. Right after faith, we must add virtue, excellence, resolution or good character. Godly or good character will keep us on the right track throughout each situation we'll face in life. The exercising of good character will help us grasp spiritual knowledge or understanding. We'll be able to apply spiritual and Scriptural principles the right way because we have the excellent character to do so. This leads to living a self-controlled life, which lends itself to steadfastness and endurance. While all of this is taking place in our inner being, godliness is becoming a reality. Then we can treat others as Jesus treated others. We'll love our Christian family as we should, extending to them meekness and patience. Then our attention will be taken to those outside of God's family. Jesus said, "Others will know that you're my disciples because of your love for each other." This type of Christian love will begin to resemble the facets developed for us in I Corinthians 13. This will be our life lived with purposeful progress.

The results of adding these qualities to our lives is quickly seen in verse 8: "The more you grow like this, the more you will become productive and useful in your knowledge of our Lord Jesus Christ." We've come full circle! Verse 3 says, "As you know Jesus better..." and as we continually add "knowledge" or spiritual understanding into our lives, we'll see our Christian lives become more and more productive and useful "in your knowledge of our Lord Jesus Christ." This is exponential growth.

However, as much as there's a positive result in adding these virtues to our faith, God presents to us two negative results, as well. In verse 9 we read, "But those who fail to develop these virtues are blind or, at least, very shortsighted. They have already forgotten that God has cleansed them from their old life of sin." The first negative result is that this person's future's best is negated. They "are blind" or "shortsighted." God's will become a secret. Then, this person's past best is neglected. They will have forgotten "that God has cleansed them from their old life of sin." Have you ever spoken to a Christian who has lost the wonder of their salvation? He has neglected Him for so long that he has forgotten what it was like when he trusted Christ.

Finally, let's read verses 10, 11: "So, dear brothers and sisters, work hard to prove that you really are among those God has called and chosen. Doing this, you will never stumble or fall away. And God will open wide the gates of heaven for you to enter into the eternal Kingdom of our Lord and Savior Jesus Christ." Verse 10 tells us that as we add these virtues to our lives, we'll experience protected paths. Then, when our time comes for us to leave this world, we'll enjoy a prominent passage into His presence!

II Peter 1 is perhaps the greatest passage of Scripture that lays out for us God's great process of setting us apart, along with all the results. Jesus Christ is going to come for us one day. We, His bride, the church, has a responsibility to fulfill. We must make ourselves ready for His return. Our stature must become "like a palm tree." We must be adding these seven virtues into our lives daily. As we do, we'll prepare ourselves for that great day of our Lord – He's coming back to take us to be with Him! When it's all said and done, what then is the climax of this entire journey? It is the simple joy of mutual possession, as proudly proclaimed in Song of Solomon 2:16, "My beloved is mine, and I am his." This is the assurance of possessing our lovely Lord and being possessed by Him.

6

REWARD
ACCOMPLISHED IN SECRET

**"But when you pray, go away by yourself, shut the door
behind you and pray to your Father secretly. Then your
Father, who knows all secrets, will reward you." Matthew 6:6**

All palm trees are known as "endogenous" plants. The term used to be "monocotyledon." This term means "growing or produced by growth from deep tissue; caused by factors inside the organism or system; produced or synthesized within the organism or system; proceeding from within; derived internally; growing or developing from within."[1] These types of plants don't display what's known as "secondary growth." Look up at a palm tree and you'll see that the growth isn't like other trees. The canopy of the palm is restricted to the crown of frond leaves surrounding the apical meristem. Lateral growth and meristems do not grow out of the main trunk. This gives palms a distinctive, paint-brush shape. The single growing meristem or trunk is surrounded by overlapping leaf bases. Palms are incapable of the ring-shaped secondary growth seen in other trees. Cut a palm tree in half and you'll see tiny circular vessels distributed evenly throughout the trunk. The "bark" of the palm tree isn't bark at all; it's made of "clarified" or hardened cells left over from the bases of previously shed fronds. **This makes a palm not unlike a column of reinforced concrete with the vessels acting as rebar.** Also, unlike other trees which grow the root system and the shoot system at the same rate, palms rapidly expand the root system so that it can significantly grow its trunk and begin to grow upward. **A palm tree grows in the same way that you might build a house. It establishes the foundation and then builds the upper stories. While all this growth is seemingly accomplished like other trees, they're actually growing upward from the inside! This is what makes the palm tree an endogenous plant.** The root system and shoot system are growing at the same rate. What this means is that their unseen growth is equal to their seen growth. The foundation is expanding underground in their root system, all the while, their frond growth is expanding right along with it! What's being done in secret, or unseen, can be viewed by the ever-increasing size of the tree itself and its leafy fronds.

In His sermon by the mountainside, Christ was very clear about doing the spiritual activities of giving, praying and fasting in secret. When it comes to our giving, He said, "Beware of practicing your righteousness before other people in order to be seen by them, for then you will have no reward from your Father who is in heaven. Thus, when you give to the needy, sound no trumpet before you, as the hypocrites do in the synagogues and in the streets, that they may be praised by others….But when you give to the needy, do not let your left hand know what your right hand is doing, so that your giving may be in secret. And your Father who sees in secret will reward you." (Matthew 6:1-4) The Pharisees would make their way into the synagogue courtyard with great pomp and circumstance. They would then grab the attention of all the people there by sounding a trumpet right before they would toss their offering into the coffers. The Lord told us never to do this. Instead, act like it's no big deal when you give. The idea of "not letting your left hand know what your right hand is doing" simply means not to worry about how it looks to others. We must remember that we're to please an audience of One.

Then Christ covers our prayer lives. "And when you pray, you must not be like the hypocrites. For they love to stand and pray in the synagogues and at the street corners, that they may be seen by others…But when you pray, go into your room and shut the door and pray to your Father who is in secret." (Matthew 6:5, 6) We're not to make a major production out of our praying in public. All of us have been present when someone wants to make a theatrical production out of their time to pray. Nope. God wants us to find a secluded place so we can be ourselves and unload our burdens to our heavenly Father! When we do this, the focus will be removed from us and placed on the right Person.

"And when you fast, do not look gloomy like the hypocrites, for they disfigure their faces that their fasting may be seen by others…. But when you fast, anoint your head and wash your face, that your fasting may not be seen by other but by your Father who is in secret…." (Matthew 6:16, 17) The times in our lives that call for some quick and radical concentration on our Lord is called fasting. When we deny our appetites from food or other necessities in life privately, don't bring it over into your public life. The Lord is saying for us to go about our daily schedules as business as usual.

The key in all of these "spiritual activities" is secrecy. Real and vital spiritual accomplishments are done in secret. As the palm tree grows inwardly or within, so too must we as Christians grow our spiritual lives inwardly or in secret. God's great intent for us all is to change good followers or disciples into loving servants who will leave an impressionable difference on people's lives. God's intention is to disturb our inner being for the purpose for us to make a huge difference in the lives of those people we touch daily. He does His greatest work inwardly, in our hearts, minds and wills. However, the Lord will not settle for any change in our lives that's less than a deep, radical change in our character. As I mentioned in the last chapter, we must make it our daily priority of adding virtue, character and excellence to our faith. As this is done in secret, in solitude or in our closets, God's radical transformation and remaking of our lives will become a reality.

The simple fact is that many Christians make it through their lives coping instead of changing. We begin to feel comfortable with a remodeling job when what we really need is a brand, new construction project. We refuse to challenge ourselves in making a difference where it matters most – in our hearts or inner being. For whatever reason we've learned to sweep issues under the rug and hide them from the Lord, or so we think. The Lord came into our world to bring about revolution to the "normal" spiritual patterns known to mankind. The religious crowd accused Him of turning the "world upside down," when He was really turning it right side up. His message was all about encountering our hang ups and issues, our besetting sins and malicious behaviors. To get this done, He hit problems head on in no uncertain terms. But the place to tackle these points of godly contentions was in our hearts.

The awesome, old-time Bible commentator, Matthew Henry, wrote these words concerning the prayer aspect of this passage in Matthew 6: "Now there were two great faults they were guilty of in prayer – vain-glory and vain repetitions. We must not be proud and vain-glorious in prayer, nor aim at the praise of men. What was the way and practice of the hypocrites? In all their exercises of devotion, it was plain, the chief thing they aimed at was to be commended by their neighbors. When they seemed to soar upwards in prayer then their eye was downwards upon this as their prey. What the places were which they chose for their devotion; they prayed in the synagogues, which were indeed proper places for public prayer, but not for personal. They prayed in the corners of the streets, the broad streets (so the word signifies), which were most frequented. It was to cause themselves to be taken notice of. The posture they used in prayer; they prayed standing; this is a lawful and proper posture for prayer, but kneeling being the more humble and reverent gesture, their standing seemed to savor of pride and confidence in themselves. Their pride in choosing those public places, which is expressed in two things: (1) They love to pray there. They did not love prayer for its own sake, but they loved it when it gave them an opportunity of making themselves noticed. (2) It is that they may be seen of men; not that God might accept them, but that men might admire and applaud them....Instead of praying in the synagogues and in the corners of the streets, enter into thy closet, into some place of privacy and retirement. Isaac went into the field, Christ to a mountain, Peter to the house top.... Instead of doing it to be seen of men, pray to thy Father who is in secret. The Pharisees prayed rather to men than to God. Do you pray to God, and let that be enough for thee. Pray to him as a Father, as thy Father, ready to hear and answer, graciously inclined to pity, help, and succor thee. Pray to thy Father in secret. He is there in thy closet when no one else is there; there especially nigh to thee in what thou callest upon him for."[2]

These three spiritual disciplines are the most beneficial of all disciplines. They raise the bar of spirituality for everyone who decides to participate in them. Fasting is a duty or discipline required of by followers of Christ. God, in His providence and wisdom, has commanded this of us, but when it comes to our personal need, we must become willing and active participants. Giving to the Lord is a regular reminder that everything we have comes from Him. It keeps our hearts soft and alive when it comes to the things pertaining to our God. Prayer falls right in the middle between giving and fasting. As giving is our physical reminder of God's blessings and that we owe Him everything, prayer is our spiritual reminder that apart from Him we can do nothing. As

Israel wasn't responsible for the daily manna that fell from God's hands, so we must go through the daily practice of prayer that will enable us to realize that we are unworthy of our daily bread. Fasting adds another layer on top of these ideas, telling God that we're serious about our present needs or situations, and that apart from Him, we have no idea how we're going to make it through our current issues. God doesn't tell us how often we're to proclaim a fast. While the Spirit of God is silent about this in Scripture, His Spirit will "bear witness with our spirit" when it becomes needed or necessary. Fasting, prayer and giving are all about the humbling of our souls. Fasting brings the other two disciplines into excellent clarity and focus. It elevates our spiritual game like nothing else can in our lives. Jehoshaphat and Israel were being overrun by the Moabites and Ammonites. They comprised a "great multitude" of mighty warriors with one goal in mind – the destruction of the nation of Israel. II Chronicles 20:3 tells us J's response to this tremendous threat, "Then Jehoshaphat was afraid and set his face to seek the Lord and proclaimed a fast throughout all Judah. And Judah assembled to seek help from the Lord; from all the cities of Judah they came to seek the Lord." Jehoshaphat then set his heart to pray in verses 5-11. His conclusion is what makes men mighty with God, "O our God, will you not execute judgment on them? **For we are powerless against this great horde that is coming against us. We do not know what to do, but our eyes are on you." (II Chronicles 20:12)** In spite of a huge amount of fear that was in his heart, he acted upon the situation that was staring him down. He proclaimed a fast. He proceeded to pray. He privately conducted himself into these spiritual activities, and then he led the nation into a public display of these two dynamic weapons we have at our disposal as Christians. What was God's answer to all this noise? The Lord's response brought about drastic change to the problem and delightful comfort to His people; "'Listen, all Judah and inhabitants of Jerusalem and King Jehoshaphat: Thus says the

Lord to you, Do not be afraid and do not be dismayed at this great horde, for the battle is not yours but God's." (II Chronicles 20:15) Notice in the Lord's answer how He addressed the people of Judah, the residents of Jerusalem and King J personally! It was the king who initiated the fast and prayer. He brought everyone together to do the same as he was doing. The Lord met each individual where he was in his own journey through this crisis. He leaves no one behind. He leaves no one guessing. He leaves no person thinking that the other person is of more value than himself. The Lord has His own way to deal with each of us, even if we're going through similar struggles or sorrows. His further instructions consisted of these simple commands, "You will not need to fight in this battle. Stand firm, hold your position, and see the salvation of the Lord on your behalf, O Judah and Jerusalem. Do not be afraid and do not be dismayed. Tomorrow go out against them, and the Lord will be with you." (II Chronicles 20:17) One of the easiest things to do when travelling through hard times is to quit on God. Troubles and trials seem to take their toll on the best of Christians. When Mark faced the reality of the Christian life in Acts 13, he left Paul and Barnabus high and dry. Here, the Lord simply says, "Stand firm and hold your position." A military leader will tell his men to "hold the line no matter what!" This is God's advice to us. And then stand back and watch the Lord work on our behalf! I believe He then speaks to King Jehoshaphat by saying, "Don't be afraid." We're told back in verse 3 specifically that he was "afraid." **But here's the piece de resistance in all of this conversation and conflict, "And the Lord will be with you."** Hebrews 13:5b, 6, "...I will never leave you nor forsake you. So we can confidently say, 'The Lord is my helper; I will not fear; what can man do to me?'" God's presence is the answer to all our conflicts or concerns, sorrows or struggles, trials or testing. A. W. Tozer wrote in *The Pursuit of God,* these words, "Why do some persons 'find' God in a way that others do not? Why does God manifest His presence to some and let multitudes of others struggle along in the half-light of imperfect Christian experience? Of course the will of God is the same for all. He has no favorites within His household. All He has ever done for any of His children He will do for all of His children. The difference lies not with God but with us."[3]

When faced with a great "horde" of horrific happenings, our response will make all the difference in the world. We can exhibit fear or we can exercise faith. We can come to our God with our heart ready to seek His face and presence, or we can flee into our problem without His aide or comfort. It's our choice.

7

RESPLENDENT SON-SHIP

"Around all the walls of the house he carved engraved figures of cherubim and palm trees and open flowers, in the inner and outer rooms. The floor of the house he overlaid with gold in the inner and outer rooms. For the entrance to the inner sanctuary he made doors of olivewood; the lintel and the doorposts were five-sided. He covered the two doors of olivewood with carvings of cherubim, palm trees, and open flowers. He overlaid them with gold and spread gold on the cherubim and on the palm trees. So he also made for the entrance to the nave doorposts of olivewood, in the form of a square, and two doors of cypress wood. The two leaves of the one door were folding, and the two leaves of the other door were folding. On them he carved cherubim and palm trees and open flowers, and he overlaid them with gold evenly applied on the carved work...He was seven years in building it." I Kings 6:29-35, 38b

According to II Chronicles 3:1, three temples stood successively on Mt. Moriah in Jerusalem. This site is today called the Haram esh-Sherif and is a Muslim holy place. The first temple was built by Solomon, the second by Zerubbabel and the Jews who returned from the Babylonian exile and captivity, the third temple, which was in use in the days of Jesus Christ, was begun and largely completed by Herod the Great. The temple was the centerpiece of religious life in ancient Israel and is greatly expressed throughout all of Scripture. The Psalms refer to it often: Psalm 42:4; 66:13; 84:1-4; 122:1, 9; 132:5, 7, 8, 13-17. Annual pilgrimages to the temple brought the citizens from every corner of Israel and even the known world at that time: Psalm 122:1-4; Acts 2:5-11. When Mary and Joseph made one of these visits to the temple, Jesus stayed behind to answer and ask questions of the religious authorities. He was only 12 according to Luke 2:41-51. Jesus, during His ministry years, often ministered in the shadows of the temple: Matthew 26:55; Luke 19:45; John 7:28, 37; 10:23.

Solomon's temple in Jerusalem was absolutely, magnificent! The great economic and cultural development of the Hebrews during the kingly reigns of David and Solomon led to the desire to build a dwelling place on earth for the God of heaven. This "house of God" was to be more complex and ornate than the temporary tabernacle the Israelites carried with them during their wilderness wanderings. The first temple, or Solomon's Temple as it became known, was noted for its lavish beauty and detail rather than for its size. It was accessible only to the priests; the average Israelite came to it, but never could enter through its door. The fact that it took the craftsmen of that day seven years to complete attests to its beauty and minute details. The temple was dedicated in Solomon's 11th year or around 950 B.C. (I Kings 6:38) The luxurious contents were carried off to Babylon as spoils of war in 606 B.C. and was destroyed completely in 587 B.C.

Most ancient religions had places of worship to their god or gods also called temples. The heathen temples of the Canaanite civilization found at Megiddo and Hazor are similar in their layout and structures. The temples themselves had floor plans that mirrored each other, while the outside grounds were also like the temple in Jerusalem. The biggest differences came in their dimensions and the pain-staking measures to the quality and details to the interior. Solomon's Temple was by far the grandest and greatest of them all!

The temple was comprised of three sections: 1. The Porch through which the temple was accessed. 2. The Holy Place, which was lighted by clerestory windows. (I Kings 6:4) These windows were placed in a raised portion of the interior of the temple, rising above the adjacent rooftops, allowing daylight to cascade down into the room they surrounded. Its dimensions were 30 feet wide, 60 feet long and 45 feet high. Its walls were covered with cedar paneling, with gold inlay to relieve the wooden monotony, as well as to provide grandeur to the room. 3. The Holy of Holies (II Chron. 3:8-11), the inner sanctuary or sanctum, was a thirty-foot cube. This room was windowless and was completely overlaid with gold. The floor was raised off the earth as to not get it corrupted in anyway with dirt or soot. This holiest place on earth was reached by steps leading out of The Holy Place. This was where the Ark of the Covenant rested. Once a year, the high priest would enter this room to present a blood atonement on the Mercy Seat, which was located on top of the Ark. When this sacrifice was accepted by God, His Shekinah glory would fill the room, and this part of the temple would have that glory resting on it, giving off the appearance of fire. It was the Day of Atonement and the holiest day to the Jewish people. (See Leviticus 16)

The temple was a prefabricated building. It was made of lime-stone finished at the quarries in or near the capital city of Jerusalem. (I Kings 6:7) When the stones were brought to the building site, they were placed into the wall according the master plan. The stone walls were covered with paneling of cedar wood from the forests of Lebanon, with gold inlay throughout and carvings of cherubim, palm trees and flowers. The building itself was built on a nine-foot high platform, which was reached by ten steps. This provided a dramatic and splendid approach for any and all religious processions. On this platform, before the entrance to the porch section of the temple, stood two pillars, called Jachin and Boaz. (I Kings 7:15-22) More than likely, these are the first words inscribed on any wall or door of the temple. Just behind these two splendid pillars, were doors that led to the porch, much like a reception area, before the real important parts of this building. The cypress doors leading into the Holy Place were carved with cherubim, palm trees and blooming or open flowers, all of which were inlaid with gold. (I Kings 6:18, 32, 35) The main descriptions of Solomon's temple are found in I Kings 5:1-9:25 and II Chronicles 2:1-7:22. Many Bibles have artists renderings of what this marvelous building must have looked like during its use. The Internet also has many sites that contain these drawings should one desire to visualize this masterpiece of architecture.

When it comes to the cost of construction, one can only speculate its value. One person calculated the value of just the building at $157,080,000,000, with the value of the gold and silver at $21,780,000,000, bringing the total to a staggering $179 billion! Another person figured it all cost much higher, with their calculation coming in at $216,603,576,000, and that's not including all the precious metals, bronze, iron, ivory or cedar wood, as well as any of the workers' wages! Based on amounts recorded in Scripture, it's been estimated that 20 tons of gold were used in Solomon's Temple. Using the value of gold in our market today, a ton of gold is worth $37.32 million. When we multiply this amount by 20, it gives us a bottom line of nearly $7.5 billion! That's just in the value of gold! When we figure the cost of wages during that time versus today's labor costs, the amount of workers required then versus what the amount would be today, the place where the raw materials were gathered and their shipping to the job site, the building techniques of that day as compared to our day, people estimate that it would take around $175 billion to duplicate this magnificent house of worship in today's world!

Everything in the tabernacle and temple was a type of the true temple – Jesus Christ. He spoke of the temple of His body in John 2:21. God Himself prepared Jesus Christ His body according to Hebrews 10:5. It is through Jesus Christ that we have the ability and authority to approach a holy God. Solomon attempted to make an earthly building that fulfilled this purpose. The design and beauty were awesome. The ornate detail was all about adorning the greatness and grace of the One true Deity of our universe. The ornaments of carved cherubim are regarded by most biblical scholars as representing the invisible Godhead, while others view these carvings as representations of the heavenly beings who surround the throne of God. Then there are those who believe they represent the highest of animal or created life. The books of Ezekiel and Revelation also mention these cherubim. The cherubim speak of royal and regal surroundings. Just as the cherubim speak of animals, so do the palms of vegetable life. They are "the princes of the vegetable kingdom."[1] (Linnaeus) "Amongst trees there is none so lofty and towering, none which has such a fair majestic growth, which is so evergreen, and which affords so grateful a shade and such noble fruits-fruits which are said to be the food of the blessed in paradise-as the palm"[2] (Bahr). Bahr also adds that it is said to have as many excellent properties as there are days in the year, and cites Humboldt as designating it the "noblest of plant forms to which the nations have always accorded the need of beauty."[3] Judaea, he further remarks, is the fatherland of the palm, so much so that the palm in later days became the symbol of Palestine (as on the well-known coin with the legend Judaea Capta). The palms, therefore, tell of the vegetable world, and of Him who fashioned its noble and graceful forms. The palm speaks of refreshment and renewal. And very similar was the testimony of the flowers. "Flowers and bloom have been, from ancient times to our own, the usual symbols of life in all its fullness .... So then by the flower work, as well as by the cherubim and the palm trees, was the dwelling of Jehovah, which was adorned therewith, designated as an abode of life"[4] (Bahr). On the earthly dwelling place of the Eternal, where everywhere within the dwelling, portrayed the various tokens of His Almighty power and goodness. And the significance of each is the same. "Thou hast created all things, and for thy pleasure they are, and were created." (Revelation 4:10, 11) They were inscribed within and without. These words, here and in v. 30, are generally taken to mean "in the oracle and in the house." These flowers speak of regeneration and revelation. Put all of these together and we have the picture of a righteous God reaching out to His created beings to redeem and reveal Himself to them, creating the freshness of renewal and refreshment!

Now we come to our day. What does all this mean to the child of God? What significance and meaning can we draw from this ancient building used for worship?

"Our fathers had the tent of witness in the wilderness (The Tabernacle – Israel's place of worship while traveling through the wilderness), just as he who spoke to Moses directed him to make it, according to the pattern that he had seen. Our fathers in turn brought it in with Joshua when they dispossessed the nations that God drove out before our fathers. It continued like this until the days of David, who found favor in the sight of God and asked to find a dwelling place for the God of Jacob. But it was Solomon who built a house for him. **Yet the Most High does not dwell in houses made by hands, as the prophet says, 'Heaven is my throne, and the earth is my footstool. What kind of house will you build for me, says the Lord, or what is the place of my rest? Did not my hand make all these things?'"** Acts 7:44-50

This was the closing part of Stephen's message to those surrounding him right before he was murdered. It's always amazing to me what people do or think when placed under the convicting hand of God. We see in these verses that the tabernacle and temple were nothing more than temporary dwellings of God's mighty presence. The nation of Israel carried the elements of the tabernacle around with them during their forty years of going nowhere because of their disobedience. After the kingdom was established in David's hand, his desire was to build God's temple. (II Samuel 7) God prohibited David from building the temple because he was a man of war. God's desire was for a man of peace to build His dwelling place on earth, and that man was David's son, Solomon. David's heart was in the exact place it needed to be. The fullness of God was deep in his heart, for David's testimony was that he was "a man after God's own heart." From an early age, David learned to trust the Lord with everything in his life. This one huge request, though, was not part of God's grand plan for his life. The Lord was greatly moved at this action from his servant, David. According to II Samuel 7, God gave the prophet, Nathan, a heart-warming and soul-stirring message to be given to David. An excerpt from that message says this, "I took you from the pasture, from following the sheep, that you should be prince over my people Israel." (II Samuel 7:8) David's humble beginning was God's starting point for the Lord of heaven to use this shepherd boy to become the greatest king in Israel's history! David desired to build God's temple in His capital city, Jerusalem. It wasn't meant to be. Instead, listen to what the Lord told Nathan to tell David, "I will give you rest from all your enemies. Moreover, the Lord declares to you that **the Lord will make you a house. When your days are fulfilled and you lie down with your fathers, I will raise up your offspring after you, who shall come from your body, and I will establish his kingdom. He shall build a house for my name, and I will establish the throne of his kingdom forever."** (II Samuel 7:11-13) <u>Resplendent son-ship is all about our desire to build a dwelling place for our God on this earth</u>. But that desire is quickly turned into God's promise of His eternal blessings upon our lives. God honors David, not for his actions, but for his intentions! The purpose and plan of God was made visible in due time, but at that moment, David was amazed at God's gracious words and actions on his behalf. Let's take in David's response to all of this in verses 18-23, "Then King David went in and sat before the Lord and said, 'Who am I, O Lord God, and what is my house, that you have brought me thus far? And yet this was a small thing in your eyes, O Lord God. You have spoken also of your servant's house for a great while to come, and this is instruction for mankind, O Lord God! And what more can David say to you? For you know your servant, O Lord God! Because of your promise, and according to your own heart, you have brought about all this greatness, to make your servant know it. Therefore, you are great, O Lord God. For there is none like you, and there is no God besides you, according to all that we have heard with our ears. And who is like your people Israel, the one nation on earth whom God went to redeem to be his people."

David's heart was in the right place. David's motives were in the right place. David totally understood who he was in the presence and sight of God. He knew that he was still the "shepherd boy" chosen among his brothers to be God's man for that time. Three words sum up all of this for us – "Who am I." That was all it took for God to see directly into the heart of his shepherd-king. It was but "a small thing" in God's eyes to elevate this boy into the man he became, who would begin the kingly line of our Lord Jesus Christ. "Therefore, you are great, O Lord God. For there is none like you, and there is no God beside you...." David couldn't build the temple of God, but David prepared with all of his being to get everything ready for its construction.

Today, God does not dwell in a building or temple made of stone, cedar and gold. Today, our God dwells in the very being of His children. We read in I Corinthians 6:19, 20 all about it: "Or do you not know that your body is a temple of the Holy Spirit within you, whom you have from God? You are not your own, for you were bought with a price. So glorify God in your body." In Paul's second letter to this church, he mentions this principle again, "What agreement has the temple of God with idols? For we are the temple of the living God; as God said, 'I will make my dwelling among them and walk among them, and I will be their God, and they shall be my people. Therefore go out from their midst, and be separate from them, says the Lord, and touch no unclean thing; then I will welcome you, and I will be a father to you, and you shall be sons and daughters to me, says the Lord Almighty.'" (II Corinthians 6:16-18)

God has chosen to indwell people instead of places. His purpose is to make His dwelling with us by living inside us in the person of the Holy Spirit. When Jesus was ready to leave our world and go back to heaven, He told His disciples that He would send them "another comforter." In the Greek language, the word "another" can be "another of a different kind" or "another of the same kind." Jesus used the latter word meaning that the Holy Spirit would do for us what Jesus did for the twelve. Jesus Christ takes up residence in our hearts in the Person of the Holy Spirit of God. Therefore, we are to be holy as He is holy. The possession of God's Spirit allows us to make this claim and assures us that we have the authority to do so. Please notice these truths taken from the verses given above: 1) Israel was the only nation on earth God redeemed to be His people. 2) Because we are the living temple of God, we are to bring glory to God through our lives or bodies. 3) Our holy living or separated living will bring us into a special relationship with our heavenly Father. In other words, we are to be holy representatives of our holy, mighty King and Lord! This is nothing less than resplendent son-ship. Solomon's temple was magnificent and awesome. It was a beautiful building almost beyond description. God's house was splendid and breathtaking. As great as it was, our lives as children of God must match its greatness! We are to glorify our God in, through and with our bodies and lives as Christians.

The "who am I" question or comment of David is answered by us with one simple, majestic statement – "I am a child of God!"

In Paul's letter to Titus he emphasizes the need to teach sound doctrine, as well as to "flesh" that doctrine out in our daily lives. Titus 2 teaches us about our earthly relationships. Paul mentions older men and women, as well as those who were young. Each demographic had certain responsibilities and qualities they were to exhibit and be an example of to the other groups. And then he comes to slaves or bondservants. In that day, slavery was in vogue and practiced throughout The Roman Empire. I want to pick up the Scripture narrative in Titus 2:9, 10: "Bondservants are to be submissive to their own masters in everything; they are to be well-pleasing, not argumentative, not pilfering, but **showing all good faith, so that in everything they may adorn the doctrine of God our Savior.**" In *The Amplified Bible*, the words of verse 10 take on a whole different level for us to consider and apply: "Nor to steal by taking things of small value, but to prove themselves truly loyal and entirely reliable and faithful throughout, so that in everything they may be an ornament and do credit to the teaching (which is) from and about God our Savior."[5] I read and re-read those words. I couldn't just pass over them without great pause and reflection. The very thought of being God's ornament in my public and private life brings me into a deep and devoted place, understanding that I am to be as resplendent as the temple, bringing credit to my God and Savior. The word "adorn" that the Holy Spirit uses here means "to arrange, to put in order, to decorate, dress with ornaments, to embellish, to render pleasing or attractive." The *New Living Translation* ends verse 10 in this fashion, "…That they will make the teaching about God our Savior attractive in every way."[6] The *Contemporary English Version* states this truth in these words, "…They must be completely honest and trustworthy. Then everyone will show great respect for what is taught about God our Savior."[7] In the *International Standard Version* we read this, "…

so that in every way they may make the teaching about God our Savior more attractive."⁸ From all of these translations, we arrive at the same conclusion: **Adornment of our God and Savior is a reflection of the mind of the giver, but it also has an influence on the recipient. We are to make that which is adorned, the teaching of our Lord, more conspicuous and better known. Adornment is nothing short than an advertisement of merit and worth. It produces a greater appreciation of the object adorned by the onlookers upon said object!** Adornment is not only a clear and plain message of the value of the object adorned, it provides that object with enhanced beauty, value, merit and worth. Solomon's temple reflected the majesty and glory of the God of heaven. Everything was to reflect His adornment. Now, today, our Savior has chosen to take up residence in our lives and bodies. How can we adorn ourselves any less than Solomon did in the building that represented our glorious God in the temple he constructed?

Resplendent son-ship is all about us paying tribute and homage of our glorious redemption. We are "showing off" to the world exactly what we think and believe about our Lord. In so doing, we make Him more attractive to a world full of ugly sin. We are forcing His beauty upon the wretchedness of a dying world. Francis of Assisi wrote, "It is no use walking anywhere to preach unless our walking is our preaching."⁹ He also wrote, "All the friars should preach by their deeds."¹⁰ When we adorn the teachings, doctrines and person of our loving heavenly Father, we become evangelists unconsciously, because we are silently proclaiming those we rub elbows with that we have received the message of heaven with grand satisfaction. After our acceptance of the Gospel and all that it entails, we must do all that we can to allow His teachings to mold and make us into Christ-like people. The people who resided in Antioch who came to Christ were called "Christians" because of their resemblance of their Lord and Master. The application and practical value of Christian virtue and values will become the focus of our lives. When this happens, when we're transformed by the power of the Holy Spirit and Holy Scriptures, His Words will "spring up in us as living springs" and give us abundant life, visible to all who are watching. The intrinsic value of the life-giving words found in God's teachings will be greatly highlighted in our lives. Down through the ages, revival has come to towns, cities and villages because of great and grand changes in sinners' lives. Men have been redeemed and transformed through the grace and mercy of God. By and through these testimonies, many others have seen God's Word adorned in these altered lives. In our passage found in Titus 2, Paul spoke of these slaves "adorning the doctrine of God our Savior." The very fact that their acceptance of God's grace would be a tribute to its majestic dignity, proving God's ability to transform any person. Their loyalty to this teaching would be a clear presentation of its total merit and value to their unbelieving and God-hating world. This is the power of God's Gospel – the complete transformation of a member of the lowest of the low classes, to the pinnacle of adorning elements relating to the glorious God of heaven! The doctrines or teachings of God are those principles and promises which He teaches and which He has revealed for our instruction in this life. It is His revelation of Himself. He is the author, giver and focus of it all. He is the purpose and end to all that is. His Word through revelation is given to us that we may know Him, love Him, serve Him and eventually live with Him. The doctrines, teachings and instructions come from One Who is infinitely holy, infinitely true and infinitely great; and yet it is capable of being adorned by those to whom it is given. Psalm 36:9 gives us this instruction, "For with you is the fountain of life; in your light do we see light." Then we read in Psalm 56:13 these words, "For you have delivered my soul from death, yes, my feet from falling, that I may walk before God in the light of life." We leave our ways of darkness and death as rebellious people living far away from a loving and holy God, to walk in His ways of light and life as redeemed people attached to a loving and holy God! Therefore, God's Word of instruction "is a lamp to my feet and a light to my path." (Psalm 119:105)

The number of slaves during this time in world history was huge. It stands to reason according to the percentages that many of the first converts to Christ and Christianity belonged to this lower class of citizens. The Gospel spread rapidly and freely among the slave population. The hope and freedom of the Good News of the Gospel gave them exactly what they needed as they lived out their meager and miserable existence. Socially they had no rights beyond what their master gave them. Chrysostom's comments on Titus 2 include the following: "They have no motive for trying to be good, and very little opportunity of learning what is right. Everyone, slaves included, admits that as a race they are passionate, intractable, and indisposed to virtue, not because God has made them so, but from bad education and the neglect of their master. The master cares nothing about their slaves' morals, except so far as their own vices are likely to interfere with their masters' pleasures or interests. Hence the slaves, having no one to care for them, naturally sink into an abyss of wickedness. Their chief aim is to avoid, not the crime, but being found out."[11]

The Gospel of Christ is now brought to meet the complete needs of everyone who is willing to accept its truth. Surely the aristocracy of the Roman Empire would embrace its doctrines. Surely the chief leaders around the then-known world would accept its teachings. Their acceptance would certainly raise the "value" and "merit" of this new- fangled religious truth, wouldn't it? One would certainly think so. But God's ways and thoughts are not the way we think things should go. After all, wouldn't we have had the Savior and King of the world be born in a palace? Not God! He chose a stable in an obscure village to an obscure couple living in an obscure town! This was one of those times that our God was demonstrating His value of "so loving the world." There must be something incredible about a "religion," or relationship as Christianity is, which, is able to raise the spiritual condition of slaves, to become obedient, gentle, honest, sober and virtuous men and women. Again, we read words from Chrysostom on this topic, "When it was seen that Christianity, by giving a settled principle of sufficient power to counterbalance the pleasures of sin, was able to impose a restraint upon a class so self-willed, and render them singularly well-behaved, then their masters, however unreasonable they might be, were likely to form a high opinion of their doctrines which accomplished this change of life....The way in which these slaves are to endeavor to adorn the doctrine of God is by cultivating precisely those virtues which contribute most to their masters' comfort and interest – submissiveness, gentleness, meekness, honesty, truthfulness, and a faithful discharge of all duties. What an amazing testimony to our world of this kind would be to the power and beauty of the Gospel; and a testimony all the more powerful in the eyes of those masters who became conscious that these despised Christian slaves were living better lives than their owners!"[12]

Think about these possible situations: the passionate master who found his slave gentle and submissive; the ferocious and angry master who had a meek and respectful slave; the corrupt master who cheated his clients out of their money, never noticed that his slave stole or told lies; the immoral master, who observed his slave as never being lewd or immodest; all these types of masters and others would at the very least take note of these drastic changes in the behavior of their slaves, then garner great respect upon their slaves for such outstanding character of life. But it went much further than just respect. Many of these owners of people came to a saving knowledge of Christ because of their slaves' honest and holy living! This new religious experience started out as a smoldering fire, but soon reached blazing proportions. The "adorning of the doctrine of God" had much to do with this phenomenal growth of Christianity in the first century. The truth that the Gospel reaches all classes of people, then and now, is beyond dispute. Every man, woman and child, rich or poor, known or unknown to many, white or black, old or young, English speaking or non-English speaking – all have the capability of receiving God's offer of salvation through faith. Then, all those who receive God's "free gift" of salvation are in turn becoming resplendent in their adorning of the doctrines and teachings of the God of heaven! One of the greatest aspects of the Lord's ministry on earth is this simple truth found in Mark 12:37, "…And the common people heard him gladly." The slave was the most common person of Christ's day.

Now comes the hard part. The Lord never tells us what to do without telling us how to do it. Once again, Titus 2:10 tells us the "what to do" – "…so that in everything they may adorn the doctrine of God our Savior." OK, so what? Now what? How do we do accomplish this amazing adornment aspect of our Christian experience?

- **Truth applied brings about our transformation into Christlikeness** – Titus 1:1 – "Paul, a servant of God and an apostle of Jesus Christ for the sake of the faith of God's elect and their knowledge of the truth, which accords with godliness." As we grow in our knowledge regarding the truths of God, we begin to behave like the One we study. I like to put it this way – **Love** the Lord because of our salvation – **Learn** about the Lord which brings about our sanctification – **Live** for the Lord by serving Him in our daily lives. Truth does us no good if we don't apply it to our lives. Belief in God's Truth with our hearts is the first step in this process of adorning His Truth. Then, that Truth must be applied to our wills so that we'll have the desire to be transformed by God's Truth. When that is done, we will then begin to behave in our daily lives according to God's Truth, thus "adorning the doctrine of God our Savior."

- **Truth adhered to brings about our triumph into Consistency** – Titus 1:9 – "He must hold firm to the trustworthy word as taught, so that he may be able to give instruction in sound doctrine and also to rebuke those who contradict it." Paul follows this thought with the truth found in verses 13, 14 "…therefore rebuke them sharply, that they may be sound in the faith, not devoting themselves to Jewish myths and the commands of people who turn away from the truth." We humans have a great tendency to forget things quickly. Christians are no exceptions. The great truths of God are eternal and are meant to be adhered to forever. However, this life often brings attacks our way from every direction, and before we know what happened, we've left the foundations upon which we once leaned. Holding firm to the doctrines and teachings of God our Savior is an essential element to the Christian remaining consistent and faithful. Perhaps one of the greatest verses on this principle is found in I Corinthians 15:58, "Therefore, my beloved brothers, be steadfast, immovable, always abounding in the work of the Lord, knowing that in the Lord your labor is not in vain." Another verse that fits this truth perfectly is Galatians 6:9, "And let us not grow weary of doing good, for in due season we will reap, if we do not give up." One of the great statesmen of the last generation was Winston Churchill. Several times throughout England's fight for survival against Hitler, Churchill had to will the people of England to keep fighting. He gave numerous inspirational speeches during WW II to get and maintain a level of optimism and hope. It was an extremely difficult task that often went unnoticed. As London was being bombarded night after night, that will to fight and that hope of victory often waned. However, events leading up to one of his greatest speeches gave the hint of optimism concerning the outcome of the war. The biggest thing was the United States began supplying vast amounts of war material to the United Kingdom. This was known as the Lend-Lease Act, which was begun in March of 1941. Also, since Nazi Germany had invaded Yugoslavia and Greece earlier in the year and invaded the Soviet Union in June of '41, it appeared that Britain was no longer the target for the main efforts of The Third Reich. It was now October 29, 1941. Churchill visited Harrow School to hear the traditional songs he had sung there as a school-boy, as well as to speak to the students. This became one of his most quoted speeches, due to many historical inaccuracies. The length of the speech was only 4 minutes and 12 seconds. The most famous lines from this speech came during his closing remarks; "Never give in. Never give in. Never, never, never – in nothing, great or small, large or petty – never give in, except to convictions of honour and good sense. Never yield to force. Never yield to the apparently overwhelming might of the enemy...Britain, other nations thought, had drawn a sponge across her slate. But instead our country stood in the gap. There was no flinching and no thought of giving in; and by what seemed almost a miracle to those outside these islands, though we ourselves never doubted it, we now find ourselves in a position where I say that we can be sure that we have only to persevere to conquer....Do not let us speak of darker days: let us speak rather of sterner days. These are not dark days; these are great days – the greatest days our country has ever lived; and we must all thank God that we have been allowed, each of us according to our stations, to play a part in making these days memorable in the history of our race."[13] An extraordinary speech, delivered by an extraordinary man, during extraordinary times. Our focus of strength must remain on "holding firm to the trustworthy word" that was delivered to us and to never give in! As we **retain** our firm hold on the teachings of our God, we then must **repeat** those teachings to others. Titus 2:1 states an obvious and great lesson for us all, "But as for you, teach what accords with sound doctrine." Then the rest of the chapter states this theme over and over: "Older men are to be…sound in faith" – v. 2 – "Older women…are to teach what is good" – v. 3 – "so train the young women…that the word of God may not be reviled" – v. 4, 5 – "Show yourself in all respects to be a model of good works, and in your teaching show integrity, dignity, and sound speech that cannot be condemned, so that an opponent may be put to shame, having nothing evil to say about us." (vv. 8, 9) Adhering to truth consistently is vital to us becoming resplendent in our son-ship. Here it is spelled out for us: **1. Retain the Lord's Teachings – Treasure Them Yourself – Hold Firm – Grasp Them Tightly 2. Repeat the Lord's Teachings – Teach Them to Others – Herald Them Faithfully – Give Them Away Tenaciously.** Read how Paul gave Timothy these truths: "You then, my child, be strengthened by the grace that is in Christ Jesus, and what you have heard from me in the presence of many witnesses entrust to faithful men who will be able to teach others also." ((II Timothy 2:1, 2) Retain God's Word Yourself – Repeat God's Word to Others.

- **Truth's assignment brings about our training into Consecration** – "For the grace of God has appeared, bringing salvation for all people, training us to renounce ungodliness and worldly passions, and to live self-controlled, upright, and godly lives in the present age, waiting for our blessed hope, the appearing of the glory of our great God and Savior Jesus Christ, who gave himself for us to redeem us from all lawlessness and to purify for himself a people for his own possession who are zealous for good works." (Titus 2:11-14) The "training" we must experience is a process that all Christians must travel through in order to obtain a godly witness. The Lord uses everything that comes our way to conform us to the image of His Son. We learn this from Romans 8:28 and 29. For those who "are the called according to his purpose," and "those who love him," will see that all elements of life work together for our good and His glory. As we travel through this holy process, we find ourselves "waiting for our blessed hope." This word "waiting" means "eagerness." While we are training toward the life God intends us to live, we wait. This is nothing less than setting our minds and hearts on His coming, which encourages us to live by God's grace, enabling us to be edified in God's Word, enlightening us to walk in God's ways in this present age! Once again, we see God's pattern of **learning God's Word in order to love God's Word so that we can live in God's Ways.**

The final conclusion of adorning the doctrine and teachings of our God is found in Titus 3:8, "The saying is trustworthy, and I want you to insist on these things, so that those who have believed in God may be careful to devote themselves to good works." Paul repeats this truth in v. 14, "And let our people learn to devote themselves to good works, so as to help cases of urgent need, and not be unfruitful." These were not preferences, but vital and core principles of the first century church. The purpose of holding firm to these foundations was to cause these early believers to make a conscious and purposeful commitment to do good deeds for others. These deeds or works would become profitable or beneficial to those served.

As God's truths are believed upon in our heart, that seed of God's truth will begin to produce fruit in our heart as we begin to put those truths into daily practice. Salvation comes to them by God's grace through their faith, then God begins His work of sanctification. As His salvation works its way to the outside, we begin to take on the characteristics of our Holy Father. We begin to adorn those teachings of our Lord when we make them living graces like ornaments on a Christmas tree. This exemplary life of living godly soon becomes the exchanged life of serving others, resulting in the excellent life of being a resplendent son of God! The splendor of Solomon's temple will have nothing on us, for we are the living temple of the God of creation, fully and completely displaying His majesty, splendor and holiness, bringing the light of heaven and Jesus Christ to a dark and dying world! Oswald Chambers said, "The golden rule for understanding in spiritual matters is not intellect, but obedience."[14] God grant to us all the obedience it takes to realize these truths in our very lives.

8

RESILIENT & SUPPLE

"So to keep me from becoming conceited because of the surpassing greatness of the revelations; a thorn was given me in the flesh, a messenger of Satan to harass me, to keep me from becoming conceited. Three times I pleaded with the Lord about this, that it should leave me. But he said, 'My grace is sufficient for you, for my power is made perfect in weakness.' Therefore, I will boast all the more gladly of my weaknesses, so that the power of Christ may rest upon me. For the sake of Christ, then, I am content with weaknesses, insults, hardships, persecutions, and calamities. <u>For when I am weak, then I am strong</u>." II Corinthians 12:7-10

"Therefore, let anyone who thinks that he stands take heed lest he fall. No temptation has overtaken you that is not common to man. God is faithful, and he will not let you be tempted beyond your ability, but with the temptation he will also provide the way of escape, that you may be able to endure it." I Corinthians 10:13

*T*elevision footage often displays palm trees valiantly standing up to the full wrath of hurricane force winds. When the crazy reporters brave the fierce driving rains and drastic winds to give us the blow by blow coverage of a hurricane making landfall, it's always intense. The constant winds and huge waves of water flooding all the coastline makes for dramatic TV. Houses and businesses are broken to pieces; regular trees are thrown about like matchsticks; cars, buses and trucks are tossed like toys to rest in weird and wacky places. However, the palm trees seem to be able to withstand the one-two punch of another horrible hurricane. The palm leaves or fronds are bending with the beating wind, but the trunk of the palm remains upright and tall. Their habitation or location along the beach seems properly suited and placed for such an event as a hurricane.

Palm trees are an example of Masterful engineering. The Creator has provided this group of vegetation with the precise makeup to withstand such tortuous winds. In studying about the palm, I've learned the reasons why palm trees mostly survive the punishing conditions of hurricanes, cyclones and even tsunamis.

First, most palm trees have numerous, short roots spread across the upper levels of the soil, which secures a large amount of soil around the base of the palm and its root ball. To begin, the soil where the palm is planted needs to be mostly dry. As it's being pounded with water via rain or even flooding, this great amount of moisture works to create a super large, heavy anchor. Since palm trees have a huge base of roots, as opposed to having just a few very strong roots, this wider network creates a bottom-heavy base that anchors the tree in place. Their roots radiate in all directions out from the center of the tree. They aren't very deep, but there are so many of them that anchors the palm securely in its place. Their roots are thin, but again, the palm tree root system is so extensive that they create a firm and solid foundation that withstands the majority of major storms that will batter them during their lifetime.

Second, the trunk of a regular or normal tree such as a pine, birch or oak grows in a radial pattern; the annual rings effectively make a series of hollow cylinders inside each other. However, the stem, or trunk, of a palm tree is made up of many small bundles of woody material, which is like bundles of wires inside a telephone cable. A plant ecologist, Dan Metcalfe, stated the following "The cylinder approach provides great strength in which to support weight (compressive strength) which means that an oak tree's trunk can support a huge weight of branches, but limited flexibility compared to the bundle approach, which allows the palm stem to bend over to extreme angles, even 40 or 50 degrees without snapping." Palm trees can snap under continuous, extreme conditions, but they have been proven much tougher in this regard than other trees. The material inside a palm tree is thoroughly flexible and bendable, permitting it to flex back and forth according to the direction of the wind.

Finally, while most trees rely on their beautiful canopy of branches, twigs and leaves to spread out and grab as much sunlight as possible, the canopy can also grab a great amount of wind and water. In a bad storm, the canopy can act as a sail and pull the entire tree over, up from its roots. The branches of regular trees can and do snap while receiving much less wind than a hurricane. Regular thunderstorms and winter ice storms can bring many trees down to size, inflicting major damage on many types of vegetation. Meanwhile, think of palm trees. They don't have wide-spreading branches or a major leaf system, but rather huge leaves with a central, flexible spine. These leaves or fronds are just like enormous feathers, resulting in much less mass to catch the wind, which would bring them down. So, as the wind blows it further sideways, the effective area that the wind can exert upon it becomes much less because it's bending with the wind and not against it. Also, because of the taper of the palm tree, the force on the top is almost always less than in the middle or even at the base of the palm. In nice weather the fronds spread out and make a fine canopy; but in instances of strong wind and water, what do the fronds do? They fold up or are discarded on purpose, making it less top heavy to catch the brunt of a storm! With less resistance against the endangering elements, they are much more likely to make it through intact. Of course, some leaves may suffer, and palm debris is part and parcel of storm clean up, but they are much quicker to grow back on the palm than a regular leaf or branch is to grow back on a pine or oak.

When a storm comes ashore, everything in its path is at its mercy. The storm cares not who or what it will ultimately and eventually affect. This is also true with people. The storm is no respecter of persons, whether rich or poor, young or old, man or woman. The storm will create chaos of some manner or fashion, with the possibility of catastrophic results. The storm will last for some time but will also be gone before one knows it. The storm will cause pain and panic, trials and troubles, but will either produce guarded fear or greatness of faith. There are three dynamics that help the palm tree survive catastrophic storms: its foundation or root system; the structure or make-up of its trunk or stem: and its configuration of fronds or leaves, minus many branches. As Christians, we have our great God and King, made up of three persons: God the Father, Jesus Christ the Son, and The Holy Spirit. Each Person of the Trinity plays an important part regarding our trials that we'll experience on planet earth. The first of these is the approval of our Father's will as it pertains to our life's storms. We read about this approval in Job 1 and 2. Then, we have the advocacy of our Lord Jesus Christ when we face trials of various kinds. Finally, the assurance that we have comfort from the indwelling Holy Spirit Who fills us with His love, grace and presence. At the end of Christ's Sermon on the Mount, we read His Words as they relate to our life's storms and subsequent choice to obey His Word or not: "Everyone then who hears these words of mine and does them will be like a wise man who built his house on the rock. And the rain fell, and the floods came, and the winds blew and beat on that house, but it did not fall, because it had been founded on the rock. And everyone who hears these words of mine and does not do them will be like a foolish man who built his house on the sand. And the rain fell, and the floods came, and the winds blew and beat against that house, and it fell, and great was the fall of it." (Matthew 7:24-27) The storm was the same – "the rain fell, and the floods came, the winds blew and beat on that house" – but the outcomes were totally different. The house built on the rock stood – the house built on sand experienced a great destruction. What were the differences? The house on the rock had a solid foundation while the sandcastle had an extremely weak one. The house on the rock is that house (or person) who obeys the Word of God; however, the house (or person) who refuses to obey God's Word will experience a horrific end. Storms come to every single person with no exceptions. Christians and non-Christians alike will go through times of trials and troubles, struggles and storms, pain and problems.

I love reading or hearing awesome quotes on any topic. So many great men and women of God have gone through life-changing and traumatic experiences, only to come out on the other side of those times with greater faith in the Lord, greater love for the Lord, and greater wisdom to use for God. I trust the Lord will use any one of these to assist you through your present or coming storm:

"No matter what storm you face, you need to know that God loves you. He has not abandoned you."[1] Franklin Graham "Trials should not surprise us, or cause us to doubt God's faithfulness. Rather, we should actually be glad for them. God sends trials to strengthen our trust in him so that our faith will not fail. Our trials keep us trusting; they burn

away our self-confidence and drive us to our Savior."[2]
Edmund Clowney

"If we see only the problems, we will be defeated; but if we see the possibilities in the problems, we can have victory."[3]
Warren Wiersbe

"Do not fear the conflict, and do not flee from it; where there is no struggle, there is no virtue."[4] John of Kronstadt

"By trials God is shaping us for higher things."[5]
Jeremy Taylor

"Don't let your trials blow you down; let them lift you up."[6]
Woodrow Kroll

"When we pray for the Spirit's help…we will simply fall down at the Lord's feet in our weakness. There we will find the victory and power that comes from His love."[7]
Andrew Murray

"Give up the struggle and the fight; relax in the omnipotence of the Lord Jesus; look up into His lovely face and as you behold Him, He will transform you into His likeness. You do the beholding – He does the transforming. There is no short-cut to holiness."[8] Alan Redpath

"Trials teach us what we are; they dig up the soil, and let us see what we are made of."[9] Charles Spurgeon

"Pain is inevitable. Suffering is optional. Say you're running and you think, 'Man, this hurts, I can't take it anymore. The 'hurt' part is an unavoidable reality, but whether

or not you can stand anymore is up to the runner himself"[10]
Haruki Murakami

"Adversity introduces a man to himself." Unknown

"The difficulties of life are intended to make us better, not bitter." Unknown

"Adversity is a fact of life. It can't be controlled. What we can control is how we react to it." Anonymous

"The greater difficulty, the more glory in surmounting it. Skillful pilots gain their reputation from storms and tempests."[11] **Epicurus**

I'm sure you've heard it said, "We are either experiencing a time of trial, have just left one, or there's one waiting around the next corner." Life's storms are not fun. Yet, we learn valuable life lessons through the storms of life that we would have never learned if we hadn't gone through the tempest. Christ came to provide salvation for our eternal soul through His sacrificial death on the cross. Christ also came to produce sanctification in our earthly bodies through His Scriptural direction and counsel. We would never have stood a chance without either of these purposes. Salvation is a "free gift" through our faith in His grace that happens in a moment of time. Sanctification is fruitful gain through our fellowship with His godliness that transpires over our lifetime. We'll never fully come to complete maturity or perfection until we see our Savior face-to-face. Our God loves us just the way we are, but He loves us too much to leave us just the way we are. In order to accomplish the working out of His salvation in and through our lives, change must take place. To accomplish this purpose and make that change to take place, He will allow circumstances that are beyond our control to enter our lives in order to transform us from who we are at the present to better resemble who He has always been. He will also take the circumstances that we did control and make them work out for the same purpose as those we cannot control.

There are many biblical illustrations that could be brought to light that would help us see the powerful hand of our God. The first story tells us all about Jesus calming a raging storm. We read this story in Luke 8:22-25, **"One day he got into a boat with his disciples, and he said to them, 'Let us go across to the other side of the lake.' So they set out, and as they sailed he fell asleep. And a windstorm came down on the lake, and they were filling with water and were in danger. And they went and woke him, saying, 'Master, Master, we are perishing!' And he awoke and rebuked the wind and the raging waves, and they ceased, and there was a calm. He said to them, 'Where is your faith?' And they were afraid, and they marveled, saying to one another, 'Who then is this, that he commands even winds and water, and they obey him?'"**

"One day he got into a boat with his disciples." One day, just like any other day, or so they thought. How many "one days" have we all had? Our morning routine was the same as any other day. We got up, got dressed, got some coffee or juice, and went off to work. Our wife or husband or kids all did their morning thing, also. A few hours into your day you receive a phone call. This is one of those phone calls that all of us have always feared might come. Whatever the emergency, put yourself back at that place and time you received that call. The violent storm has begun. A tempest of circumstance that you didn't see coming and even now can't believe or accept that it did is upon you. Nonetheless, the "one day" has become today. Four of these men getting into the boat with Jesus were expert and experienced fishermen. They knew what could happen because it happened to them at other times. They just didn't expect it to happen to them, not then, with Jesus being RIGHT THERE WITH THEM! How could anything go wrong?

But notice what He said to them, "Let us go to the other side of the lake." His direction or command to everyone who was with him was simple: get in; we're going to the other side of the lake. Case closed, end of story. He didn't tell them what was going to happen while they on their way, though, did He? He didn't give orders and say, "Now, there's going to come a brutal storm. I want you, Peter, to grab a firm hold on the helm. John, you man the sails. James, here's a bucket to bail water. Andrew, make sure you keep a steady eye on where we're going." Nope. Nothing. He just said, "Get in; we're going to the other side."

The Lord, in His love, spares us all the details from the time we get into the boat with Him at salvation, until we reach the other side of the lake. If He told us what's going to transpire in our lives between those two events, we'd all live our lives in fear and dread, knowing that on that "one day" this or that was going to come down on us, beating against our very souls! Did Jesus know what He was getting them into? He sure did. He knows all things and so He fully knew what they were going to experience while rowing across The Sea of Galilee. Although, as I said, four of them were experienced fishermen, and they had been on that body of water so many times before that they couldn't tell you that number. So they knew the weather conditions on that body of water and they probably didn't anticipate that particular storm. If they had seen ominous weather conditions, they more than likely would've said to Jesus, "I don't think we should be going out there right now because it look as though a storm is brewing." The Sea of Galilee is about 13 miles long and 7 miles wide at its widest point. It lies in a low spot in that area that is almost 700 feet below sea level. On the eastern side of the sea, there are mountains that reach almost 2,000 feet. When the right conditions meet, the winds will swirl at great speeds down from those mountains, creating an instant and quick storm that will be on you in a flash. It was one of those greatly feared and unexpected storms that trounced on them that day. I say "unexpected" storm. It was unexpected to the disciples, but not Jesus. He was tired from the day's events of ministry, so he fell asleep. His humanity was on full display after a busy day of service. However, His Deity would shine through as it had at no other time up to this point. But now, He was exhausted from all the activity of the day. The violence of the storm was immediately felt as the Scripture tells us that "they were filling with water and were in danger." Everyone knows that the water is supposed to stay out of the boat and remain in the lake or river or ocean. But Luke tells us that they really feared for their lives when he penned the words, "and were in danger." But were they really? Danger to the children of God is an opportunity for God to display His delight in delivering us from that danger. Jesus was fast asleep, seemingly unaware of all that was taking place. But we must remember, even though those seasoned fishermen feared for their lives, the Lord and His sovereignty led them right into it!

The Word of God is clear when speaking of God's matchless love and His marvelous sovereignty. We cannot obtain comfort in life's storms by turning away from God's perfect sovereign will for us. I've often explained that our loving, heavenly Father has His eye on His Son. He looks at Him, then at us. His desire is for us to "be conformed to the image of His Son." (Romans 8:29) He will then work on us to mold and make us into that awesome and amazing image of Jesus Christ. It's the story of Jeremiah when the Lord asked him to learn a lesson from the potter. Jeremiah 18 gives us the dialogue between the Lord and Jeremiah. We're told that the clay "was spoiled in the potter's hand, and he reworked it into another vessel, as it seemed good to the potter." The "potter" is the Lord and we're the "clay." As it seems good to the Father or potter to make us, so be it. The clay's responsibility is to sit on the potter's wheel and allow him to do his work. So too is our responsibility. The forming may hurt, and we may have to become a different shape, but we're still loved by the potter and are still in His hands! Listen to these words found in Isaiah 45:8-11, "I am the Lord, and there is no other, besides me there is no God; I equip you, though you do not know me, that people may know, from the rising of the sun and from the west, that there is none besides me; I am the Lord, and there is no other. I form light and create darkness, I make well-being and create calamity, I am the Lord, who does all these things." All of us, every one of us, will discover comfort during a storm only if we understand and affirm God's absolute sovereignty overall, and accept this storm as coming from His awesome love! An essential element we all must have during any storm is an anchor. Hebrews 6:13-20 gives us these assurances, "For when God made a promise to Abraham, since he had no one greater by whom to swear, he swore by himself, saying, 'Surely I will bless you and multiply you.' And thus Abraham, having patiently waited, obtained the promise. For people swear by something greater than themselves, and in all their disputes an oath if final for confirmation. So when God desired to show more convincingly to the heirs of the promise the unchangeable character on his purpose, **he guaranteed it with an oath, so that by two unchangeable things, in which it is impossible for God to lie, we who have fled for refuge might have strong encouragement to hold fast to the hope set before us. We have this as a sure and steadfast anchor of the soul, a hope that enters into the inner place behind the curtain, where Jesus has gone as a forerunner on our behalf....**" God called Abraham to pick up his belongings and family and move far, far away. The only person to guarantee Abraham that all was going to come to pass was God Himself. Abraham believed God, and the Lord gave him His righteousness. He obtained or received the promise from God. Now the Lord wanted to show the heirs a more convincing proof of His Lordship and Being. God stakes His reputation on two unchangeable truths: the impossibility of

God telling a lie and the shelter we have in the Lord when fleeing to Him as our refuge. We have the authority of taking away from this "strong encouragement" of holding fast "to the hope set before us," taking these truths as "a sure and steadfast anchor of the soul," knowing that Jesus entered the Holy of Holies on our behalf, and is safely on the other side of the lake! Jesus Christ is our Anchor. He made it safely to the other side. One day, He's coming back for us to safely take us to where He is.

Storms pounce upon us suddenly and oftentimes without any warning. How often have you come upon a tragic accident on your way to work, or heard about one on the radio? That person or those people went about their normal, morning routine. They kissed a loved one goodbye, got in their car, stopped by their favorite coffee shop, only to meet a horrible fate. Life's storms are often like that. The disciples climbed aboard thinking all was great for a smooth sail across the lake. It wasn't meant to be. Right now, everything in our lives is nothing but blue skies and smooth water. In a matter of hours or even minutes, without warning, a quick, moving storm creates havoc on us and everyone residing within our circle of family and friends. Mark's account of this story in 4:36 provides us with some additional, interesting facts: "And leaving the crowd, they took him with them in the boat, just as he was. And other boats were with him." The huge crowd that came under His ministry in that day was left standing on shore. His work was done with them on that day. The disciples "took him" with them in the boat, "just as he was." Jesus gave the command, "Let's go across to the other side." The disciples "took him with them into the boat." Their way of getting across the Sea of Galilee was by boat. Christ's way may have been different than their way, but He got in the boat with them. Then they took Him "just as he was." No prep time needed. No extra gear was necessary to stow away. They had Christ and that was all they thought they needed. All we ever need in life is Jesus. Salvation consists of Jesus plus nothing, Jesus minus nothing. Jesus alone is all we'll ever need in our lives, no matter what storm may come our way. However, there were other people who got into boats to travel across the lake with Christ. When storms batter our tiny boats, the other boats in our lives will experience the storm, as well. But did you notice this vital truth? The verse says, "And other boats were with him." Jesus gave the command. The disciples took Jesus into their boat to be with them, just as He was with no additional props. The "other boats" decided to go – "with him!" They weren't following a group of men who were following a famous rabbi or teacher. This storm came down upon them all! Jesus was in only one boat – physically – but He was in all the other boats, also. This tells me that storms may come quickly and without any heads up, but also that storms come to everyone. The disciples were with Christ. The disciples were being obedient to Christ by setting out to get to the other side. The simple fact is that Christians, obedient Christians, aren't exempt from the storms of life. Just because you're in Jesus' boat doesn't mean that it's going to be a smooth trip across to the other side.

I've found in my life that the most severe times of testing or storms have come right after I have taken a fresh step of obedience. My ministry has been marked by serving people in churches that experience a variety of major storms. Without going into a great amount of detail, suffice it to say that the storms experienced weren't pleasant for anyone. At one church in which I was privileged to serve, the pastor asked me to lead our Christian school. I was only 25. I told him that I would do my best and get some additional schooling for the task ahead. We faced many storms during our ministry days at that church and school. Some were personal storms, while many others took place within the ministry itself. On one occasion, we were coming down to the start of school and our staff wasn't filled. We needed a fourth- grade teacher. The entire staff was in prayer as we sought the Lord's choice for that class. One day, as I was spending time with the Lord in my office, my secretary tapped on the door. When I opened the door, she was standing there with tears in her eyes. She then simply said, "A teacher just walked into the office who is moving from Florida." I replied, "She teaches fourth grade, doesn't she?" "Yes." We reached the other side of the lake. At the beginning of another year, we were in our second day of orientation and preparation for that school year. One of our first-grade teachers, who was under contract, told me that her dad, a superintendent of a local school district, got her a job. I told her that I was glad for her and didn't want to keep her in our school if she desired to be elsewhere. The winds began to blow. Here we were just a few days from the first day of school and I had to find another teacher. After praying over the matter, the Lord laid a name on my heart. I called this person who had decided not to teach that year so she could assist her daughter who was in her last year of college obtaining a teaching degree. When I called her and asked if she thought of anyone, she said, "Let me tell you what I'm doing right now. I'm laying out bulletin board materials so my daughter can use them in class. I got so excited doing it that I just thought how fun it would be to teach first grade. I guess my recommendation would be me." Again, we reached the other side of the lake! The Lord mightily blessed our time in that ministry as we saw spiritual growth within our student body and numerical growth as the Lord brought us kids and families to minister to via the tool of a Christian school. There are many stories of God's hand of protection and prosperity during my two terms of ministry at that church. We then went to a church that eventually experienced the falling away of their pastor. It's a sad and great difficulty to over-come to be sure. But, despite that storm, God blessed us with many people coming to know Him. The Lord gave us wisdom to navigate that ministry through those tempestuous waters, but we reached the other side of the lake. In another ministry, the church experienced two major church splits. This was after a six-year period of great growth spiritually, numerically and financially. After the second split, the Lord gave us understanding of holding onto the helm to navigate strategically that church through the boisterous winds and we reached the other side of the lake. On that first Sunday, several people came up to me essentially saying all the same thing, "It seems like a dark, black cloud has been lifted off our church." And it did! I preached a simple sermon on the Great Commandment. My points were just two: 1. Love God Supremely 2. Love Others Sacrificially. A few months after this storm, the national storm of 9-1-1 happened. We decided to hold a prayer and memorial service for our community on that Thursday. The auditorium was filled with people from all walks of life. This often occurs after a national emergency and tragedy. Many people came to a saving knowledge of Christ as Savior that day, with many of them becoming faithful members! That same year, we were planning our second missions' trip to Bolivia. The funds hadn't come in like the first time we had gone a few years earlier. I preached on Memorial Day weekend on our great county. A lady, unknown to me, was in the audience that morning. I was getting very close to canceling our trip because of a lack of funds. A few days later, while I was praying in my office about this very issue, telling the Lord that unless I heard from Him that day, I was going to cancel the trip, one of our secretaries knocked on my door. I told her that I was with someone. Anyway, she opened the door, looked around my office and saw no one with me. She informed me that there was a lady on the phone from Chicago. I asked her to take a message and that I would call her back after I had finished my conversation with the Lord. I did. The woman's name was Nicole. She told me she had been visiting a cousin in the area over the weekend and heard me preach, saying how encouraged she was by my message. She told me that she and her husband wanted to help us get to Bolivia. They set aside part of his income to help ministries as the Lord lays them on their hearts. I said that would be awesome. But the funny thing was that the more she talked, the more I realized who her husband was. I then asked the 64-million-dollar question, "Wait a minute. Is your name Nicole Graffanino?" She said, "Yes." "Is your husband Tony Graffanino?" I asked. "Yes," she replied. Tony Graffanino was playing for the Chicago White Sox at that time. During his playing days with the Atlanta Braves, first base coach, Glen Hubbard, led Tony to Christ. Nicole told me that they wanted to give us some money for our trip. She asked me how much. I told Nicole that I wanted them to pray about it and send what the Lord laid on their heart. They sent $3,000. That was the exact amount we needed to get back to the mission field! Later in the conversation, we set up a time for Tony to come and give his testimony at church. And once again, we reached the other side of the lake!

Time and space will not allow me to share all the stories of how God helped us through the storm in enabling us to reach the other side of the lake. At the same time, the last thing the disciples thought Jesus was going to do was to go to sleep! But He did! Mark 4:38 tells us that He was fast asleep on a cushion in the back of the boat. For the longest time prayer was being made for that fourth-grade teacher. He didn't answer and didn't answer. I thought He was asleep because He didn't answer our prayers – when we thought He should've answered them. I can't tell you how many times the storms that have come my way that have seemingly gone unnoticed by my God and Savior. I'm confident you've experienced the exact feeling. The storm comes down on us suddenly and the Lord seems as though He has no idea what's going on, completely oblivious to our present woes. We shout to the heavens, "Where in the world are you, Lord? Don't you care that we're dying here? We're in great danger – NOW!" However, He's always there, with us by our side as we travel through the storms of life. But He often waits until we are at the end of our rope, then He meets our earnest needs. We read in Hebrews 13:5 "I will never leave you, nor will I ever forsake you." In the original Greek language, we read this verse as, "I will never, never, never leave you, nor will

I ever, ever forsake you." In our English language, double negatives cancel each other, but in the Greek language, double negatives add depth and meaning as the words layers itself upon each word of emphasis.

Allow me to remind you of the story of the three Hebrew children – Shadrach, Meshach, and Abed-nego. These Hebrew children also obeyed the Lord as they didn't bow down to the image of Nebuchadnezzar. For their faith, they were thrown into a burning, fiery furnace, stoked seven times hotter than any other time before. The guards who threw them into the fire were instantly died due to the fierce heat. But soon, right after they were tossed inside this blast furnace, someone said to the king, "Look! I see four men loosed and walking around in the midst of the fire without harm, and the appearance of the fourth is like a son of the gods!" That was Jesus Christ with those three servants. As Jesus was in the boat with everyone on the water that day, so Jesus stood with these guys in the flames. When they came out of the furnace, their clothes didn't even smell like smoke. The only thing that burned were the ropes tied around their wrists. Whatever boisterous winds we may be facing, or fiery furnaces in which we may find ourselves, it may not at first appear that the Lord is with us; but rest assured, He is!

In Mark's account of this story, Jesus said, "Peace! Be still." Luke tells us that He "rebuked the wind and the raging waves." Through their accounts, this command by the Creator resulted in an instant calm. Mark says, "There was a great calm." The natural elements of our world are under the authority of the real Master of the universe – Jesus Christ. According to John 1, everything that was created was done so by Jesus Christ. If He could speak the universe into existence in six days, then this miracle wasn't anything at all. He spoke – He rebuked – and the storm stopped immediately. The Lord is quick to respond to our urgent needs during our storms. When my dad went to heaven in 1987, I had one of my church members tell me that she was sorry that the Lord didn't heal my dad. I knew what she was saying, but then I recall telling her that the Lord answered our prayers and healed him perfectly. The raging waves and tempestuous winds battered my dad for nearly ten years as he battled the storm of cancer. The Lord called his name one day and said, "Peace, be still. I rebuke you, cancer," and He healed him completely by taking him to live with Himself, and my dad reached the other side of the lake. I fully realize that many of you have had dear ones in your life leave in this fashion. Age isn't a factor here. Our beloved family members leave us at 10, 29, 52, or 94. The storm of death will eventually come to every family member should the Lord tarry His coming. But be assured that God's perfect plan is being fulfilled in their lives, as well as every family member who is left heartbroken. Therefore, we all must trust Jesus the Lord during and after the storms of life. The lesson comes to us all as Jesus asked the question, "Where is your faith?" (Luke 8:25) We all can navigate the still and calm waters. We all can skip the Bible time and prayer time while sailing under pleasant and blue skies. But when the winds begin to blow and waves begin to rock our boat back and forth, we must take hold of our faith. The storm that the disciples went through that day brought them to the end of themselves. Four of them were master sailors. They made their living being on that body of water. But they were all brought to the edge with this storm. Their expertise and abilities were no good against such a gale force. Often, a crisis or storm shows us a side of ourselves we were blind to and had no idea those kinds of thoughts or actions could ever exist in our heart. David asked the Lord in Psalm 19 to deliver him for those known sins and for the secret sins that he didn't know was in him. The Lord often uses the stormy season of life to reveal new areas where we need to trust Him more. Storms will show us our lack of faith and trust, as well as show us how distorted a view we often have regarding storms. The disciples yelled, "Master, Master, we're perishing! We're going to go down with the boat, and you're going with us!" Mark adds, "Don't you care that we're going down?" It was absurd for them to think that Christ's life was going to end in this fashion; but in their panicked condition, they had a foggy and distorted view of the circumstances in which they found themselves. If we become so focused on the storm that we can't see that our God is in complete and total control, then our faith has been replaced with fear. This is when we become the end of the story and not Christ. We begin to exalt ourselves by throwing ourselves a great big pity party. Any time we become excessive in feeling sorry for ourselves, we're much too fixated on ourselves. We need to pull back, wait for the Lord to act, and recapture God's perspective on the storm. Remember when the twelve spies came back to report on the promise land? All of them told about how awesome the land was for growing crops and the largeness of the grapes. However, ten of them told the others that there were giants in the land, and they felt and looked like mere grasshoppers in comparison to them. But Joshua and Caleb stilled the crowd to remind them that God had this. They realized what the giants were in comparison to God! That's putting everything in its proper perspective.

I believe, though, that the worst distortion was that of the disciples' view of Jesus. After the storm was stilled and peace restored, they asked, "Who then is this, he even commands winds and water, and they obey him?" Their perspective of who Christ was fell off the proverbial cliff. We often do the same thing when a storm or fiery furnace comes our way. We endeavor to solve our own problems by figuring out the natural formula, instead of having faith in our supernatural Lord and King! I Peter 5:6-11 gives us so much insight into any storm that may fall upon us: "Humble yourselves, therefore, under the mighty hand of God so that at the proper time he may exalt you, casting all your anxieties on him, because he cares for you. Be sober-minded; be watchful. Your adversary the devil prowls around like a roaring lion, seeking someone to devour. Resist him, firm in your faith, knowing that the same kinds of suffering are being experienced by your brotherhood throughout the world. And after you have suffered a little while, the God of all grace, who has called you to his eternal glory in Christ, will himself restore, confirm, strengthen, and establish you. To him be the dominion forever and ever. Amen." Let's just admit it – anxiety is miserable. Anxiety and panic are caustic feelings that bring destruction to our minds and personalities. The word "anxiety" used in I Peter means "a painful or apprehensive uneasiness of mind, usually over an impending or anticipated ill." Anxiety is nothing more than our normal feelings clothed in fear and intensified by anger and clamoring for control. We lose it when we don't have control over a situation or storm. As we cast (literally throw them, as the word means) at the feet of Jesus, we're displaying the greatest act of humility we can show the Lord. We're literally making Him responsible for our worries and cares. Proverbs 12:25 says it all, "Anxiety in a man's heart weighs him down, but a good word makes him glad." The cares of this life can quickly become anxieties that pull us down in our mouth and spirit, weighing heavily upon our hearts that the joy of the Lord is only a pleasant memory. In this miracle, all Jesus had to do was speak to the wind and waves and they were absolutely and immediately quiet. Not a single drop from the boisterous waves or one wisp of wind can be defiant against the sovereignty of the Almighty God! This horrific storm was sent to reveal the glory of Christ in a way that would have been withheld had there not been a ferocious event in the lives of these men on that day.

The natural elements obey their Master and Creator without reservation or question, but, we on the other hand, have a choice. The disciples first feared this great storm. Then, that fear was transferred to the Lord. Their fear of that horrific storm was due to their absence of faith. Their fear of the Lord was a direct result of their new awareness of His awesome faithfulness displayed through His mighty power.

Now we come to us in "our day." The disciples went through this storm and I'm sure many others that we're not told of in Scripture. But what does this do for us today? There are many biblical texts that we could turn to at this point. I know you probably have those favorite passages in which you turn to during your storms. I want to turn to James, the half-brother of Jesus. (Matthew 13:55) He became the leader of the church in Jerusalem in the years following the great Day of Pentecost. He became known as "James the Just" or "James the Righteous," on account of his awesome testimony of right living. It's likely that James was the first New Testament book written, probably around 47 or 48 A.D. We know this because it was written before the Council of Jerusalem, which was held in 49 A.D. According to the Jewish historian, Josephus, James was put to death in 62. The martyrdom of Stephen in Acts 8 caused a great dispersion of the Jews from Israel. These people were to be the recipients of this book. (James 1:1) The killing of Christians, especially those Jews who came to accept Christ as Messiah, was growing greatly throughout the Roman Empire. The phrase that says, "The blood of the saints is the seed of the church" became more than a saying; it became a daily reminder of the price that many of the early Christians paid for their faith in Christ. Well, word got back to Pastor James of some of the extreme measures and difficulties that these scattered, Jewish Christians were experiencing. James wanted to get the message out to them of living a true faith that shows itself in a practical, godly life. Throughout this little book, he developed many major themes: enduring in spite of trials; the pitfalls of riches; the encouragement of the poor; the contrast and comparison of law and love; the relation of faith with works; the coming of Christ; and the meaning of real humility. His main focus, however, was the simple truth that real, true biblical faith works in our daily lives, no matter what we're going through, good or bad.

For us in this context, let's focus our attention on James 1:2—8, 12: **"Count it all joy, my brothers, when you meet trials of various kinds, for you know that the testing of your faith produces steadfastness. And let steadfastness have its full effect, that you may be perfect and complete, lacking in nothing. If any of you lack wisdom, let him ask God, who gives generously to all without reproach, and it will be given him. But let him ask in faith, with no doubting, for the one who doubts is like a wave of the sea that is driven and tossed by the wind. For that person must not suppose that he will receive anything from the Lord; he is a double-minded man, unstable in all his ways....Blessed is the man who remains steadfast under trial, for when he has stood the test he will receive the crown of life, which God has promised to those who love him."**

The word "count" or "consider" means "to think, to regard something based on the weighing and comparing of facts." It implies a deliberate and careful judgment as a result of observing external proof, not subjective judgment based on our senses or feelings. After the extreme emotional effects that we feel when entering a storm, we need to think or regard this storm from a biblical perspective and God's viewpoint. Therefore, we're to receive this storm with the attitude of joy. Peter stresses this vital point in I Peter 4:13, "But rejoice insofar as you share Christ's sufferings, that you may also rejoice and be glad when his glory is revealed." Paul adds this viewpoint in Philippians 4:4, "Rejoice in the Lord always; Again I will say, rejoice!" We're not rejoicing in the storm. We're not joyful because we seem as if we're in a fight for our very lives. No, we're told to "rejoice in the Lord" and to "rejoice because we're partnering with Christ in His sufferings," so that we can "rejoice and be glad when his glory is revealed," fulfilling the Scripture that says, "Those who weep now will rejoice." After being beaten and jailed, Paul demonstrated this principle as he and

Silas sat in a Philippian jail cell, unable to sleep, but were heard singing praises at midnight! (Acts 16:25)

Then James uses the word "when," not "if." We're not going to be spared living through mild or mighty storms throughout our lives. The storms we navigate through will be varied according to His sovereign purpose and plan for our individual life. Peter chimes in on this point as we read these truths in I Peter 4:12, "Beloved, do not be surprised at the fiery trial when it comes upon you to test you, as though something strange were happening to you." Both James and Peter used the word "when" as they described the trials that the children of God will experience. I've learned that trials in life aren't an elective, but a mandatory course requirement in Christ's school of faith. We may not readily know why He sends certain storms our way; but however strong or mild they may be, we can be certain that they are sent from Him with love and a purposed ending.

Another lesson I've learned while going through my own difficulties is that we must not deny our deep, emotional pain. Mary wept over the death of her brother Lazarus. There's nothing wrong with that. In fact, one would think something was strange or unusual if she hadn't wept. Jesus didn't condemn her for her show of great emotion, either. Instead, when He saw her weeping, He also wept. (John 11:33-35) The joy that James speaks of isn't about putting a fake smile on the outside, while we are weeping on the inside. All of us have stood by the casket of a dear friend or loving family member and cried. If that person knew the Lord, we rejoice for him, but feel the loss in our hearts because of his absence. I Thessalonians 4:13 states, "That we do not grieve as those who have no hope." Through and in it all, as we cry and grieve, we should have complete confidence that our God is in total control. Our faith is being stretched as we live through the sovereign plan God has for our individual life. Our God has NEVER uttered the phrase, "Oh, oh! What do I do now?" He's never taken by surprise or off guard. He holds our future in His hands for He is the essence of eternity. He sees where our lives are going and is conforming us to His Son as we travel from birth to death. His purposes reign in creation and He's after the same result with us, His crowning work in creation. He is making Himself a people after His own heart.

According to Matthew 6:33, we are to make the seeking of the Kingdom of God and His righteousness our life's priority. In order to accomplish this command, God has given us two dynamic essentials we all must develop: endurance and wisdom.

- **God Uses Trials to Test Our Faith to Produce Endurance**

James 1:3 says, "For when your faith is tested, your endurance has a chance to grow."[12] *The New Living Translation* Precious metals are refined by fire and in so doing, the fire produces a better product through the process. The KJV uses the word "patience" instead of endurance. The word that is better translated here is the word "endurance." It means "to stand fast or persevere." R. C. Trench makes this point in his book, *Synonyms of the New Testament,* "The Greek word translated 'patience' is used with respect to persons, whereas 'endurance' refers to things. Thus the man is patient who is not easily provoked or angered by difficult people, whereas the man endures who does not lose heart under great trials."[13] When speaking to people through the course of my ministries, I've often told people that the storm or trial that you're experiencing right now is growing your faith in greater depth in order so you can better endure what's coming next. Our God knows that we're all going to face death, either that of our most precious people we love on earth, and, of course, one day, ourselves. This will be our final test or storm. As we journey toward that day, our loving, heavenly Father is preparing us to cross over to the other side of the lake. We know that we can endure the coming storms because we've endured the "nasty" storms in the past. We must understand the reassuring truth that our sovereign Master and Lord is using all of them to develop an enduring and lasting faith that can and will stand up to anything, even our own death. So, let's allow the process of equipping us with endurance to have its complete work, making us mature and complete children of God, lacking nothing when it comes to faith and hope.

- **God Uses Trials to Train Our Focus to Prudent Foresight**

"If any of you lacks wisdom, let him ask God, who gives generously to all without reproach, and it will be given him." (James 1:5) In the original Greek, this is a conditional sentence. What that means and implies is that all of us lack wisdom when we face difficulties, trials and storms. The problem comes to light when we don't see our need for wisdom that comes from above. In the context of James 1, wisdom refers to the wisdom that we must have to endure trials with the attitude of God's joy, in order that we will be "a people perfectly and fully developed with no defects, lacking in nothing."[14] (*The Amplified Bible*) Instead of surrendering to our natural inclination of asking God, "Why me, God?", or "Why is this happening to me?", the wisdom of God will lead us to ask these vital questions: "How can I view this storm from God's viewpoint?"; "How can I navigate these stormy waters in such a manner as to bring glory to the Lord?"; "How can this storm help me mature in my faith?"; "Is God trying to get my attention for one reason or another?"; and "Is there a sin in my life that needs to be confessed?" We Christians from the United States often pray for the Lord to deliver us from the storms of life. Many Christians in other lands pray for God to strengthen them during the storms of life. Old Testament wisdom comes into play here. James is well read in the Old Testament. The main idea of Old Testament wisdom is that of "skill or expertise." It includes the skill of workers who made the high priest's garments and those who worked with metal, stone and wood during the making of The Tabernacle (Exodus 28:3; 31:3-5; 36:1,2), to those who were able to draw up a battle plan (Isaiah 10:13), leadership in a government capacity (Deuteronomy 34:9), possess the ability and skill set to know what to do during a difficult situation and lead others to take action to change course (II Samuel 20:22), for those who speak prudent words to others (Psalm 37:20), and for those who used their time carefully and discreetly (Psalm 90:12). Biblical wisdom focuses on practical living in obedience to God's revealed will. So, by wisdom, James is speaking about the needed skill that enables us to live obediently before God as we navigate the choppy waters and howling winds in which we often find ourselves.

To ask God for the wisdom that we need to have joy during our storms implies that He can provide the exact wisdom we need for that specific storm. Proverbs 2:6 states, "For the Lord gives wisdom; from his mouth comes knowledge and understanding." God's Word also warns us with these words found in Proverbs 21:30, "There is no wisdom and no understanding and no counsel against the Lord." Therefore, if the world's wisdom contradicts God's wisdom, it is, by definition, false wisdom. God's all-encompassing wisdom doesn't appear from nowhere. He doesn't write in great big, bold letters in the sky for us to read on our way to work. He has already written it out in His Word. The revealed Word of God doesn't contain all that God knows. Not by a long shot. The Bible contains all that God wants us to know for now, and, all that we need to get to the other side of the lake, even though terrifying storms will pop up from time to time. We're told in Colossians 2:3 about the knowledge of Christ, "in whom are hidden all the treasures of wisdom and knowledge." So, the first step in gaining God's wisdom is to know His Son, Jesus Christ. God also reveals His wisdom by and through His Holy Spirit to those who are spiritual. Take a moment and read through I Corinthians 2:6-16. James adds another important element to this mix. He says that we must ask God for wisdom "in faith without any doubting." (James 1:6) The word used here for "ask" is in the present tense, stressing that we'll need to ask more than once to obtain all the wisdom we'll need to meet the various number of storms that will come our way. This isn't a magic formula or the need for repeated incantations. God simply says, "Let him ask God." Every child of God is a priest who can approach the Lord directly. We don't have to go through a pastor, minister, preacher, priest or rabbi in order to ask God for wisdom. Faith is essential in approaching God for whatever our needs might be. Hebrews 11:6 says, "Without faith it is impossible to please him, for he who comes to God must believe that he is and that he is a rewarder of those who seek him." As we seek the Lord to obtain the necessary wisdom needed to navigate the many boisterous storms during life, we must conclude that God has engineered all the circumstances within that specific storm. In so doing, He has proven Himself faithful and has desired to use them to promote greater faith in my heart. When we understand these truths, we can relax in Him, receive His substantial comfort as only He can give, and gain huge doses of wisdom for our coming days.

"Consider it a sheer gift, friends, when tests and challenges come at you from all sides. You know that under pressure, your faith-life is forced into the open and shows its true colors. So, don't try to get out of anything prematurely. Let it do its work, so you become mature and well-developed, not deficient in any way. If you don't know what you're doing, pray to the Father. He loves to help. You'll get his help and won't be condescended to when you ask for it. Ask boldly, believingly, without a second thought. People who 'worry their prayers' are like wind-whipped waves. Don't think you're going to get anything from the Master that way, adrift at sea, keeping all your options open."[15] *The Message*

Storms are a fact of life for believers and unbelievers alike; no one is exempt. The important element through all of them is how we're going to react. We will either become better people or bitter people. During each storm, no matter the severity or lightness, we can choose to work out the details ourselves or we can choose to ask Him for His instructions and directions. But just know this – the storm is coming ashore and we all must face it, one way or another. As the palm tree is ready to face the howling winds and battering water, so too must we be ready. Ryan Stevenson wrote and sings a song entitled "Eye of the Storm." Here are those lyrics:

In the eye of the storm, you remain in control.

And in the middle of the war, you guard my soul.

You alone are the anchor, when my sails are torn.

Your love surrounds me, in the eye of the storm.

When the solid ground is falling out from underneath my feet,

Between the black skies, and my red eyes, I can barely see,

When I realize I've been sold out by my friends and my family,

I can feel the rain reminding me, in the eye of the storm, you remain in control,

In the middle of the war, you guard my soul,

You alone are the anchor, when my sails are torn,

Your love surrounds me, in the eye of the storm.

When the test comes in and the doctor says, I've only got a few months left

It's like a bitter pill I'm swallowing, I can barely take a breath.

And when addiction steals my baby girl, and there's nothing I can do.

My only hope is to trust You, I trust You, Lord.

When the storm is raging, when the storm is raging,

And my hope is gone, and my hope is gone, Lord.

When my flesh is failing, You're still holding on.

135

When the storm is raging, and my hope is gone.

When my flesh is failing, You're still holding on.

The Lord is my Shepherd, I have all that I need.

He lets me rest in green meadows. He leads me beside peaceful streams.

He renews my strength. He guides me along right paths, bringing honor to His name.

Even when I walk through the darkest valley, I will not be afraid.

For You are close beside me.[16]

GOD IS SOVEREIGN OVER EVERY STORM THAT OCCURS IN OUR LIFE.

GOD IS USING STORMS TO TEST OUR FAITH IN ORDER TO PRODUCE ENDURANCE FOR OUR LIFE.

GOD IS USING STORMS TO TURN OUR FOCUS TO HIS PRUDENT FORESIGHT THROUGH OUR LIFE.

> "Our sorrows are all, like ourselves, mortal. There are no immortal sorrows for immortal souls, they come, but blessed by God, they also go. Like birds of the air, they fly over our heads. But they cannot make their abode in our souls. We suffer today, but we shall rejoice tomorrow."[17]
> Charles Spurgeon

9

REFRESHED SOJOURNERS

"Then Moses made Israel set out from the Red Sea, and they went into the wilderness of Shur. They went three days in the wilderness and found no water. When they came to Marah, they could not drink the water of Marah because it was bitter, therefore it was named Marah. And the people grumbled against Moses, saying, 'What shall we drink?' And he cried to the Lord, and the Lord showed him a log, and he threw it into the water, and the water became sweet. There the Lord made for them a statute and a rule, and there he tested them, saying, 'If you will diligently listen to the voice of the Lord your God, and do that which is right in his eyes, and give ear to his commandments and keep all his statutes, I will put none of these diseases on you that I put on the Egyptians, for I am the Lord, your healer.' Then they came to Elim, where there were twelve springs of water and seventy palm trees, and they encamped there by the water." Exodus 15:22-27

When I was a kid, many, many years ago, I heard a missionary say, "I asked a little boy in the last church what he wanted to be when he grew up. He told me, 'I want to be just like you, a missionary on furlough.'" After reading this passage of Scripture, I want to live in Elim, encamped by the water.

There really isn't a hard choice to make at this point in the game. The nation of Israel had just experienced one of the greatest miracles in all of God's Word – the crossing of the Red Sea on completely dry ground! Three days out from that monster miracle, they begin to gripe and complain to Moses about not having any fresh water to drink. They came to a place of plentiful water, but it wasn't any good, hence the name "Marah" or "bitterness." The Lord gave Moses the solution of throwing a tree into the water, changing it from disgusting, bitter water, to delightful, sweet water. He then proceeded to present three statutes, rules or test questions. Finally, this magnificent truth presented to us in v. 27 says it all, "Then they came to Elim, where there were twelve springs of water and seventy palm trees, and they encamped there by the water." This nation of people had lived through the dramatic event called The Exodus. I'm sure they had a million thoughts running through their collective minds in those closing days of their time spent in a foreign land. All these people had ever known was slavery. They didn't have lives that belonged to them. They were at the mercy of the pharaoh and all the leaders of Egypt. A man by the name of "Moses" showed up one day and said, "Pack up, we're moving!" He claimed to be their new leader and emancipator. He claimed to be a man called by God to do the job of leading an entire nation of people to freedom and to start a brand-new life, back in the land God gave them. But it wasn't a piece of cake to get these people moving and out of Egypt. It took several mighty acts of Jehovah to help convince them that Moses was legitimate. The plagues that devastated the mightiest country on earth of that day were all targeted on the false gods of the Egyptian people. The judgment that was brought upon the Egyptians wasn't meant for God's people, so the plagues had little or no effect on them. Lastly, God's feast of Passover was introduced. They were to take blood and sprinkle some on the side posts and door header, letting the death angel know that that house was a confirmed believer in Jehovah. The Lord said, "When I see the blood, I will pass over that house so that no harm will come to it." If there was no blood on the door in this fashion, the firstborn male child and the firstborn of the animals would die. The blood made the difference as it does today! They were to prepare a special meal, also. As all of this was done, they were to be ready to move out. After this feast or meal, they gathered up all their belongings and they were on their way. Pharaoh had changed his mind over and over regarding the release of God's people. He finally told them to get out after the horrific night of death that touched every part of the land of Egypt. They did. After they left, Pharaoh got to thinking about his decision and once again changed his mind. He mustered his army and set out to recapture the people of Israel. The estimates of the number of Jews leaving Egypt falls somewhere between a million and half to three million! This was a huge undertaking that required great planning and leadership. As they made their way down the road, they were surrounded by obstacles and hardships. One side of the road were cliffs, while on the other side stood gigantic mountains. The Red Sea was in front of them and the world's most powerful army was hard on their heels behind them. To the natural, human mind and heart, this presented an impossible situation. Certain death was to their right if they chose to go over the cliff. The mountain wall presented an absolute barrier for them to climb. Maybe a few of them could scale the mountains, but not all of them, and certainly not the children. The Red Sea was right in the center of their escape route, but it offered nothing but drowning. While all of this was in plain sight, the danger and destructive force of the formidable Egyptian army was in their rearview mirror, bearing down upon them and getting closer by the hour. They had nowhere to turn and nowhere to hide as this seemed to be their destiny, literally surrounded by hurdles, obstacles, danger and destruction. This is a terrible place for us to be, but a terrific place for our God to be! How often have we felt as these people were feeling? How often have we gone to bed, only to wake up a few hours later worrying about this, that or the other? How often have we scratched our heads trying to figure out how we're going to make ends meet? God has His people exactly where He wants them. He isn't taken off guard or surprised by any of these turn-of-events. All that the nation of Israel needed was faith in their God. Tim Keller said, "As many have learned and later taught, you don't realize Jesus is all you need until Jesus is all you have."

The main lesson through this entire ordeal is that God was in all of this. We read in Exodus 13:17 these dynamic truths, "When Pharaoh let the people go, God did not lead them by way of the land of the Philistines, although that was near. For God said, 'Lest the people change their minds when they see war and return to Egypt.'" For us, the nearest or quickest way to get someplace is the very best way. Didn't we all learn in geometry class that the shortest distance between two points is a straight line? We're always looking to do something faster or get the newest gadget to save us time. Efficiency seems to be the greatest factor in every business decision. We live according to a time schedule. But not our God. He knows exactly what we need and when we need it. He knows what He's doing, and He sees His purposes accomplished according to His time and schedule. This shoots down any plausibility of the instant health and wealth aspect of life, does it not? There never has been or will there ever be a quick way to learn life's lessons from the hand of God. In this life lesson, Israel wasn't ready to face the terrible conditions of war. They were only slaves with no military training whatsoever. Men, women and children who had to learn a whole new way of thinking and living made up this great mass of people. God was teaching His people the valuable lesson of trusting Him and His direction for their lives. The other way was guaranteed shorter, but this way was under the guidance of Sovereignty.

The Sovereign Way always takes a bit longer but is always the absolute best way to travel. God's Word is crystal clear in telling us that He IS NOT in a hurry like us. He takes His time. The Sovereign Way isn't very efficient, either. As we go through storm and trial one after another, we look at the reasoning behind it and oftentimes it doesn't make any sense. Why didn't the Lord deliver John the Baptist? Why did Joseph unjustly spend those years in prison in Egypt? Why did Moses spend those forty years on the back side of the desert? Why did the Lord have Abraham and Sarah wait twenty-five years to see the promised seed? Why wait? Why not be more efficient with our time, Lord? I've also learned that the Sovereign Way is oftentimes the extreme way. We're always looking for the "easier way" out of the storm or path through the wilderness. Pain, suffering, trials and storms aren't on our agenda of things to do today. But the Lord is looking at what's around the next bend that we will face so the Sovereign Way is the best, howbeit an extreme way to journey through life. However, God's Sovereign Way is the ABSOLUTE BEST WAY WHEN ALL IS SAID AND DONE!

The reason and purpose for us taking the Sovereign Way is because of God's abiding presence. There is no life that is comparable to a life that is lived in the very presence of Almighty God. Israel could've been led straight into the Promise Land, but that wasn't God's Sovereign plan for them. And it's not God's Sovereign plan for us, either. As it turned out, this great nation of Israel spent forty years learning to lean on God by camping out with Him, considering His ways of doing things, counting the blessings of daily manna and being led by the fire by night and pillar of cloud by day. This people of Israel had gone from living a life subjected to slavery to living a life of submission to Sovereignty! That's what I meant by saying a few paragraphs ago that there really isn't a hard choice to make at this point of the game. They had been through so much. They had lived through daily drudgery and virtual vulnerability all their lives. Their personal powerlessness was a way of life. They were now free from that dreadful dungeon of feeble-ness and failings. They were now ready to move on and create a brand-new chapter in Israel's history. Little did they realize what this all meant. After all this proclivity to pain, they were ready for passionate prosperity as they would learn what their God desired for them to learn following these initial struggles on the other side of the Red Sea.

"But God led the people around by the way of the wilderness toward the Red Sea…." (Ex. 13:18) "The way of the wilderness toward the Red Sea" doesn't sound very appealing to me. Faith in the Lord requires us to recognize our own weaknesses, resulting in us telling Him our specific needs, then realizing His power and provision as He declares them in His promises. They were in the middle of nowhere going to a body of water with no human way possible of getting from one side to the other. When we find our-selves "trapped," we often look to our right, our left, before and behind us; but we often fail to look up. God is never trapped or cornered. He knows the end from the beginning and everything in between. He knows the way that we take because He has pro-vided the way for us. One of the greatest claims of Christ was His statement, "I am the Way, the Truth, and the Life," in John 14:6. The early Christians were called "people of the Way." Therefore, if, for the time being, He leads us "by the way of the wilderness toward the Red Sea," so be it. He's the Leader and I'm to follow the Leader. However, the rest of verse 18 states, "And the people of Israel went up out of the land of Egypt equipped for battle." We fall in step with the Lord and follow Him wherever He leads us, but we're also to prepare ourselves for whatever may come our way. Even though the Lord didn't lead them into a possible war, He did want them to get ready to meet any obstacle that stood in their way. This literally meant that they went up "harnessed." They had orga-nized themselves to fall in rank and be responsible for the person on their right and on their left. They were the first group of people to have the meaning of leave no one behind. Moses and the Lord had organized them into large groups to care for one another. They were to be there for the other person in case anything would happen. Thus, they were "harnessed or equipped to face any struggle they may have faced during their journey." The answer to the age-old question, "Am I my brother's keeper?" is a resounding "YES!" This biblical principle is also found in Ecclesiastes 4:9-12, "Two are better than one, because they have a good reward for their toil. For if they fall, one will lift his fellow. But woe to him who is alone when he falls and has not another to lift him up! Again, if two lie together, they keep warm, but how can one keep warm alone? And though a man might prevail against one who is alone, two will withstand him – a three-fold cord is not quickly broken." This is an extremely valuable lesson when travelling through the wilderness toward an experience like the Red Sea. I know we have our God safely keeping us and strongly defending us, but sometimes it sure helps to have someone tell us they love us and give us a great big hug. God is always there securing and sustaining us, but we all take comfort when we have a person who is wearing flesh to just hang out with us during our wilderness trip. Praise God for loving family members and caring, wonderful friends to walk with us through life's ups and downs!

The purposes of God are clearly seen in and through His promises. We read these amazing words in v. 19 of Exodus 13, "Moses took the bones of Joseph with him, for Joseph had made the sons of Israel solemnly swear, saying, 'God will surely visit you, and you shall carry up my bones with you from here.'" On top of everything else, Moses had to make sure this item was checked off his "have to do list." I find that somewhat amusing, and at the same time amazing. We remember the wonderful story of Joseph and how God secured the safety of His people through a world-wide famine. Joseph is a whole other story with so many valuable lessons for us to learn and live. But in Genesis 50:24, 25 we read Joseph's last words, "And Joseph said to his brothers, 'I am about to die, but God will visit you and bring you up out of this land to the land that he swore to Abraham, to Isaac, and to Jacob.' Then Joseph made the sons of Israel swear, saying, 'God will surely visit you, and you shall carry up my bones from here.'" Then Joseph died at the ripe old age of 110. The end of v. 26 reads, "…they embalmed him, and he was put in a coffin in Egypt." "I am about to die, BUT GOD!" Two of the greatest words put together are these: "But God!" If it were not for Him, how many situations would end up in desolate dreariness? "But God" provides another chapter to an otherwise sad ending to any of our life's stories. Even though Joseph was facing his final moments on earth, he knew the promises of God would be fulfilled and he wanted in on the action. They mummified him as they did in Egypt in those days and placed his body in a coffin. The word "coffin" has the complete meaning of "hope chest." At the bleakest moment of one's life, the refreshing idea of "But God" comes into play. The people are reminded of God's promise of returning His people to their homeland, and Joseph is the leading cheerleader. We turn some pages in our Bibles and read that Moses followed the promise of God and plea of Joseph. Packing up the nearly 400-year-old mummy back to their homeland was a visible proof that the God of Heaven keeps His loving promises to His people! During their 40-year test in the wilderness, the men in charge of Joseph's coffin would put it on a wagon before they travelled and take if off that wagon when they camped. Each time, people would be reminded of this one vital truth: taking Joseph's coffin back to the Promise Land displays God's faithfulness to us by keeping His promise to Abraham, Isaac, and Jacob.

Verse 20 tells us "And they moved on from Succoth and encamped at Etham, on the edge of the wilderness." The exact location of Succoth is unknown. Its meaning is "booths" or "huts." It was the first place mentioned on their trip out of Egypt. The Bible says in I Corinthians 5:1, "For we know that when this earthly tent we live in is taken down (that is, when we die and leave this earthly body), we will have a house in heaven, an eternal body made for us by God Himself and not by human hands." One of these days, we are going to move from living in "Succoth" or the booths of our bodies and take up residence where God lives. Verse 2 further elaborates on this truth, "For in this tent (booth, tabernacle) we groan, longing to be clothed with our heavenly dwelling." When facing storms and trials, we begin to long for God to move us away from "Succoth." Paul further explains this truth in greater detail in II Corinthians 4:7, "Now we have this treasure in jars of clay to show that this surpassingly great power is from God and not from us." As the nation of Israel had to learn this life-changing lesson, so too must we. We live life as best we can, living in frail, weak bodies. We may have awesome health in our youth, but soon we'll begin to experience the ravages of time taking that youth away. Our outward body starts dying the moment we're born, with the Bible describing our bodies as nothing but clay or dirt pots. When life is over, we'll once again return to the dust of the earth. The quicker we understand and learn this truth, the quicker we can lean and rely on the eternal, all-powerful King of Kings!

"And they moved on from Succoth (booths, huts, tents) to Etham…" Etham means "solid, enduring, fortress." Isn't it like our God to move us from a temporary dwelling that can be blown down from mighty storms, to camping out in a fortress like-structure that will endure all kinds of storms and remain a solid habitat in which to reside! One day we'll lay aside our feeble and frail frames we call bodies and He will give us a brand-new body, exactly like His! But until that day, we must run to a solid, enduring, fortress during the time of earthly sojourn. Christ is that fortress. Proverbs 18:10 reveals the truth that "The name of the Lord is a strong fortress; the godly run to him and are safe." This "running to him" is explained in the Lord's instructions found in Matthew 11:28-30, "Come to me, all who labor and are heavy laden, and I will give you rest.

Take my yoke upon you, and learn from me, for I am gentle and lowly in heart, and you will find rest for your souls. For my yoke is easy, and my burden is light." "Come to me" is the invitation of salvation. "Take my yoke" is the invitation for sanctification. The yoke of the Middle East has room for two animals. After I come to Christ to be saved, I accept the task of placing myself in the yoke neck right next to His! From that point I'm never alone. As I work, He's right alongside me, carrying the heavy load. "I can do all things through the One (Christ) who provides the strength." (Philippians 4:13) "I am the vine; you are the branches. Whoever abides in me and I in him, he it is that bears much fruit, for apart from me you can do nothing." (John 15:3) I come, and He gives me rest. I take His yoke (not my own agenda, His will and plan for my life) and I find rest. I come – I take – He gives – I find – as I learn from Him. If I'm yoked in with Him, what else can I possibly do, but learn from Him? He is the Master and I am the servant. He is the Potter and I am the clay. He is the Teacher and I am the student. He is the King and I am the subject. Jesus told people, "Follow me, and I will make you become fishers of men." I learn from Him and place my life behind His by following Him. When I do, He simply says, "I will make you..." We live in "Succoth" every single day. As we do, we recognize our urgent need for something much more solid and enduring. He then moves us to "Etham" – Himself! Why? The answer is right in front of us – we're going to be living "on the edge of the wilderness." Etham was on the edge of the wilderness, or literally on "the edge of civilization" or "the edge of cultivated land." This marked the start of their wilderness journey. As we venture out on our own personal journeys, we stand at our own Ethams. What better place to begin this arduous journey but from a place of solid fortitude that will stand the test of time. A few chapters from now, the people will again complain about not having water to drink. The Lord instructs Moses to strike the rock and water will come out of the rock. I Corinthians 10:1-5 reads as follows, "For I do not want you to be unaware, brothers, that our fathers were all under the cloud, and all passed through the sea, and all were baptized into Moses in the cloud and in the sea, and all ate the same spiritual drink. For they drank from the spiritual Rock that followed them, and the Rock was Christ. Nevertheless, with most of them God was not pleased, for they were overthrown in the wilderness." Edward Mote lived from 1797 to 1874. He learned the family business of cabinetry making. Mote was called into Christian ministry, becoming a Baptist minister and faithfully served the Lord and His people for 26 years. Perhaps he was better known for writing some 150 Christian hymns. While he was working on a sermon entitled, "Gracious Experience of a Christian," a poem came to his mind which included the following lines: "On Christ the solid Rock I stand; all other ground is sinking sand." After delivering this message to his church, one of his church members came to Mote and asked prayer for his very ill wife. He had these words in his pocket and told the man that he could come and sing them to his wife. He would like that and so they went to this church member's home. She enjoyed this new poem or song very much and asked if she could have a copy. He left that copy with her. Mote returned to his own home, sat down by the fireplace and composed the rest of the song, "My hope is built on nothing less,"[1] returned to the church member's home, and sang the rest of the song to her. Psalm 61:1-3 tells us, "Hear my cry, O God; listen to my prayer. From the end of the earth I call to you when my heart is faint. Lead me to the rock that is higher than I, for you have been my refuge, a strong tower against the enemy." We then read Psalm 62:2, "He alone is my rock and my salvation, my fortress; I shall not be greatly shaken." After spending more time with the Lord, David writes in v. 6, "He only is my rock and my salvation, my fortress; I shall not be shaken." After David reminds himself of this great truth that "God alone, O my soul, wait in silence, for my hope is from him," that he takes note that security is found not just "in" Him, but it ultimately comes "from" Him. He writes in v. 2 the words "I shall not be greatly shaken," and then writes in v. 6, "I shall not be shaken." He moves from "not so sure about this" to "I have absolute confidence in my God, and I SHALL NOT BE SHAKEN!"

Here is the guidance by which they were blessed, "The Lord went before them by day in a pillar of cloud to lead them along the way and by night in a pillar of fire to give them light, that they might travel by day and by night. The pillar of cloud by day and the pillar of fire by night did not depart from before the people." (Exodus 13:21, 22) "The Lord went before them" in His "shechinah" glory. This glory appeared to be a huge cloud in the daytime but changed in appearance at night as a form of fire. God's "shechinah" glory appeared over the tabernacle and filled the temple's holy of holies when that was built. Moses wore it on his face when he came off Mount Sinai after he spent 40 days in the presence of God while receiving God's 10 Commandments. It is the visible expression of Divine Majesty! This majestic glory would be fulfilled in the Person of Jesus Christ. John exclaimed in John 1, "We have seen his glory, the glory of the only begotten of the Father, full of grace and truth." God's glory, literally meaning "tabernacle among us," performing miracle after miracle, or sign after sign as John describes them, for people journeying in their own wilderness. I love what Matthew Henry says regarding this passage of Scripture, **"Those whom God brings into a wilderness he will not leave nor lose there but will take care to lead them through it. Those who made the glory of God their end, and the word of God their rule, the Spirit of God the guide of their affections, and the providence of God the guide of their affairs, may be confident that the Lord goes before them, as truly as he went before Israel in the wilderness, though not so sensibly; we must live by faith. They all saw an appearance from heaven of a pillar, which in the bright day appeared cloudy, and in the dark night appeared fiery. God gave them this ocular demonstration of** his presence, in compassion to the infirmity of their faith. They had sensible effect of God's going before them in this pillar. It led the way in that wilderness in which there was no road, no track, of which they had no maps, through which they had no guides. When they marched, this pillar went before them, at the rate that they could follow. It sheltered them by day from the heart. It gave them light by night and at all times made the wilderness they were in less frightful." This magnificent presence of the great God of the universe is doing the same for us in our wilderness journeys. Henry continues with these thoughts about this truth; "The pillar of cloud...fire...did not depart from before the people" – "These were constant miracles. It never left them, till it brought them to the borders of Canaan. It was a cloud which the wind could not scatter. There was something spiritual in this pillar of cloud and fire. Some make this cloud a type of Christ. The cloud of his human nature was a veil to the light and fire of his divine nature. Christ is our way, the light of our way and the guide of it."[2]

God was leading His people to something much larger than they had ever experienced. They, of course, had no idea how He was going to deliver on His promises. We, on the other hand, have heard their story preached and taught so much through the years that we have a "ho-hum" attitude concerning their deliverance from Egypt using the least obvious way possible. I want to pick up the Scripture narrative in Exodus 14:1-4, "Then the Lord gave these instructions to Moses: 'Tell the people to march toward Pihahiroth between Migdol and the sea. Camp there along the shore, opposite Baalzephon. Then Pharaoh will think that those Israelites are confused. They are trapped between the wilderness and the sea! And once again I will harden Pharaoh's heart, and he will chase after you. I have planned this so I will receive great glory at the expense of Pharaoh and his armies. After this, the Egyptians will know that I am the Lord!' The Israelites camped there as they were told." Israel was led every step of the way as they made their journey from place to place and from event to event, but take great notice that the Lord told Moses, "I have planned this so I will receive great glory." This leading by God to have His people make camp on the beach of the Red Sea in a seemingly vulnerable and defenseless position was at the very heart of God's purpose and plan. The Lord knows man's thoughts and end from the beginning. He changed Pharaoh's mind after three days, and they went to attempt to capture their slave labor and bring them back to Egypt.

Those of us who have placed our faith and trust in Jesus Christ as Savior are God's heritage and children. Because of this blessing, we have freedom and liberty from our enemies. That liberty becomes a heavy burden to our enemies, and they want to pursue us with all their strength and vigor. This rage inside the enemies of God becomes a torment to their hearts and souls. Their intent is to reduce us to nothing, or seek revenge against us, or just plain re-enslave us back to our way of life in Egypt to live alongside them, doing their bidding. No, a thousand times, NO! This is not God's intentions with us from the moment we leave Egypt. Egypt, in the Bible, is a type of the world. God's children have no business being enslaved in the world. Jesus Christ came to free us from living a life of slavery to the weak and beggarly elements found in this old world. But what we don't see or know is how our God is working on our behalf, behind the scenes, to ensure that we don't have to return to slavery in our world! We may seem completely out in the open with no place to turn, but our God has this. We have become traitors to our three enemies – the world, our flesh and Satan. Therefore, we who have become children of the King of heaven and who have decided to live godly and righteous lives for the cause of Jesus Christ, must expect to be pursued and attacked by Satan's temptations and terroristic ways. None of our enemies will calmly go away. They will gather "all the forces in Pharaoh's army" (Exodus 14:9) and pursue us with all their might.

Now, here's the thing. How often did the nation of Israel think and say, "We had everything we ever wanted living in Egypt. We ate and drank what we pleased. If we could just go back and pick up where we left off!" God had greater and larger plans for His people than being enslaved in a foreign land. We can be held in bondage in our minds, bodies and souls if we allow it. The crossing of the Red Sea marks the end of one way of life and the beginning of a new way of life. If it were so easy to release the worldly elements of the former life in order to embrace the future life, we wouldn't have to go through all these situations that life throws at us. But the main and key elements in all of this are these truths:

- **"So God led them along a route through the wilderness toward the Red Sea..." 13:18**

- **"And the Lord did not remove the pillar of cloud or pillar of fire from their sight." 13:22**

- **"I have planned this..." 13:4**

- **"So I will receive great glory..." 13:4**

- **"After this, the Egyptians will know that I am the Lord!" 13:4**

- **"So the Israelites camped there as they were told." 13:4**

God's leading is the best. We may not think so at the time, but His leading is the best way to take. It may be through a wilderness experience where we learn to depend and trust on Him for our sustenance, but it's the best way. We may be heading to a Red Sea crossing, but what a miracle we're going to see and tell others about when it's over. God's Sovereign Way is best. He has plans for us. Jeremiah 29:10-13 captures this truth perfectly, "'The truth is that you will be in Babylon for seventy years. But then I will come and do for you all the good things I have promised, and I will bring you home again. For I know the plans I have for you,' says the Lord. 'They are plans for good and not for disaster, to give you a future and a hope. In those days when you pray, I will listen. If you look for me in earnest, you will find me when you seek me.'" We all want to place our attention on the words, "…For I know the plans I have for you…they are plans for good and not for disaster, to give you a future and a hope…" We often fail to read the first part of this passage which tells us, "The truth is that you will be in Babylon for seventy years." Ouch! No one wants to realize that reality in their lives. What we must realize, regardless of what we may be going through at the present, God's plans are the best. The truth is that we can't fully enjoy the sunny days without the rainy and stormy ones mixed in. Israel was on their way out of living the grudge and grunt existence as slaves to living lives under the guidance and guardianship of Almighty God. Slavery versus liberty were the choices of the day. However, they were exchanging one form of hardship to another form of hardship. The difference was their masters of Egypt forced their hands to labor, while their Master of heaven framed their hearts to love Him. Hardships found in the land of Egypt leave one dissatisfied, discouraged, and disappointed at the end of the day. Hardships found living under the hand of God leave one delighted and encouraged when the day is over. The road may be long and bumpy; but we know that the Lord is guiding us every step of the way, and that makes it all great. The comfort and relief that one has when knowing that the person leading the way understands exactly what we need, what we can deal with, and how to get us to that absolute best place for us to be, then we're good with whatever may come our way.

Exodus 14 speaks of the red-letter day for this generation of God's people, for it tells us about the crossing of the Red

Sea. **"Stand still and see the salvation of the Lord." The New Living Translation simply says, "Just stand where you are and watch the Lord rescue you...The Lord himself will fight for you. You won't have to lift a finger in your defense!"** When our world comes crashing down on our heads, God's orders stand tall and true: Leave it to Me! In our extremities, it becomes our delightful duty to get out of our own way and allow God to be God, for our God is about ready to go to work for us! This garnered the results God is always looking for in our lives and hearts, "When the people of Israel saw the mighty power that the Lord had displayed against the Egyptians, they feared the Lord and put their faith in him and his servant Moses." (Exodus 14:31) The fear of the Lord is the first step in gaining wisdom according to Proverbs 1:7 and 9:10. Trusting in the Lord and His might is the first step in receiving God's promise of direction according to Proverbs 3:5, 6. Following God's leader falls in line with receiving His very best from His hand for our lives. The people of Israel found themselves on the other side of the lake, or, in this case, the Red Sea. God was now ready to teach them some more valuable lessons.

"Then Moses led the people of Israel away from the Red Sea, and they moved out into the Shur Desert." (Exodus 15:22) I'm sure that it was with some great difficulty and mixed feelings that they picked up their belongings and moved off the beach. They had never, ever seen anything like what they just saw crossing that body of water. By now, their thoughts had to be that of safety and security, ready to become sojourners on a long, long journey back home. With the Egyptian army history, surely blue skies were the only skies they were going to see on their way back to Canaan. We're told in Deuteronomy 1:2, 3 these sobering words, "Normally it takes only eleven days to travel from Mount Sinai to Kadesh-barnea, going by way of Mount Seir. But forty years after the Israelites left Mount Sinai..." These people thought they were going to spend less than a month in the wilderness as sojourners.

What they didn't know was that it was going to be home for the next forty years! They were going to spend forty years taking the longest possible route known to man. I've heard it said this way, "It would only take eleven days for Israel to get out of Egypt, but it would take God forty years to get Egypt out of Israel." As much as we would love to spend extra time basking in God's wonderful workings and miracles, the time does come for us to move forward.

"They traveled in this desert for three days without water." (Exodus 15:22) We all know that water is the sustenance of life; for it is life's necessity. Water is one of our basic needs. Animal and plant life must have water to make it through each and every day. But this mass of people walked for three, long, grueling days without the much, needed substance of water. We all understand that nothing in Scripture is by accident or there without purpose or reason. Israel walked precisely for three days. Numbers in the Bible have significance and deep meaning. Every word is inspired or "God-breathed" so why wouldn't we take into great consideration the use of numbers throughout God's Sacred Text? The number "3" is used 467 times in the Bible. It represents completeness. The meaning of this number derives from the fact that it's the first of four spiritually perfect numerals, with the others being "7," "10," and "12." There were three righteous patriarchs before the flood: Abel, Enoch and Noah. After the flood there was the righteous fathers of the nation of Israel: Abraham, Isaac and Jacob, or Israel as God changed his name. There are twenty-seven books in the New Testament, which is 3x3x3, or completeness to the third power. Jesus prayed three times in the Garden of Gethsemane before He was arrested and crucified. He was placed on the cross at the third hour of the day, or 9 A.M, and died at the 9th hour, or 3 P.M. There were three hours of darkness that covered the earth while Jesus was suffering from taking our sins upon Himself. The Father, being holy and righteous, had to turn away from looking at His Son because God cannot look at sin. So, from the 6th hour until the 9th hour there was darkness covering the land as creation was mourning the dying and eventual death of the Creator. Three is the number of "resurrection." Christ was dead and in the grave for three days and three nights. There were only three individuals who witnessed Jesus' transfiguration on Mount Hermon: Peter, James and John. There were three gifts offered to the new King, the young child, Jesus, on that first Christmas. God is described, in the very beginning of the book of Revelation, as a Being "which is, and which was, and which is to come." (Revelation 1:4) There are three Persons of the Holy Trinity: God the Father, God the Son, and God the Holy Spirit. There are so many other illustrations of the number "3" in Scripture. This three-day trek to begin Israel's journey is all about the Lord conveying to His people that they were completely clear of the threat from Egypt, signaling complete victory over this enemy. This marked the end of this tragic chapter in their history and the beginning of a new one. It was time to close the book on their days as slaves. The number "3" speaks to us of harmony, God's presiding presence and of completeness. This number also speaks of eternal life, as Jesus was resurrected after three days and nights. When Israel came upon this body of bitter water, God was instantly telling them that their new lives were on the horizon and He was going to be with them throughout their long journey.

"When they came to Marah, they finally found water. But the people couldn't drink it because it was bitter. (That is why the place was called Marah, which means 'bitter.' Then the people turned against Moses, 'What are we going to drink?' they demanded." (Exodus 15:23, 24) Many biblical scholars believe that this location is known today as Ayun Musa. It fits the description in Scripture and is commonly referred to as the "The Springs of Moses."[3] There are a great number of wells that have created pools of water and much vegetation surrounding those wells, springs and pools. In this usage of the name "Marah," it's spelled with a "hey" or "h" at the end of it in the Hebrew. This is the fifth letter of the Hebrew alphabet, with the number "5" in Scripture being the number of "grace." It's the same letter that was added to Abraham and Sarah's name as a God-given sign of His covenant grace bestowed on each of them. When Naomi, in the book of Ruth, asked to be called Mara, it was spelled without this "h." In the fact of her calling herself Mara, she was announcing her complete bitterness to everyone. This inner bitterness was felt by her as she considered herself outside the Lord's covenant provision, thus immersed all alone in her own bitterness. Does this not represent us much of the time? After a great victory by our God performed for our benefit, a problem surfaces right afterwards that causes us to lodge a complaint against God, or against anyone close enough that we can cast blame. In this case, it was lodged against their human leader. We're so very quick to cast blame on someone else when our lives take a turn for the worse. We're so very quick to complain if our needs aren't meant right then and there. We're so very quick to forget God's provision of complete victory over our enemies. And we're so very quick to lose sight of our focus on God's Sovereign Way as being the best way we can take.

But Moses knows where to go to find answers. "So Moses cried out to the Lord for help, and the Lord showed him a tree. Moses took the tree and threw it into the water. This made the water good to drink...." (Exodus 15:25) There was nothing special about this tree. The only thing special was "and the Lord showed him a tree." The Lord was the One who made these bitter waters turn sweet. Having been shown this tree and without any further discussion between Moses and the Lord, we next read that Moses simply threw it into the pool. The verb for "made sweet" is used for the first time here but is further used just four more times in the Bible. In each passage where it appears, it's used to contrast something with something else. Here, the bitter waters are contrasted with those waters becoming sweet. In Job 20:12, the sweetness of wrong and evil is contrasted with utter sourness in the stomach.

Job uses it again in chapter 21 as the bitterness of life is contrasted with the sweetness of being in the grave. Psalm 55 speaks of the sweet advice of a friend being contrasted with a betrayal later in life by that same friend. Finally, Proverbs 9:17, 18 tells us of the temporary sweetness of stolen water being contrasted with the consequences of the action itself. What we see before us in this little snapshot hidden away in this big story is that water pictures life; and without fresh and satisfying water, people will die. So, the tree that the Lord specifically directs Moses to throw into the pool of bitter water pictures the life-giving freshness that only the cross of Christ can provide mankind! He is the only hope we have in turning our bitter "state of affairs" into a sweet abundant existence. For the nation of Israel, He was once again reminding them that He's in complete control and that He will supply all their needs. Faith and trust are two lessons that will forever be present for us to learn. Their depth of meaning and breadth of use are elements that we can never exhaust or gain full and complete comprehension. God must teach us over and over and over of their value in our day-to-day endeavors.

"...It was there at Marah that the Lord laid before them the following conditions to test their faithfulness to him: 'If you will listen carefully to the voice of the Lord your God and do what is right in his sight, obeying his commands and laws, then I will not make you suffer the diseases I sent on the Egyptians; for I am the Lord who heals you.'" (Exodus 15:25, 26) It's no mistake that the Lord calls Himself "Jehovah-Rapha" at this point. He had just performed the miracle of healing the waters so they could drink it, so He calls Himself the One that will heal them. Then, for good measure, He assures them, "I will not make you suffer the diseases I sent on the Egyptians." However, this promise was conditional. If Israel would do something first, then the Lord promised this massive promise upon His people. Here are those conditions He laid out before them as they camped at the waters of Marah:

- **Diligently Listen – To God's Voice – Follow the Word of God – "If you will listen carefully to the voice of the Lord your God"**

- **Do Life – According to God's Vision – Obey the Will of God – "And do right in His sight"**

- **Determine to love God for the Long Term – Love God's Values – Seek The Worship of God – "Obeying his commands and laws"**

The biggest word in this passage is the word "IF." That makes God's promise conditional. This little word of "IF" implies that if someone agrees to a stated plan or he complies with it, then there will be one result. If it isn't agreed upon or complied with, then there will be a completely different result. If we want and desire God to hold up His end of this verse, then we must perform this mighty word of "If." This was God's great lesson for His people at this moment: moving forward from this moment for them and in their historic journey, after this first testing that ended in God's grace and mercy, that all other further testing will have rewards of gain or result in losses. Right after God turned this water from bitterness and death to sweetness and life, He lays out these three orders to be followed, obeyed and sought. "If you will…" "Then I will" was extremely clear to His people that day. The listening part literally means, "Listening you shall listen." In other words, God is clearly saying, "Sit up and pay attention. Take notes and hear My Word." The next command uses the word "upright." This is the first time this word appears in Scripture. Essentially, God is saying, "I am telling you to do what is moral, honorable and proper in My sight, not yours. I am setting the standard and it's up to you to accept it and do it." The last of this trio of commands raises the bar to a whole other level. Remember Jesus said in The Sermon on the Mount, "Be perfect like my Father in heaven is perfect." "Be mature and strive to be just like the Father." This is God telling His people to value Him in their lives so much that they were to honor Him through every detail of their lives. Valuing the Lord is recognizing His "Worth-ship," where we get our word "worship." The entirety of our lives is to be "a reflection" of our God and King. It is the same for us today. As we follow the principles found of God's Word, we'll begin to realize His awesome promises in our lives. As we obey the will of God, we'll begin to recognize His awesome presence in every step we take in our daily lives. As we seek to worship our God, we'll begin to recall our God's greatness in past victories in which He has provided every need on our behalf!

"Then they came to Elim, where there were twelve springs of water, and seventy palm trees, and they encamped there by the water." (Exodus 15:27) The next place the children of Israel came to was a place called "Elim." This place is thought to be identified in our day as the Wadi-Ghurandel. It still is a modern- day oasis with many types of trees, including palm trees. The water in this place is cool and fresh because there's a stream that runs through the middle of the settlement. Barnes describes Elim as about a mile in breadth, but its length stretches a long way to the northeast. It wasn't a little resort. It had to be large enough to accommodate the many thousands of Israelis during their journey. The name Elim seems to come from a root word with a meaning of "to protrude or stick out, such as a porch on a house, a ram in a flock, or a large tree." The word "wells" is better read as springs, since the Hebrew word used here means "eyes of water" or "sources of water." Elim was an extremely welcomed sight for these weary sojourners. They had already been through so much, but little did they realize what they were to face in the coming decades.

They encamped by the twelve springs. You'll find the number twelve used in 187 verses in our Bibles. The number twelve seems to have some significance with the Lord, as it represents, in most situations, the number of authority and completeness. The number twelve is mentioned 22 times in the book of Revelation. There were twelve tribes of Israel, which symbolizes the completeness of the nation of Israel and God's authority runs through those twelve tribes. Moses sent twelve spies into the promise land to spy out the land and bring back a report on that land. Solomon had twelve administrators in his kingdom. Jesus chose twelve disciples or apostles, teaching them directly to assimilate His Word into their lives, then taking that Word to the world after Jesus went back to heaven. Jesus' very first words that are recorded in Scripture were spoken at the age of twelve. The woman with the issue of blood who Jesus healed had the disease for twelve years. Jairus' daughter was twelve years old when she died, and Jesus raised her back to life. There are many other significant uses of this number in the Bible. It's evident that the Lord has ascribed the number twelve to have great meaning and purpose, which is governmental authority, completeness or perfection, and authority that has been given to man by God. According to Bible scholars, 12 is the product of 3, which signifies the divine, and 4, which signifies the earthly.

Then we come to the seventy palm trees. Seventy also has a significant meaning in Scripture. It's made up of two perfect numbers, seven which represents perfection, and ten, which stands once again for completeness and God's law. Therefore, the number seventy symbolizes perfect spiritual order that is performed with complete and perfect power. The first occurrence of the number seventy is seen with the family line of Shem, Japheth, and Ham as they repopulated the earth after the flood. When you add their descendants in Genesis 10, it reveals that there were seventy. Numbers 11:16 tells us that Moses appointed seventy elders. While in Egypt, the nation of Israel had its beginning with Joseph coming to second in command only to Pharaoh. During the seven years of famine, Jacob moved his entire family to Egypt. Joseph was already there, and we're told that the total number of Israelites that resided in

Egypt at that time was seventy. (Exodus 1:5) According to Isaiah 23:27, seventy years is the duration of days of a king. Man is promised seventy years of life on earth. (Psalm 90:10) Daniel prophesied of seventy weeks of judgment on God's people of Israel in Daniel 9:24. Israel spent seventy years of captivity in Babylon for not keeping seventy Sabbath years. The Egyptians mourned the death of Jacob for seventy days. (Genesis 50:3) Jesus sent seventy disciples out into the harvest field to reap the souls of men. (Luke 10:1) There are two main views of the meaning of the number seventy. 7 x 10 signifies perfect spiritual order and is carried out with all spiritual power and significance. Second, the number seventy is considered the number of universality or the restoration of all things. When God's complete and perfect spiritual order comes, everything will be restored as God ordered in the beginning. Jesus Christ came to give His life to redeem all the Father's creation back to the Father. Acts 3:19-21 reveals God's plans for the ages, "Repent therefore, and turn back, that your sins may be blotted out, that times of refreshing may come from the presence of the Lord, and that he may send the Christ appointed for you, Jesus, whom heaven must receive until the time for restoring all the things about which God spoke by the mouth of his holy prophets long ago." Repentance always comes before refreshing. Refreshing always comes from the presence of God. Jesus Christ, when finished with His work on earth the first time, returned to heaven. When He returns at His second coming, not the rapture of the church, He will begin to restore all of creation back to the original intention of the Father in the beginning.

The nation of Israel needed a great deal of rest and refreshing. The numbers three, twelve and seventy speak to us of the Father's complete renewal and refreshing of His people. The finality of the Egyptian army was complete. The crossing of the gigantic hurdle, The Red Sea, was complete. Their first big test at Marah was complete. Their long, difficult years spent in the land of Egypt was

161

complete. They had spent some harrowing hours in the past several days and weeks, preparing for their great exodus. The time to "encamp by the waters" for some time had come. Please allow me to refresh our memories of the story concerning the disciples' busyness in ministry. We're told in Mark 6:30-32, "The apostles returned to Jesus and told him all that they had done and taught. And he said to them, 'Come away by yourselves to a desolate place and rest a while.' For many were coming and going, and they had no leisure even to eat. And they went away in the boat to a desolate place by themselves." We often get so busy in going about "doing good" that we end up only to find ourselves weary in the battle. We may not be weary of the battle, but we certainly grow weary and tired in the busy seasons of life. But because they were so awfully busy, they forgot the Lord's instructions that He gave them back in Mark 3:14, 15. When Christ called His disciples, notice why He called them, "And he appointed twelve (whom he also named apostles) so that they might be with him and he might send them out to preach and have authority to cast out demons." Here's the exact order as to the why of God's call on our lives:

- **To Meet With Christ Personally – "So that they might be with him" – Learn From Christ Ourselves**

- **To Receive Our Message From Christ – "And send them out to preach" – Lessons To Teach About Christ For Others**

- **To Perform Ministry For Christ – "And have authority to cast out demons" – Live Out Christ's Message To Others**

As we put this in other ways, we might say that the Lord was putting together His TEAM, TRAINING them to go out from Him to perform TASKS for and to others, especially when He wouldn't be there with them. The greatest element in all of this is the COMPANIONSHIP they would have and enjoy with the Lord Himself. The vital and valuable lessons they would learn from Him directly would be the difference between life and death, between them moving forward or quitting when He would return to heaven, and between the world having a Christian witness after Jesus was gone, or not knowing anything about the salvation He provided through His death on the cross. From these intimate times as a TEAM, He would teach and instruct them about the day's events. Can you imagine the talks and discussions they must've had? After they would learn spiritual truths from the mouth of Jesus, they would then go COMMUNICATE those truths to others. He sent them out to teach and preach the Word of God. Then came ministry or COMPASSION toward others. They MET With Christ – Received their Message from Him – then went and did Ministry. We read Mark 6:12, 13 that they did just what they were told to do, "So they went out and proclaimed that people should repent. And they cast out many demons and anointed with oil many who were sick and healed them." However, when they got back to Jesus, Luke records what they said to Him, "The apostles returned to Jesus and told him all they had done and taught." They put what they "had done" first and then what they had "taught." That was the wrong order. I realize that oftentimes ministry is much more thrilling and exciting than "mere" teaching, but the main thing of the two is teaching. Jesus essentially said, "OK, we've been real busy with so many people and helping them. I want to get back to the main thing, and that is for you all to be with Me." They boarded a boat and went to a desolate place – by themselves. Remember, the very first instruction He gave these men was "to be with Him." When the people saw them leaving, they couldn't let Him go, so they followed Him and them. But notice what He did in verse 34, "When he went ashore, he saw a great crowd, and he had compassion on them, because they were like sheep without a shepherd. And he began to teach them many things."

Then He ministered to them by feeding them! If we are to experience flourishing souls and refreshment the way the Lord intends for us to experience and have, then we must follow His order of doing things. Our time with Christ is vital and essential. It is our daily sustenance of spiritual vitamins that is needed to face all our Red Sea crossings and Egyptian armies!

Psalm 103:2-7 provides some backdrop for God's renewal process, "Bless the Lord, O my soul, and forget not all his benefits, who forgives all your iniquity, who heals all your diseases, who redeems your life from the pit, who crowns you with steadfast love and mercy, who satisfies you with good so that your youth is renewed like the eagle's. The Lord works righteousness and justice for all who are oppressed. He made known his ways to Moses, his acts to the people of Israel." All these words represent God's very best that He has for us: benefits, forgives, redeems, crowns, satisfies, renewed, righteousness, justice and made known. The holy God provides all of these incredible actions upon His people, making "His ways" and "His acts" fully known, or "received in reality," to His people. Everything that comes from God results in His ultimate glory and our utter good. Nothing is wasted on us. The issues we view as obstacles that result in a predicament God views them as an opening that results in His peace. Our complications of life are God's certainties of His love for us. As it has been said, "Man's extremities are God's opportunities." All the difficult encounters that Israel would face as they travelled from Egypt to Canaan were nothing more than activities that displayed Divine encouragement. There are many lessons in our earthly journey that we can never learn aside from dipping our toes in some Red Sea before we experience the eye-opening and exuberating crossing of that Red Sea! **HE WILL MAKE HIMSELF KNOWN TO US AS WE REST IN HIM!**

The Lord gives us His promise of renewal and refreshment for our totality. Our hearts or inner self, our minds and bodies all need

His touch of renewal daily. It's His desire and design for us to find Him at our Elim.

- **For Our Heart – "So we do not lose heart. Though our outer self is wasting away, our inner self is being renewed day by day. For this light momentary affliction is preparing for us an eternal weight of glory beyond all comparison, as we look not to the things that are seen but to the things that are unseen. For the things that are seen are transient, but the things that are unseen are eternal." II Corinthians 4:16-18** The key to life's battles is to keep our inner being or soul refreshed, ready to face the next storm that must be calmed by the Master. In the light of eternity, everything in this life will become nothing but a fleeting memory after the Lord is finished bringing us to Elim. The second after we set foot on heaven's shore, all storms and trials of this life will be instantly vaporized!

- **For Our Mind – "Now this I say and testify in the Lord, that you must no longer walk as the Gentiles do, in the futility of their minds....to put off your old self, which belongs to your former manner of life and is corrupt through deceitful desires, and to be renewed in the spirit of your minds, and to put on the new self, created after the likeness of God in true righteousness and holiness." Ephesians 4:17, 22-24** Paul gives us a list of how the unsaved mind works in verses 18 and 19, and then he says in v. 20, "But that is not the way you learned Christ!" in verse 20. This renewing of our minds is a God-process that begins with "Let this mind be in you which was also in Christ Jesus." Romans 12:2 speaks to us of "Be not conformed to this world, but be transformed, by the renewing of your mind." As it took the Lord forty years to get Egypt out of His people, it'll take our lifetime for Him to transform our minds into one like His. He removes the worldly philosophies and replaces those with His wonderful principles.

- **For Our Body – "Put to death therefore what is earthly in you...But now you must put them all away: anger, wrath, malice, slander, and obscene talk from your mouth. Do not lie to one another, seeing that you have put off the old self, which is being renewed in knowledge after the image of its creator." Colossians 3:5, 8-10** As we allow and apply the knowledge, instruction and wisdom of God to our inner being and minds, it will have a holy effect on our bodies or actions. Our lives will change from the inside out, conforming us to the image of His dear Son.

Our entire being can be renewed and refreshed as we allocate God's principles into our presence and have them work themselves out through our practices. Almighty God is in the business of making all things new. God's design for all His creation is to be completely restored to Himself. He begins by saving our eternal souls at salvation. He continues to save us as He sets out to send trials and storms our way to bring us to the realization that we must have Him to make it across to the other side of the lake and to make the Red Sea crossings in our lives. We will face obstacles and hardships. There is no doubt about that. But for every storm we have His promise that He'll be in the boat with us. We have His Word to rely on as we journey from place to place, experiencing all that the wilderness can throw at us. Then we have His promises of times of renewal at Elim, for it's there we can rest assured we'll enjoy His twelve springs of refreshing water and seventy palm trees to change our perspective from doubt to delight, and to crystallize our persuasion to our duty and the Divine!

10

REJOICING IN OUR SAVIOR

"The next day the large crowd that had come to the feast heard that Jesus was coming to Jerusalem. So they took branches of palm trees and went out to meet him, crying out, 'Hosanna! Blessed is he who comes in the name of the Lord, even the King of Israel!' And Jesus found a young donkey and sat on it, just as it is written, 'Fear not, daughter of Zion; behold, your king is coming, sitting on a donkey's colt!' His disciples did not understand these things at first, but when Jesus was glorified, then they remembered that these things had been written about him and had been done to him. The crowd that had been with him when he called Lazarus out of the tomb and raised him from the dead continued to bear witness. The reason why the crowd went to meet him was that they heard he had done this sign. So the Pharisees said to one another, 'You see that you are gaining nothing. Look, the world has gone after him.'" John 12:12-19

"After this I looked, and behold, a great multitude that no one could number, from every nation, from all tribes and peoples and languages, standing before the throne and before the Lamb, clothed in white robes, with palm branches in their

hands, and crying out with a loud voice, 'Salvation belongs to our God who sits on the throne, and to the Lamb!' And all the angels were standing around the throne and around the elders and the four living creatures, and they fell on their faces before the throne and worshiped God, saying, 'Amen! Blessing and glory and wisdom and thanksgiving and honor and power and might be to our God forever and ever! Amen.'" Revelation 7:9-12

These two passages portray both similar and contrasting reactions to the Lord. The passage in John provides us a glimpse to the past of different people's reactions when Jesus entered Jerusalem a week before His crucifixion. The Revelation passage reveals to us a great scene in heaven yet to come of a cosmopolitan and vast crowd worshiping God the Father and God the Son around the mighty throne of God! The similarities are that many people are praising the Lord holding palm branches and crying out their words of worship. The contrasting elements consist of the place of worship, earth versus heaven. The people in Jesus' day didn't really grasp or comprehend who He really was. The raising of Lazarus made headlines in the newspapers around Israel and this miracle, or sign as John calls Christ's miracles, was the benchmark of all His miracles up to that point. Another major contrasting element between the two passages is the reason for their worship. Jesus was certainly their King and they wanted to recognize Him as King at that moment in time, but only for their own purposes. They wanted to throw off the Roman rule so badly, and they thought Jesus was going to be the person to do just that; however, He had come to serve and give His life as a ransom for them. The time of His authority and rule on earth will be for a time in the future. The innumerable people in heaven were there for the coronation of King Jesus forever. The people gathered in Jerusalem were there for various reasons while the vast crowd of people in heaven were focused on their praise of almighty God. The enormous crowd in heaven was praising the Lord for salvation provided by the Lord and His incredible, majestic Person! What we have before us is the listing of the sevenfold character of God, denoting His universal, all-embracing and all-encompassing Person! John records these words in Revelation 5:11-14, "Then I looked, and I heard around the throne and the living creatures and the elders the voice of many angels, numbering myriads of myriads and thousands of thousands, saying with a loud voice, 'Worthy is the Lamb who was slain, to receive power and wealth and wisdom and might and honor and glory and blessing!' And I heard every creature in heaven and on earth and under the earth and in the sea, and all that is in them, saying, 'To him who sits on the throne and to the Lamb be blessing and honor and glory and might forever and ever!' And the four living creatures said, 'Amen!' and the elders fell down and worshiped." Here, the four living creatures respond, "Amen" to the praises voiced by the angels; in Revelation 7:12, in response to the praise uttered by the earth's redeemed the angels say, "Amen." These two dramatic scenes, yet to come, are nothing more than preparatory to what's going to take place throughout eternity! The adoration of Jesus in Jerusalem on that first Palm Sunday was nothing more than a minute version of adoration, praise and worship for Jesus Christ. Many people had no idea why they were there. They had heard about the raising of Lazarus and that Jesus was going to make an appearance in Jerusalem during Passover, but the magnitude of the moment was missed by most. Not so in heaven. There will be such praise and worship happening to and for our glorious King that the only responses will be "Amen" and "Amen!" The last great contrast between these two events of praise is that nothing is mentioned of the clothing worn by the people that day in Jerusalem. I'm sure many wanted to look their finest and best for the coming of the King of Israel. Most people didn't have a great amount of clothing to choose from for their daily attire. They did, however, have those clothes that were for special occasions, so I'm sure they wore those for this great festival of Passover. I'm sure the Pharisees had on their usual attire that made them stand out from the rest of the crowd, to draw attention to themselves. But we're told that the enormous crowd of people in heaven were wearing white robes. These robes are robes of righteousness, which have been placed on these people because their sins had been cleansed by the blood of Christ! Revelation tells us, "All who are victorious will be clothed in white. I will never erase their names from the Book of Life, but I will announce before my Father and his angels that they are mine." We then read in 4:4 these words, "Twenty-four thrones surrounded him, and twenty-four elders sat on them. They were all clothed in white and had gold crowns on their heads." Let's move forward to chapter 15 and verse 6 to read this, "The seven angels who were holding the bowls of the seven plagues came from the Temple, clothed in spotless white linen with gold belts across their chests." We read in 19:14, "The armies of heaven, dressed in pure white linen, followed him on white horses." This is Christ returning to set up His earthly kingdom with us! It seems that the attire of heaven will be basic white, and this will be all the time. Obviously, the symbolism is great in all these situations. White is the color for cleanliness and holiness. When Christ was transfigured before Peter, James and John, the Bible says that His garment became whiter than any cleansing agent could clean it on earth. The idea of all peoples wearing white speaks of the majestic and glorious environment that heaven will be. The very presence of the holy God requires purity and holiness, and white captures this theological point perfectly. Would we expect anything less than people wearing white garments to express God's holiness? On the other hand, the white references may just be pointing out the appearance of shining holiness coming out from these people because they are now perfected and made completely holy! Follow Paul's language in I Corinthians 15:40-45, "There are bodies in the heavens, and there are bodies on earth. The glory of the heavenly bodies is different from the beauty of the earthly bodies. The sun has one kind of glory, while the moon and stars each have another kind. And even the stars differ from each other in their beauty and brightness. It is the same way for the resurrection of the dead. Our earthly bodies, which die and decay, will be different when they are resurrected, for they will never die. Our bodies now disappoint us; but when they are raised, they will be full of glory. They are weak now; but when they are raised, they will be full of power. They are natural human bodies now; but when they are raised, they will spiritual bodies. For just as there are natural bodies, so also there will be spiritual bodies." Many key elements about our heavenly bodies are discovered in this passage. Our heavenly bodies and earthly bodies will be totally different. That's obvious, but the differences given in this passage are major. Our earthly bodies decay and are weak and will die. Our heavenly bodies "will be full of glory" and "will be full of power." We then discover that just like the difference between sunshine, the glow of the moon and the twinkling of the stars, our resurrected bodies will reflect that same difference. In other words, part of God's reward program will be to give us shining or glowing bodies in heaven! Some people will be lit up like a 100-watt bulb, while others will be glowing at a 25-watt power. Could this be why all the people referenced in heaven are wearing white? Is that white color the glow of their resurrected bodies? Whatever it may mean, the appearance of all will be a majestic and glorious sight to be sure!

Now let's focus on one of the similarities between the praise given to Jesus in Jerusalem and that of the Father and Son in heaven. The crowd in Jerusalem laid palm branches before the Lord as He rode down the street. The crowd in heaven had palm branches in their hands as they praised God. Palm branches represent victory, peace and eternal life. Let's put ourselves right in the middle of that group of Jews as they began their journey after the Red

Sea crossing and their victory over Egypt. They had been walking for three days through unknown lands, while the blazing sun was beating down upon them. All these people had ever known was familiar to them. It may have been doing something that someone else wanted them to do, but they knew what they were going to do each day. It's like our routines we get ourselves comfortable with doing daily. We know that most weeks we're going to get up and go to work. We spend the 8 or so hours working, and we go home. We may have some daily chores to do around the house, but then we settle in for the night, maybe watch some game on TV and go to bed, getting ready to repeat the routine that next day. We get adjusted to our schedules and settle in. On this day we do that. On that day we do this. On the weekends we do such and such. The only difference comes if we take a vacation or a day off here or there; but for the most part, we have daily and weekly habits and routines that are followed as if we're doing something that someone else wants us to do. We're really not that much different than the nation of Israel was during their days in Egyptian captivity. Our routines and habits keep us captive to the task at hand. Now this great number of people were free. They were on their way home, back to the land the Lord had given to them. Their minds and hearts might have been back to those days they had spent in Egypt, just because of the security that it meant for them. Now they faced the unknown, and I'm sure their hearts began to melt with anxiety of some level or another. Now comes that day when Israel, already weary and worn out after their victory over Egypt through the Red Sea crossing, comes around the bend of the trail or over that hill and there lies Elim right in front of them! Our God knows precisely where we are. He knows exactly what we need and when we need it. The fears and anxieties of His people must have been great. They didn't have fresh water to drink. They really didn't know if the complete army of Egypt was destroyed, or maybe some had escaped and would be upon them before they know it. What about tomorrow? What's going to happen then? How are the moms and dads going to care for their children out in the middle of nowhere? Their hearts and minds surely were filled with such thoughts and fears. Then there's Elim.

I didn't have the opportunity to travel much outside my home area of Michigan until I was older. I was born in Indiana and moved to Michigan when I was ten. Those were the only two states I knew in my life until my mid-twenties. I had the opportunity to go to Florida for more education and my school senior trips at that time. I had never seen a palm tree in my life until my times spent in Florida. I couldn't stop looking at them. I had seen pictures of them in books and on TV shows, but to see them in person was amazing to me. I felt as if I were on another planet. It gave me such a feeling of relaxation and refreshment. I had an almost euphoric feeling that today was going to be a fantastic day and a brighter hope for tomorrow. The thought of being in an exotic place capable of growing palm trees was something that I had never experienced before in my life. I realize that I was there for just a few days to either watch over a group of students or gain some knowledge, but when I went outside and walked in the midst of such vegetation, my outlook shifted from a sense of work to that of ease and relaxation. The duties of life seemed to fall from my shoulders onto the ground for someone else to pick up. It was a feeling like no other feeling I ever had. Then our middle son moved to California. We visited him twice before he moved to Texas. Those two trips to Cali were met with the very same feelings I had during my trips to Florida. Again, I realize I was there on vacation, but southern California is a different world than the one I'm used to. I really don't know how a person can get any work done living in such a beautiful environment. It's so laid back and such great weather day after day to enjoy that I really don't know how anyone can go into an office building, do their jobs, all the while knowing what's outside! Lord help me if I'm ever able to go to Hawaii! Right now, if I close my eyes, I can go to Florida or California in my mind and recapture all those feelings I had while visiting those two beautiful states. I can return and relive some of those feelings and thoughts, taking a brief vacation, if only in my mind. But it refreshes and renews me just the same. My routine day can be changed into a refreshing day as I allow my mind to take me away to a beach in Florida or Cali, lined with palm trees and enjoying a nice, warm, tropical breeze!

Now comes Elim. Elim had twelve springs or pools of cool, refreshing water for a weary and worried people to drink and enjoy. But God also had seventy palm trees to refresh their weary and worn out souls! I can only imagine what that oasis in the middle of nowhere meant to this people. And God knew that, too. Those springs of water and palm trees refreshed and renewed their bodies and spirits like nothing else could have done. God knew exactly what they needed to meet the needs of a tired, weary and discouraged people. Our lives are no different. He knows us and calls us by name. He understands that we are frail and weak, weary from our daily routines and grind of life. He brings us to an Elim in our life, springs of cool, refreshing water to quench our thirsty hearts and palm trees to quiet our trying souls.

The scene at Jerusalem that first Palm Sunday and the innumerable crowd of people in heaven as seen by John at some future date are praising the King of kings with palm branches in their hands. The nation of Israel came to a place filled with palm trees. The symbolism speaks to us of a giant victory and gigantic celebration! We read at the end of Exodus 14 these words found in verses 30 and 31, "Thus the Lord saved Israel that day from the hand of the Egyptians, and Israel saw the Egyptians dead on the seashore. Israel saw the great power that the Lord used against the Egyptians; so the people feared the Lord, and they believed in the Lord and in his servant Moses." We then read the massive song of victory by Moses in Exodus 15. For eighteen verses we read of God's might and power against the enemies of His people, and for their behalf. It's all great, but read the highlights from this declaration of victory:

> **"Then Moses and the people of Israel sang this song to the Lord, saying, 'I will sing to the Lord, for he has triumphed gloriously... The Lord is my strength and my song, and he has become my salvation; this is my God, and I will praise him, my father's God, and I will exalt him. The Lord is a man of war; the Lord is his name.... You have led in your steadfast love the people whom you have redeemed; you have guided them by your strength to you holy abode.... The Lord will reign forever and ever."**

The time had come for Israel to celebrate God's mighty victory over their foe and enemy, Egypt. He was busy redeeming His people back to Himself and back to their homeland. He had eliminated their main threat to their liberty and peace and the time to kick back and have a victory party was on! This is what Elim was meant to be for Israel. Moses captured the tone of the day in his song and Israel sang right along with him.

The truth is that we can always celebrate and rejoice in our Lord. When my dad went to heaven in 1987, we were serving the Lord in Massachusetts. I said in my sermon at church the Sunday I returned that we Christians can rejoice in the Lord no matter what comes our way. A lady in my church took a little exception with my statement and asked to speak with me after church. I listened to her and went back through my text of that day, "Rejoice in the Lord always; Again, I will say, rejoice." I simply explained that I wasn't rejoicing in the fact that my dad had died and would no longer be with us, but that I was still rejoicing in MY Lord and what He meant to my family and what He did for my dad and family during that difficult time. I went on to say that while we were sad for our loss, we were happy for him because he didn't have to suffer any longer with his cancer. I further explained that I wanted to remain focused on the Lord and His deep care for me and my family, rejoicing in His care, compassion and comfort. I took it to the next step by telling her some of the lessons He had taught me during those hard days that led up to his passing. Finally, I led her to the truth that while our earthly relationships experience dramatic and a seemingly tragic end, our relationship with the Lord will remain constant because our Lord remains faithful to us week after week, month after month and year after year. The Lord reminds us throughout Holy Scripture of this wonderful truth. Look at these marvelous passages that should leave His mark on your life all along your life's journey:

"Rejoice in the Lord, O you righteous…" Psalm 33:1

"I will bless the Lord at all times: his praise shall continually be in my mouth…" Psalm 34, 1, 2

"I will extol you, my God, O king; and I will bless your name for ever and ever…" Psalm 145:1, 2

"While I live will I praise the LORD: I will sing praises to my God while I have any being." Psalm 146:1

"Sorrowful, yet always rejoicing…" II Corinthians 6:10

"Finally, my brothers, rejoice in the Lord…" Philippians 3:1

"Rejoice at all times…" I Thessalonians 5:16

"Rejoicing in hope; patient in tribulation; continuing instant in prayer…" Romans 12:12

We must be careful to read each word in the Bible thoughtfully and pay close attention to all that the words mean and are saying. That little word "in" in Phil. 4:4 is a preposition, denoting "position and instrumentality, a relation of rest such as "in" or "on" or "by." What the Lord is telling us is to find ourselves resting in our position as a child of His, relying on the instrumentality of all that He is and all that He can do. Therefore, no matter what happens to us, our family, our friends or our situations of life, the Lord will always be there, positioned to act on our behalf, so we can confidently rest in Him and relax knowing that He has us in His care. Israel needed to be reminded of this awesome care by their God at the wells and palm trees found in Elim! We need to recall that Paul wrote this letter to the church at Philippi from prison. It was in prison that he and Silas were heard singing God's grace at midnight, and the Philippian jailor came hurriedly in and asked what he needed to do to be saved! Joy is the overriding theme in the book of Philippians, but here in 4:4, Paul is telling us that it is the joy found in the Lord as the only way possible for a thoughtful mind or a feeling heart to make it through a Red Sea crossing or the ability to arrive on the other side of the lake! I believe Paul is emphasizing joy in the Lord so much throughout this book that Christian joy is our chief duty. Chrysostom said, "He who rejoices in the Lord is always rejoicing, for we have Him with us always."[1] Matthew Henry writes, "Joy in God is of great consequence in the Christian life; and Christians need to be again and again called to it. It more than outweighs all causes for sorrow. Let their enemies perceive how moderate they were as to outward things, and how composedly they suffered loss and hardships."[2] Rejoicing in the Lord comes down to us making a choice to do so or not. The time may be difficult. The situation may be a matter of life and death. The sun may be setting too fast on an issue and darkness with confusion may be coming when it does set. However, none of these issues alter the fact that our God is still on His throne and Jesus is still making intercession for us to the

Father! Our relationship with Him hasn't been severed or broken. He's still there. As the song says, "He's only a prayer away," and He's ready, willing and able to listen. As Peter walked across those boisterous waves, Christ was there. In fact, He was the One who asked him to get out of the boat and walk to Him! It was when Peter took his eyes off the Lord that he began to sink. The next words out of Peter's mouth were simply, "Lord, save me!" And Jesus did. So, have you arrived at Elim? Are you there in your heart, mind and soul? Go ahead, encamp there by the water, for "The Lord is my shepherd; I shall not want. He makes me lie down in green pastures. He leads me beside still waters. He restores my soul…" It's OK. It's alright. Sit back and enjoy the cool, springs of water, allowing them to refresh your spirit. Visit Jesus at the well in Samaria as He spoke with the woman there. Listen to His words He gave her that warm day, "If you knew that gift of God, and who it is that is saying to you, 'Give me a drink,' you would have asked him, and he would have given you living water." (John 4) So drink. Spend time with the living waters found in God's Word. Allow those waters to clean and comfort your weary soul. Then close your eyes and see yourself surrounded by numerous palm trees. Do you hear the wind softly blowing through their leaves? Are you seeing yourself lounging and relaxing in this exotic setting? Israel was ready for such a time of renewal and refreshment. Are you?

The more I read the Old Testament the more I see the one cycle Israel went through most often. It was seen in the book of Judges as a new judge would come to rule over the nation. The cycle went something like this: sin, slavery, supplication, salvation, spiritual lethargy, back into sin and so on. When it comes to the kings of Israel and Judah, they were known for their relationship with God or the lack of one. The northern ten tribes of Israel never did have a righteous king, while Judah would often go back and forth between kings who did right in the sight of God and those who left the ways of God. In our churches today, many Christians will react to the Lord accordingly. If things are moving forward in the right direction, which is the direction they think their life should go, then they're walking in step with the Lord. However, if life takes some sideways turns, then their warmth for and walk with the Lord cools off dramatically. The prophet Habakkuk prophesied during a rough stretch in Israel's history. Nothing is much known about this man of God. The very fact that the prophet is only known to us by name highlights the unimportance of the messenger and the vast importance of the message he brought. The key figure is always the Lord and what He wants us to know. Habakkuk's name means "embracer" or "wrestler," thus providing us the window of focus into this book. These three chapters reveal the heart of Habakkuk as he wrestles with God over his beloved Israel. We see that he embraces God by faith, embraces his nation with great national empathy, and relays God's message of encouragement coming through the eventual judgment on Babylon. When Habakkuk delivered his message to the people of God, the southern kingdom of Judah was mired in its sin of disobedience and rejection of God as their King, experiencing great political turmoil because of the sins of the king and people. Idolatry was the preferred sin of this day. Habakkuk himself is seen contending with the Lord, while chapter three shows him submitting to the Lord's authority. He doesn't know if his prayers and pleas will help change the mind of God or not, so he continues to discuss alternative ways to get around the coming doom on his beloved Israel. We can begin to see the work of the Lord on Habakkuk's heart in 2:20, "But the Lord is in his holy temple; let all the earth keep silence before him." He recognizes the mighty work of God in everything that comes man's way. He's beginning to really understand that the Lord is on His throne in heaven and we're to remain silent before Him when it comes to His perfect will and planned ways. Habakkuk goes to prayer in chapter three, "O Lord, I have heard the report of you, and your work, O Lord, do I fear. In the midst of the years revive it; in the midst of the years make it known; in wrath remember mercy." He has come to the point that all of us must come to in our lives: God's reputation and resume is awesome, and we must respond with revered fear. God's works are an amazing list of unbelievable actions that are for the benefit and betterment of those who leave their life's choices with Him. We may have made some choice that has gone against the will, way or Word of God, which has resulted in our relationship with the Lord to be strained or even severed. We may have had some life experience that hasn't been fully processed in our hearts and minds that has brought us to the doorstep of bitterness. One episode has been within our control and choice, while the other event has been outside the bounds and power of our control or choice. Either way, we find ourselves right where Habakkuk found himself – praying to the Lord to revive His work in our lives, then to reveal that work to others. Then comes the main element in this short prayer – "Lord, in wrath remember mercy." Habakkuk is essentially saying these words, "OK, OK. The people of Israel have turned their collective backs on the work, will and Word of God. OK, OK. Lord, you must punish and discipline your children. I get it. But, please, please, please, in your wrath upon Your people, please, please, please remember that you are a God of mercy, also." We always want to remind God of His matchless mercy and greatness of His grace!

Now we come to the pivotal point in Habakkuk's message. The inevitable day of God's judgment is coming and there isn't anything that anyone can do about it. From what he knows and from what he's been told, Habakkuk responds to this Word from the Lord as any one of us would have responded. Habakkuk 2:16 brings so much of humanity into this whole scene, "I hear, and my body trembles; my lips quiver at the sound; rottenness enters into my bones; my legs tremble beneath me. Yet I will quietly wait for the day of trouble to come upon people who invade us." The prophet was experiencing a total meltdown. He wasn't prepared to face all that was going to come upon himself and his fellow citizens. The panic was beginning to settle in, and he was living through a constant panic attack. Fear grabbed hold of his mind, heart and soul. The "hearing" and "sound" of the words of God was too much for him to handle. He describes his body as "trembling" and his "lips quivering" for all the horrific days that lay ahead. The "rottenness" that entered his bones was more than likely a great sense of anxiety, which brought on this feeling of great weakness in his legs. This is letting us know that the strongest parts of his body had become so weak that he couldn't stand, let alone walk. The coming disaster that was war and the devastating effects of captivity that would follow was becoming too much for even God's man at this point. Then he makes this statement, "Yet I will quietly wait for the day of trouble." The actual thought presented to us here is "to rest and settle down." When episodes of our making or events that lie outside our control happen and are unpreventable, our anxieties and stresses must be swept aside based on our joyful and overpowering confidence in our Savior and God! When the lake that is our life becomes stormy, let's rest and settle down in Him. When that storm becomes of hurricane force and we think that we'll never make it to the other side, let's rest and settle down in Him.

Habakkuk, however, takes all of this to whole other level. Read carefully the words found in Hab. 3:17-19, "Though the fig tree should not blossom, nor fruit be on the vines, the produce of the olive fail and the fields yield no food, the flock be cut off from the fold and there be no herd in the stalls, yet I will rejoice in the Lord; I will take joy in the God of my salvation. God, the Lord, is my strength; he makes my feet like the deer's; he makes me tread on my high places. For the choir director: This prayer is to be accompanied by stringed instruments." The prophet is describing the aftermath of an enemy invasion, which would cause the human, frail heart to despair even of life. The utter devastation of an invading army would most assuredly leave the countryside barren of all natural, food sources. We're told in Deuteronomy, Isaiah and Jeremiah that the Chaldeans, Assyrians and Egyptians cut down and burnt the fruit-bearing trees of the countries which they conquered. The trees that were part of the basic food group and economy are the ones mentioned by the prophet in this passage. The olive oil industry dries up because of it. Anyone who is familiar with Middle East cooking knows how vitally important olive oil is to the preparation of his meals, as well as selling it on the world market. That's all gone. The fields of corn as well as the other crops fail. This desolation and defoliation causes, the meat industry to fold because livestock has nothing to eat. The first and foremost effect of war then is famine, especially if it's done on purpose as it was in this case. Nothing will cause a society to collapse as fast as famine. When a country cannot feed its citizens, then that country will become vulnerable and fall prey to all kinds of evil. Hunger will lead to theft, which would lead to murder, which would lead to anarchy, which would result in the total breakdown of all that is civil. We see this happening in the time period the Bible calls The Great Tribulation. Food will become so scarce that a person will have to work all day in order to buy a piece of bread. There is nothing that a hungry man won't do in order to eat. Habakkuk knew this was coming upon his country and people. And then he writes, "Yet, I will rejoice in the Lord…" One translation has this verse saying, "Yet I will triumph in Yahweh; I will rejoice in the God of my salvation!" Others put it, "As for me, I will rejoice in the Lord;" "I will rejoice because of the Lord;" "Even then, I will be happy with the Lord." Job says in 13:15, "Though he slay me, I will hope in Him." Several Psalms come to mind here: "Guide me in your truth and teach me, for you are the God of my salvation; all day long I wait for you." 25:5; "The Lord is my light and my salvation – whom shall I fear? The Lord is the stronghold of my life – whom shall I dread?" 27:1; "God is our refuge and strength; I will trust and not be afraid. For the LORD GOD is my strength and my song, and he also has become my salvation." 46:1. Please allow me to offer some other verses in Psalms that could've been mentioned here, but please take note of their locations and add them to the three that were given: Psalm 5:7; 13:6; 17:14, 15; 31:19. The literal rendering of Habakkuk's words found in 3:18 tells us, "I will SHOUT for joy, expressing it outwardly." The prophet then goes in the totally opposite direction. He begins with a lament over the fact that there won't be enough food to feed everyone. He continues by saying that he's going to visibly praise the Lord and rest or settle down, all based on that "God remains his salvation." He proceeds to look at the end of all things and realizes that his God will bring him to experience of the heights of his salvation once again! This is an adaptation of Psalm 18. Throughout this majestic Psalm we read of God being our rock and fortress, our shield and stronghold, our deliverer and defense. Listen to the wording of verse 19, "He brought me out into a broad place; he rescued me, because he delighted in me." Then verse 36 states, "you gave a wide place for my steps under me, and my feet did not slip." Finally, verses 39, 46, 49 and 50 tells us, "For you equipped me with strength for the battle;" "The Lord lives, and blessed be my rock, and exalted be the God of my salvation;" "for this I will praise you, O Lord, among the nations, and sing to your name. Great salvation he brings to his king, and shows steadfast love to his anointed, to David and his offspring forever." Right in the middle of invading armies and ferocious enemies, David, the psalmist in this case, praises the Lord for all His help and aid in delivering David from his enemies, especially King Saul. The significance of "walking in high places" speaks of the ultimate victory God's people will enjoy. It literally denotes the victorious possession and government of a country. The truth is that all believers, believing Israel here, shall once and for all overcome all opposition and dwell in safety within its own borders. Then Habakkuk orders this to be given to the chief musician to be sung by stringed instruments! Really? Even though war and famine is coming, we're to rest and settle down in the presence of our great God. While our world is being destroyed around us, we're to SHOUT praises to our God! The Lord wants others to see our inner rejoicing outwardly. Once again, let me turn to the wise words of Matthew Henry: "When we see a day of trouble approach, it concerns us to prepare. A good hope through grace is founded in holy fear. The prophet looked back upon the experiences of Israel in former ages and observed what great things God had done for them, and so was not only recovered, but filled with holy joy. **He resolved to delight and triumph in the Lord; for when all is gone, his God is not gone.** Destroy the vines and fig-trees, and you make all the mirth of a carnal heart to cease. But those who, when full, enjoyed God in all, when emptied and poor, can enjoy all in God. They can sit down upon the heap of the ruins of their crea- ture-comforts, and even then, praise the Lord, as the God of their salvation, the salvation of the soul, and rejoice in him as such, in their greatest distresses. Joy in the Lord is especially seasonable when we meet with losses and crosses in the world. Even when the provisions are cut off, to make it appear that man lives not by bread alone, we may be supplied by the graces and comforts of God's Spirit. **Then we shall be strong for spiritual warfare and work, and with enlargement of heart may run the way of his com- mandments and outrun our troubles.** And we shall be successful in spiritual undertakings. Thus, the prophet, who began his prayer with fear and trembling, ends it with joy and triumph. And thus, faith in Christ prepares for every event. The name of Jesus, when we can speak of Him as ours, is balm for every wound, a cordial for every care. It is as ointment poured forth, shedding fragrance through the whole soul. **"In the hope of a heavenly crown, let us sit loose to earthly possessions and comforts, and cheerfully bear up under crosses. Yet a little while, and he that shall come will come, and will not tarry, and where He is, we shall be also."**[3] Habakkuk took some time getting to this place in his soul, but he got there. Each one of us will take our own route in getting to this place of resting and settling ourselves in our God. Life is filled with monstrous events that will take just about everything from us. We really don't know if we'll see tomorrow in the aftermath of life's biggest ordeals. Honestly, we may not even want to see tomorrow. This is when our faith raises our focus to the God of our salvation. He's there. He'll always be there no matter what befalls us. We may not want to sing right now, but our song will return as we turn our complete focus on our loving and caring heavenly Father. "Sing to the Lord, O you his saints, and give thanks to his holy name. For his anger lasts only a moment, but his favor lasts a lifetime! Weeping may last through the night, but joy comes with the morning." Psalm 30:4, 5

Although I've been discussing the idea of rejoicing in the Lord when situations may not warrant it and we really don't have any desire to do so, there are so many examples in God's Word to rejoice in Him because it does warrant that response from us. In the days before Christ, young women knew the theology behind the birth of the coming Messiah. They prepared themselves by remaining pure sexually. Mary was one of those young girls. One day, the angel Gabriel was sent by the Lord to the little town of Nazareth in Northern Israel. All we're told about Mary was that she was a virgin, engaged to a young man named Joseph. As it turned out, Mary and Joseph, were both from David's ancestral line. He opens the conversation by saying, "Greetings, O favored one, the Lord is with you!" Gabriel continues to explain all that's going to happen to her and Joseph. Mary's first response is that of humility and submission, "Behold, I am the servant of the Lord; let it be to me according to your word." She essentially signed the contract and is ready for this amazing event. Mary took a trip to visit her cousin, Elizabeth, who was pregnant with John the Baptist, to discuss all of this with her. When the baby heard the news in her womb, he couldn't help himself from rejoicing! Then Mary wrote a song of praise to the Lord. She began with, "My soul magnifies the Lord, and my spirit rejoices in God my Savior, for he has looked on the humble estate of his servant." (Luke 2)

When things turn south for us, it's not our natural tendency to offer the Lord praise and to rejoice in Him. When things take a major upturn, oftentimes we fail to look up and offer the praise that's due His wonderful work on our behalf, but to look at ourselves as the cause of our successes. Not Mary. She was quick to recognize her "humble estate" and ready to let everyone know that it was her "soul" that was magnifying the Lord at this glorious news! She would be the one that would birth the Savior of mankind into the world! The rest of Mary's song recounts God's awesome faithfulness to His people throughout their history. She begins this section with the words, "For he who is mighty has done great things for me, and holy is his name." She's very quick to get the attention off her and back on the Person responsible for this great news – the holy name of her God and Savior!

After the birth of Jesus in Bethlehem, shepherds were told about this momentous event. After the angels left them, "they went with haste and found Mary and Joseph, and the baby lying in a manger." They began to do the only natural thing they could do at that point, they told everyone they saw about what they had seen. Then we read in Luke 2:20, "And the shepherds returned, glorifying and praising God for all they had heard and seen, as it had been told them." Rejoicing in the Lord should be our first response after seeing the work of God in action.

In Acts 3, we see Peter and John going to church at the hour of prayer. A lame man was lying outside begging from people as they walked into church. This man had been crippled from birth. When Peter and John walked by him, he asked them for some money. Peter simply said, "We don't have silver or gold, but what I do have I give to you. In the name of Jesus Christ of Nazareth, rise up and walk!" Peter then reached down and took him by the hand

and helped him to stand. Remember, he had never walked before so he had no idea what it felt like to get up by himself. The Bible tells us that his legs and ankles immediately received the strength they needed to support him "and leaping up he stood and began to walk, and entered the temple with them, walking and leaping and praising God." I guess he would! I know I'd be shouting and jumping around if that had happened to me! It was his natural response after the working of God in his life.

We read the story of Philip and the Ethiopian Eunuch in Acts 8. This eunuch was worshiping the Lord in Jerusalem and was on his way home to Ethiopia. The Lord had everything arranged for this impromptu meeting. The man was reading Isaiah 53. The Holy Spirit told Philip to get over and speak with the man who was riding in this "specific" chariot. Philip heard him reading this Scripture out loud and then simply asked him, "Do you under-stand what you're reading?" The eunuch told him that he needed someone to explain it to him. Philip did and the man came to Christ for salvation. Now, this weary traveler who just came to Christ saw his need to be baptized, so they stopped the chariot, got down, walked into some water that was by the road, and Philip baptized him right then and there! We pick up the story in Acts 8:39, "And when they came up out of the water, the Spirit of the Lord carried Philip away, and the eunuch saw him no more, and went on his way rejoicing." Again, we see a person's natural response to the Lord working in his life.

Here's the bottom line in all of this. We tend to think and believe that anything "bad" or "terrible" isn't from God and should not be met with us rejoicing in the Lord. We have come to experience and even expect the "good" or "great" things come from the Lord, and we often respond accordingly with praise, worship and rejoicing in the Lord. However, we need to grasp the full meaning of Romans 8:28 within the entire context of that amazing truth. To get a com-plete and total picture of where the Apostle Paul has gone at the end of chapter 8, we need to capture the overall intent of this marvelous chapter. The first seventeen verses speak to us of living life in and through the Spirit of God. It is essentially teaching us to live the Divine life through our life. Of course, this all begins with verse one that teaches us, "So now there is no condemnation for those who belong to Christ Jesus." Besides John 3:16, it's hard for me to imagine any more encouraging and inspired string of words put together as those found in this verse. In God's mind and through His viewpoint, those who have claimed Christ as Savior stand in complete exoneration of all their sins before a holy and righteous God! Christians may be disciplined of the Lord after salvation for unconfessed sin, but we will never be condemned with the world! The Law of Moses could not accomplish this act of being set free from judgment. It is only through the grace of Christ found in the Gospel of Jesus Christ that can ever produce this freedom and liberty. The next sixteen verses explain to us that this freedom is our present reality, and that reality is produced in and through the indwelling Holy Spirit. After Paul finishes this section regarding living life in and through the Spirit of God, he now turns his attention to the larger picture of God's working in us during our lives, which will eventually end up receiving God's full glory. Please read through these verses carefully in order to understand the Spirit's full intentions for every one of us:

> **"Yet what we suffer now is nothing compared to the glory he will give us later. For all creation is waiting eagerly for that future day when God will reveal who his children really are. Against its will, everything on earth was subjected to God's curse. All creation anticipates the day when it will join God's children in glorious freedom from death and decay. For we know that all creation has been groaning as in**

the pains of childbirth right up to the present time. And even we Christians, although we have the Holy Spirit within us as a foretaste of future glory, also groan to be released from pain and suffering. We, too, wait anxiously for that day when God will give us our full rights as his children, including the new bodies he has promised us. Now that we are saved, we eagerly look forward to this freedom. For if you already have something, you don't need to hope for it. But if we look forward to something we don't have yet, we must wait patiently and confidently. And the Holy Spirit helps us in our distress. For we don't even know what we should pray for, nor how we should pray. But the Holy Spirit prays for us with groaning that cannot be expressed in words. And the Father who knows all hearts knows what the Spirit is saying, for the Spirit pleads for us believers in harmony with God's own will. And we know that God causes everything to work together for the good of those who love God and are called according to his purpose for them. For God knew his people in advance, and he chose them to become like his Son, so that his Son would be the firstborn, with many brothers and sisters. And having chosen them, he called them to come to him. And he gave them right standing with himself, and he promised them his glory." Romans 8:18-30

There are impurities and infirmities which have been cast upon God's creation because of the fall of man. I can't help to think that Paul is recalling of all his own personal setbacks and sufferings.

We can read of these infirmities in Acts 19:23-41, II Corinthians 6:4, 5, and 11:23-28. But in the final analysis, he would count all of this as "dung," according to Philippians 3:8. In his last will and testament found in II Timothy 4, he tells us, "I have fought a good fight. I have finished the race, and I have remained faithful. And now the prize awaits me - the crown of righteousness that the Lord, the righteous Judge, will give me on that great day of his return." What we have laid out for us in the Romans 8 passage is telling us that the sufferings of God's people through the ages hit us no deeper or harder than the element of time, will last no longer than this present day and age, are nothing more than light and momentary infirmities, and that they are nothing in comparison to our future glory with the Lord! The Lord is telling us that the momentary impurities and infirmities of our human race is declaring to the rest of creation that our world will not continue as it is in its present "state of affairs." God is coming again to redeem man and His entire creation back to Himself! Therefore, having received God's Holy Spirit as our own, this should enliven our spirits, encourage our hopes, and electrify our expectations. Sin is the culprit in man's destructive spirit and creation's demise from perfection. While the sins of man are many, we would be without hope and power if left to ourselves. But God, in His mercy, has given to us His Spirit to make intercession for us. He enlightens us and teaches us what to pray. He comforts and encourages us as travel along life's road. We have the confidence knowing that our infirmities and impurities are temporal, and we'll eventually be in glory with our Savior. But then we have the confidence that God's Spirit is fighting for us, even to the point of praying to the Father for things we may not have even thought about. And the capstone in all of this comes to us as the Lord confirms that ALL situations that are experienced by those who love God and are called according to His purpose happen for their good. This child of God knows that whatever happens, everything is working together as God has purposed for that child of

His. In the earliest manuscripts found, the rendering of this verse could read like this, "God works all things with" or "cooperates in all things." The very trials that we find ourselves must be met with our understanding that our God Himself is working in them for our eventual good. Every test and trial is a sign that the providence and sovereignty of God is for our spiritual good, breaking the bondage of sin in our lives, bringing us nearer to Himself, making the world less attractive, and getting us ready to live in glory with Him! His grand and glorious purpose is to conform us to His Son, Jesus Christ. With Christ as the model, there's much work to be done in our hearts, minds and bodies to accomplish the goal of transformation and conformation to Christ. The final product the Lord has in mind is our glorification. He starts with justification or salvation. Justification is a word that means "just as if I had never sinned." In the Lord's perspective of my life, He views me as if I had never committed one sin. What a Savior! What a Redeemer! But He also sees the Christian as already be glorified and living in His very presence.

The world is in travail and it will remain so until Jesus redeems it back to Himself. Many people are experiencing so much anxiety in their souls. Unless they are redeemed by Christ, they will continue to live so. The entire universe is groaning and moaning because of sin. God's intentions and will is to bring everything back to its original condition, which is in right relationship with Himself. Until that time, we, as Christians, must fully understand the purposes of God for all that comes our way. The way may be hard and difficult, but the way will always be His way if stay in love with Him and are following His call and purpose for our lives. Therefore, we are to find ourselves rejoicing in our Lord and Savior, no matter what. When life is exciting and thrilling, rejoice in Him. But when life is excruciating and tempestuous, rejoice in Him, also. This is the Word of the Lord. This is the command of the Lord. This will be our comfort and confidence. "Always be full of joy in the Lord,

I say it again – rejoice!"[4] *New Living Translation* "Celebrate God all day, every day. I mean, revel in him!"[5] *The Message* "Rejoice in the Lord always (delight, gladden yourselves in Him); again I say, Rejoice!"[6] *The Amplified Bible* **There's a reason why the Lord repeats this command of rejoicing in Him: it's because we fail at doing it over and over again whenever we think that life takes a wrong turn! HOLY JOY IS A CHIEF CHRISTIAN DUTY – NO MATTER WHAT!** The reason why the book of Psalms end with these words should be a command and celebration to the child of God:

"Praise the Lord! Praise God in his sanctuary; praise him in his mighty heavens! Praise him for his mighty deeds; praise him according to his excellent greatness! Praise him with trumpet sound; praise him with lute and harp! Praise him with tambourine and dance; praise him with strings and pipe! Praise him with sounding cymbals; praise him with loud clashing cymbals! Let everything that has breath praise the Lord! Praise the Lord!" (Psalm 150)

11

RETREATING FROM OUR OUTSIDE STRENGTHS

"And the descendants of the Kenite, Moses' father-in-law, went up with the people of Judah from the city of palms into the wilderness of Judah, which lies in the Negeb near Arad, and they went and settled with the peole. And Judah went with Simeon his brother, and they defeated the Canaanites who inhabited Zephath and devoted it to destruction. So the name of the city was called Hormah. Judah also captured Gaza with its territory, and Ashkelon with its territory, and Ekron with its territory. And the Lord was with Judah, and he took possession of the hill country, but he could not drive out the inhabitants of the plain because they had chariots of iron. And Hebron was given to Caleb, as Moses had said. And he drove out from it the three sons of Anak. But the people of Benjamin did not drive out the Jebusites who lived in Jerusalem, so the Jebusites have lived with the people of Benjamin in Jerusalem to this day." Judges 1:16-21

"And the people of Israel again did what was evil in the sight of the Lord, and the Lord strengthened Eglon the king of

Moab against Israel, because they had done what was evil in the sight of the Lord. He gathered to himself the Ammonites and the Amalekites, and went and defeated Israel. And they took possession of the city of palms. And the people of Israel served Eglon the king of Moab eighteen years."
Judges 3:14-16

"Then Moses went up from the plains of Moab to Mount Nebo, to the top of Pisgah, which is opposite Jericho. And the Lord showed him all the land. Gilead as far as Dan, all Naphtali, the land of Ephraim and Manasseh, all the land of Judah as far as the western sea, the Negab, and the Plain, that is, the Valley of Jericho the city of palm trees, as far as Zoar." Deuteronomy 34:1-3

I played sports throughout my junior high and high school years. I recall in very vivid terms all my coaches talking to the team about our opponents' strengths and weaknesses. The coaches put together a game plan for our next game based on that team's upside and downside. We, of course, wanted to stop their strengths and exploit, as much as we could, their weaknesses. Sometimes we were successful and sometimes not so much. After my playing days, I tried my hand at coaching. We had the privilege of enjoying some successes at my school in Michigan in the game of basketball. During my coaching years, the Lord blessed me with some very talented players, which led to many victories. Let me say this about those times; I was less nervous as a player than I was as a coach. My school had a great team in the early 80s when I was there, and then once again in the early 90s. I can honestly say that those were some of the best days of my life! The joy I saw on the faces of my players after winning a tough game was priceless. The amount of hard work they displayed during our practices paid off when the final horn blew to end the game. Before each game, I would write out on the chalkboard my game plan for that night. It would include what we needed to do as a team to win the game and what we needed to do to counter what the other team wanted to do against us. Then, during the game, adjustments had to be made according to the actual game experiences. At the end of the game, when we had the ball and needed a basket, I would always draw up a play to get the ball to my best player. This was a no brainer. The Detroit Pistons had a promotion (I'm sure they still do) to have local basketball teams play on their floor. The catch was that you needed to see a certain amount of tickets for that night's game. On one of these occasions, we had the awesome experience to play in the Pontiac Silverdome. This is where the Detroit Pistons used to play their games before The Palace of Auburn Hills was built. It was awesome! I was just as excited as my ball players were! The guys were able to dress in the Pistons' locker room with their jerseys hanging in their locker stalls. Well, it came to the last shot of the game. We were down a point (to a team that we should've beaten handily but didn't do our game plan very well that game) and we had the ball. I drew up the play, got the ball to my best player, he took the shot and it came up just short. A great experience didn't end the way we wanted it to end, but the guys still had an experience that will last them a lifetime. Another time we were in the state championship game. We were down three points to a very well coached team. The game was tight the entire way. We had the ball for the last shot. I called a time out and gathered the team on our bench. One of my players began to chew his fingernails. I asked him, "Are you nervous?" He responded, "Coach, of course I am." My simple response was this, "But isn't this fun!" That broke the ice. They all laughed and smiled. I told them what I wanted them to do. Of my five players, I drew up a play for each guy, but one. We got the ball in, but the other team did a great job and took all four options away. My point guard was the only one not in my original play, and he was all alone at the three-point line. My strengths were all taken away and my weakest three-point shooter was left standing without a defender anywhere close to him. The clock was winding down to zero. I simply yelled, "Shoot the ball!" He did and it went in, tied the game, and we won in overtime. Sporting events are great teaching tools for many events that happen in life. The attempt that's made by coaches to have their teams always play to their strengths and exploit the weaknesses of their opponents is masterful. The end in all of it is to win the game. The end to the season is to win the league. The end to the playoffs is to win the championship.

One of the questions that is most often asked during job interviews is, "What do you believe are your strengths and weaknesses?" I've never really known how to answer that question in the best possible way. On the one hand, you want to display some form of self-confidence, but not to appear conceited or arrogant. As far as the weakness part, when do you stop telling about all your mistakes you've made along the way or you can't do this or accomplish that? At one of my jobs, we had a vacancy in the management area. A person came walking into the office and gleefully said, "Hey, my name is ___ and I'm your new ___!" He hadn't been hired as far as we knew, but, in his mind, he was, and he came to tell us all about it. Well, he got the job. He's since left the position, but he must've had just the right amount of conceit, or confidence, or whatever.

All of us have something we do that's good or great, and all of us have something that we could never do if we tried for a hundred years. But let's focus on our positives or strengths. Obviously, God has gifted us with talents and abilities or gifts. His desire is to have us use them for service to Himself and the people of God. When a person comes to Christ at salvation, the Holy Spirit brings with Him a gift. That spiritual gift is to be used to honor the Lord through serving others. These gifts aren't for the purpose of self-glorification or advancement. They aren't to be used for any selfish gain whatsoever. These spiritual gifts are to be used as tools in the building of God's church and kingdom and in the lives of other people. Remember the admonition found in I Corinthians 10:31, "So, whether you eat or drink, or whatever you do, do all to the glory of God." This is absolutely an essential part of the Christian life, and this area is no exception.

However, just like answering the question in the job interview regarding strengths and weaknesses with the right amount of abasement and arrogance, and just like utilizing your strengths as a team and exploiting the other teams' weaknesses, we must capture the balance between these two opposites. As Christians, we need to be bold in our faith and speak up for the cause of Christ. And yet, as Christ said, we must display a spirit of wisdom as serpents, but to be harmless as doves. I heard it once said, "I must be willing to make a man my enemy over my position, but never my disposition." The very definition of truth means that every other opinion that's opposite truth must be a falsehood or a lie.

This brings me to the passage in Judges 1. We're told that the descendants of the Kenite went up with the people of Judah "from the city of palms into the wilderness." The picture presented here is one of leaving a place of rest and refreshment to one of restlessness and roving. The context actual tells us this group of people gathered together in order to continue their campaign against the Canaanite people, endeavoring to capture their cities and lands. It becomes a total description of leaving surroundings that provided a great sense of security and into an uncertain place of severities. In fact, Judges tells us of the many struggles Israel had in defeating and conquering the people of the land. We come to a very paradoxical truth in verse 19, "And the Lord was with Judah, and he took possession of the hill country, but he could not drive out the inhabitants of the plain because they had chariots of iron." In warfare, the army that controls the high ground usually ends up winning the battle. The army possessing the higher aspects of the battlefield can more easily defend an approaching army coming up its slopes. This is one of the reasons Picket's Charge was a miserable failure during the Battle of Gettysburg. 10,000 Southern troops began their charge up an open field trying to reach the top. It turned out to be one of the reasons the Confederacy lost that battle that turned our horrible Civil War around. It's like the game we all used to play as kids, "King of the Hill." A person would stand on top of a hill and defend his position against all the other kids trying to push him off. Here, in this verse of Scripture, the Holy Spirit is quick to point out that "the Lord was with Judah, and he took possession of the hill country." He seems to be telling us that the presence of the Lord was the key to this victory in obtaining this high ground during this fight for "king of the hill." Now the reason I point this out is the drastic change midstream in the verse with the word "but." The people of Judah took the portion of the land known as the hill country, "but they could not drive out the inhabitants of the plain." Wouldn't you think that the "people of the plain" would be easier to dispose of than those in the hill country? But just like we had the defining statement of "the Lord was with Judah" in the first part of the verse, we have another defining statement in the second part of the verse, "because they had chariots of iron." Had this new generation not heard about the Lord taking care of the Egyptian chariots 40 years earlier? And if they were able to defeat a people holding on to the strategic high ground because "the Lord was with them," then why run in defeat now? Where were the Calebs and Joshuas to remind them of the power and strength of the Lord? Where were their minds and hearts in not believing that the Lord could take care of these iron chariots with the breath of His mouth? All they had to do was to ask Him, trusting in His presence to carry them on to total victory instead of partially taking care of the enemy. God never does things "partially." The Lord wants us to experience total victory.

But then we see the next two verses, which gives us more of a preview of things to come. "And Hebron was given to Caleb, as Moses had said. And he drove out from it the three sons of Anak." Caleb is once again brought to our attention. The city and surrounding land of Hebron was to be given to Caleb and his descendants as per the command of Moses. This was a promise stated followed by the promise delivered. But Caleb had to fight the three sons of Anak. The name "Anak" means "long necked." This nation of people were descendants of Arba, Joshua 15:13. We're told that "Arba" was "the greatest man among the Anakim," Joshua 14:15, and that their ancestors were the Anakim of Numbers 13. This was a fierce, fighting people that didn't mess around when it came to war. This is why Joshua ended verse 15 of chapter 14 in his book with these words, "And the land had rest from war." It wasn't just because that the tribes of Israel had fought their way to victory, but that this was the last stronghold, at that time, to fall. Caleb had defeated this fierce foe and was ready to claim his possession given to him by His God and Moses! Caleb had the reputation of upholding his duty to His God and discarding the strengths of God's enemies.

We all know the story of the Lord telling Moses to send spies into the land of Canaan. He was asked to choose twelve representatives from each tribe. The tribe of Judah was represented by Caleb, while the tribe of Ephraim chose Hoshea, who was renamed Joshua by Moses. After the spy mission, which lasted forty days, the twelve returned to Moses in order to issue their report. Numbers 13:26-29 provides the record of that report: "...They brought back word to them and to all the congregation and showed them the fruit of the land. And they told him, 'We came to the land to which you sent us. It flows with milk and honey, and this is the fruit. **However, the people who dwell in the land are strong, and the cities are fortified and very large. And besides, we saw the descendants of Anak there**. The Amalekites dwell in the land of the Negeb. The

Hittites, the Jebusites, and the Amorites dwell in the hill country. And the Canaanites dwell by the sea, and along the Jordan.'" The blessing of this new land was going to be something to behold. The physical aspect of the land was described in glowing terms and detail. What they witnessed while spying was something that the rest of the people just wouldn't believe so they had to bring back some physical evidence of the fruit. It was most assuredly everything that God had promised them. But did you notice the one word that changed the entire mood and feeling of them giving Moses and the leaders their oral report? It's the word "however." Yes, the land was awesome. Yes, the fields were overflowing with plenty of food. Yes, the trees were bearing tremendous amounts of fruit. Yes, the grapevines grew such HUGE grape clusters that two men had to carry! **However, the people were strong, the cities were fortified and very large, and the descendants of Anak lived in the area.** Caleb spoke up quickly, "But Caleb quieted the people before Moses, and said, 'Let us go up at once and occupy it, for we are well able to overcome it.'" His response was rapidly shot down by ten of the spies saying, "We are not able to go up against the people, for they are stronger than we are." They would continue this evil report, "The land, through which we have gone to spy it out, is a land that devours its inhabitants, and all the people that we saw in it are of great height. And there we saw the Nephilim (the sons of Anak, who come from the Nephilim), and we seemed to ourselves like grasshoppers, and so we seemed to them.'" Without going into detail here for our purposes, the Nephilim simply means "giant." They were a certain group of people that came from the antediluvian period of Genesis 6. They were giants much like Goliath from Gath and his relatives whom David's mighty men disposed of later in Israel's history. In the very least, though, they were imposing figures to these men and caused great panic and fear among ten of the twelve spies. This entire fiasco caused a tremendous amount of grumbling, complaining and backbiting among the people of Israel against Moses and the Lord. They even wanted to stone Joshua and Caleb to shut them up. The tenor of the crowd became so opposed to moving forward that the people said that life was a whole lot better for them while they lived as slaves in Egypt. They decided to choose another leader to take them back to Egypt! Why would anyone desire the life of servitude and subjugation to slave masters, as compared to living under the direction of a loving and generous Master in the Lord? That just doesn't make sense. Caleb and Joshua had enough of this foolish talk. They tore their clothes as a sign of humility and brokenness and spoke to them once again: "The land, which we passed through to spy out, is an exceedingly good land. If the Lord delights in us, he will bring us into this land and give it to us, a land that flows with milk and honey. Only do not rebel against the Lord. And do not fear the people of the land, for they are bread for us. Their protection is removed from them, and the Lord is with us; do not fear them." There are several key principles that speak to us about retreating from our strengths as mentioned in the story and fallout from the report of the twelve spies. Their drastic example gives us clear consequences of what will happen when our fear is misplaced. Those vital principles are as follows:

- **Discern the actions of God in the direction He leads.**

- **Distinguish the difference in the size of our problems faced versus the Sovereign power God furnishes.**

- **Discover God's favored blessings when we obey the direction of God, becoming His delight.**

- **Diagnose God preparing the way for us to receive His very best.**

The command came from God to Moses to send these spies into the land. It just stands to reason and makes logical sense that our God isn't going to lead us down the wrong path. I don't think these people had fully bought into that concept enough to follow the explicit directions of God. If God is leading us specifically, then His actions will back up that leading. When we obey His guidance and direction, we then must place any obstacles that are in front of us and compare them to the size of our God, not to us. I heard a message by Billy Graham in which he said, "If God was small enough to be understood by man, He wouldn't be big enough to meet man's deepest and eternal needs."[1] A truer statement has never been made. The ten spies with a bad report compared themselves to the giants of the land instead of comparing the giants of the land to God! When we take our eyes off the Almighty God and on to the giant issues of our lives at any given time, then we'll live defeated lives and endeavor to overcome those giants in and through our own strengths. However, when we follow our God's directives and Word, He takes great delight in our faith and obedience, resulting in His provisions that have been promised to us from the very beginning. Charles Stanley has often said, "When you obey God, the consequences of your obedience becomes His problem."[2] God was at work in bringing His people into the land He gave them hundreds of years earlier. The land hadn't known the mighty working of God for many, many years, so it had been overgrown with great unbelief and gross ungodliness. It was time for righteousness to reign in the land once again and God was going to use His people to accomplish this task. Joshua and Caleb told the rest of their countrymen these astounding words in no uncertain terms: "Only do not rebel against the Lord. And do not fear the people of the land, for they are bread for us. Their protection is removed from them, and the Lord is with us; do not fear them." Caleb and Joshua were telling everyone that God will prepare Israel's way to capture the land He had promised them! God desires to give His people His very best. Remember, everything works together to bring about God's greatest good in and for us, and God's greatest glory for the whole world to see. "Their protection is removed from them" is simply relying on God's mighty power and sovereignty. The situation they faced in their day and the situations we face in our lives in our day all fall under the care, concern, consideration and compassion of a Sovereign King who loves His people unconditionally and desires to load them daily with benefits – "Blessed be the Lord, who daily loads us with benefits, even the God of our salvation. Selah." (Psalm 68:19) The *New Living Translation* of this verse puts it this way, "Praise the Lord; praise God our Savior! For each day he carries us in his arms."[3] There isn't a day that comes and goes that our Father and God doesn't know our every step, directing and steadying them no matter what happens during that specific day. Louis Gigleo stated, "When we are constantly and consistently in God's presence, we become deep in a shallow world, we become constant in a changing world, we become confident in a fearful world, we become spiritual in a material world, and we become patient in an instant world."[4] As we're sent out into our daily world to bear witness of our loving and gracious God, we must understand that there will be "giants" and "fortified cities" that will challenge our faith. What we must keep in the forefront of our minds is that our God has gone before us, preparing the way for the defeat of those "giants" and "fortified cities," fully comprehending the strength and size of those obstacles compared to the strength and size of the One going before us, ready to defend us in each situation and circumstance!

"And the descendants of the Kenite, Moses' father-in-law, went up with the people of Judah **from the city of palms into the wilderness of Judah**, which lies in the Negeb near Arad, and they went and settled with the people." (Judges 1:16) Jericho is located five miles west of the Jordan and seven miles north of the Dead Sea, 740 feet below sea level, and is considered by many archaeologists as the oldest city in the world. Its climate is tropical, with an average temperature of 88 degrees in the summer, with it dropping to 59 degrees during the winter months. With averaging only 6.4 inches of rainfall, one would think it would be a desert area, but it has deep and plentiful wells everywhere. According to Genesis 13:10, this area "was well-watered everywhere" and Lot chose this area for himself and family during the dispute between him and his Uncle Abraham. During the winter months it became a resort for people who wanted to escape the colder weather of the Judean hill country. In ancient times date palm trees flourished everywhere around the city, thus garnering the nickname "the city of palm trees." The fruit from these palms, along with its strategic site by a ford of the Jordan, enabled the inhabitants of the city to control the ancient trade routes from the East, which brought the city great wealth. After crossing the river, the smaller rivers branched out, one going towards Bethel and Shechem in the north, another westward to Jerusalem, and a third to Hebron in the south. Jericho controlled the access to the hill country in the region known as the Transjordan. The city's location made its capture the key to the invasion of the central hill country. It was regarded as a formidable obstacle by the Hebrews, requiring Divine intervention. Its walls were high and thick, which made penetration into the city virtually impossible. It was a formidable fortress of a city to say the least.

Even before the preparations for the battle of Jericho were finalized, the Lord was at work in all lives surrounding this momentous event. Just as the people of Israel came to the banks of the Red Sea, they were once again facing a natural obstacle to reaching their God-given promises. We're told in Joshua 3:15 that "the Jordan overflows all its banks throughout the time of harvest." The time had come for God's people to enter the Promise Land. Specific directions were given to the priests carrying the ark of the covenant of the Lord, as well as to the people of Israel. They were told that as soon as they saw the ark being carried, they were to rise to their feet and follow it. As the priests carried the ark into the waters of the Jordan, the waters would stop flowing and the riverbed would dry up. The key phrase in all of this was simply, "...in order that you may know the way you shall go, for you have not passed this way before." (Joshua 3:4) Joshua's response to this directive was incredible, "Consecrate yourselves, for tomorrow the Lord will do wonders among you." These "wonders" or miracles or signs will demonstrate how our God will work on our behalf, seeing that we haven't "passed this way before." This is how we discern the actions of our God as He provides direction for us. The ark represented the guidance of His presence. It's where He met with the people, displaying His glory above the mercy seat. The directive was given: As soon as you see the ark of the covenant of the Lord your God being carried by the Levitical priests, then you shall set out from your place and follow it." Now the time for God to act on that directive had come. Our task is to follow always the directions God provides for us. We are to "consecrate" ourselves to those directions. It had begun. The priests stood up and went before the people. The Jordan River parted and "Now the priests bearing the ark of the covenant of the Lord stood firmly on dry ground in the midst of the Jordan, and all Israel was passing over on dry ground until all the nation finished passing over the Jordan." (Joshua 3:18) The Lord then instructed Joshua to have twelve stones taken from the middle of the Jordan River in order to set up a memorial on the other side. These stones were to be specially taken from the place where the priests stood as the people of Israel were crossing over. The purpose of this monument or memorial was to help the people in future generations to remember EXACTLY how the Lord preserved, protected and provided for them. On the day their children would ask their parents, "What do these stones mean?" They would point to that time in their life that God brought them across the river and into the land He promised to give them. I see some other spiritual principles for this part of the story for our lives today. All of us stand on the banks of the Jordan River at one time or another in our lives. God has victory waiting for us on the other side. We must follow His instructions and directions exactly. For our crossing of that specific "Jordan River" in our lives during that difficulty, issue or circumstance, is our:

- **The Peak of our Vulnerability**

- **The Path to our Victory**

- **The Plan for God's Visitation**

The stones were to be taken from "the midst of the Jordan." This was at the most vulnerable time of their crossing – right in the middle of the river. So much could've happened, but it didn't. God had won the day for His people and brought them over to the other side without any difficulty. When we find ourselves at our weakest and most vulnerable, our God is there with us. We can rest assured that He has everything well under control. But this was also their pathway to victory. In order to conquer the land of promise, the Jordan River had to be crossed. To my knowledge, there wasn't any Corps of Engineers to throw up a quick bridge to make this happen. I also don't think they had enough boats to ferry the mass of people across the swollen, fast currents of the river that day during this season when the Jordan would overflow its banks. Nope. All they had to do to get over to the other side of the Jordan was to follow God's explicit directions. They followed those directives and God brought them across just as He had told them. I don't know why God takes us down the paths He takes us at times. All I know is He's the One doing the leading and I must follow that path and direction as He sees best. By no means does His path mean it's going to be the fastest or easiest. By no means does His path mean it's going to be without any troubles or tragedies. But it's His path, not ours, and that makes all the difference in the world. Finally, the crossing that day lays out the plan He had to visit His people. Just think of all the victories God's people were going to experience in the next few years! Just think of all the future blessings the world was going to see because of the nation of Israel! The prophets and kings, the miracles and ministry, all culminating in the birth of the Savior – Jesus Christ! For these courageous and conquering people, their destiny was in their own hands as they submitted themselves to the directions of God, realizing His very best outcomes for them would become their eventual realities.

Through all of this and in all our circumstances, including successes and struggles, they and we must fully comprehend God's reasoning for dealing with His people as He does through all ages. That answer is found in Joshua 4:24, "so that all the peoples of the earth may know that the hand of the Lord is mighty, that you may fear the Lord your God forever." God's stated purpose for the crossing of the Red Sea and now the Jordan River was twofold: for the people of our world to know God's might and for the people of God to know the meaning of fearing Him. In Matthew Henry's words we read, **"The power of God was hereby magnified. The deliverances of God's people are instructions to all people, and fair warnings not to contend with Omnipotence. The remembrance of this wonderful work should effectually restrain them from the worship of other gods and constrain them to abide and abound in the service of their own God."** J. Sidlow Baxter states, **"Entering, overcoming, occupying! If these are the three movements recorded in Joshua, then there can be no doubt as to what is its key thought, or central message. Clearly, it is** *the victory of faith.* **In this, the Book of Joshua stands in sharp contrast to the Book of Numbers, where we see the failure of unbelief – failure to enter, failure to overcome, failure to occupy. Spiritually interpreted, the exploits of Israel under Joshua proclaim the great New Testament truth – 'This is the victory that overcometh the world, even our faith.' (I John 5:4) Each of** the victories in the program of conquest was ordered so as to exhibit that victory was due to faith in God, not to the arm of man. To quenching unbelief, the overthrow of giants and great cities was an *impasse,* but to the eye of faith it was a *fait accompli.*"[5] The crossings of the Red Sea and Jordan River are more than just mere miraculous happenings. They represent a crisis of faith. Two generations faced the same type of obstacle which lay straight in their path to obtaining victory. To the one generation, they were escaping a land and life of servitude. To this new generation, they were facing the excitement of a land and life of service for God. The Red Sea crossing was an escape; the Jordan River crossing was an entrance. It's one thing to be "brought out" in one fell swoop; it's a totally different issue to "go over this Jordan" and become committed, without any probability or even possibility of retreat, to the struggles against the awesome powers of the armies of Canaan, their iron chariots and large, fortified cities. To the natural eye, and ten out of the twelve spies, this entrance was to risk everything: their lives, the lives of their children, and any hope of building a nation of their own! J. Sidlow Baxter continues this discussion, **"The same crisis comes in one way or another to all the redeemed – that intense crisis of the soul in which we are forced to the supreme choice whether there shall be an utter once-for-all abandon of ourselves to the will of God, so that henceforth God is absolutely first in the soul's love and life, or whether we shall take what seems to be the easier way, that is, of continuing in the Christian life, but with a reservation in our love to God. It is one thing to take Christ as Savior from the guilt of our sin. It is another thing to make Him absolute Master of our will and life. It is one thing to be brought out from the Egypt of our unregenerate life and to join God's redeemed Israel. It is another thing altogether to bury all our self-born aims and desires in Jordan's swift-flowing flood, and to pass through to that higher life where no desires or purpose** are tolerated but those of our blessed Lord Himself. It was one thing for Abram to leave Ur of the Chaldees and go out in faith at God's behest. It was another thing – a far bigger and costlier and sublime thing – for him to climb Moriah and lift the knife to slay his beloved Isaac. Yet the crisis must be. There was no other way of decisively determining whether God was to be supreme in the life and love of the soul. There was no need for further testing after that… Abraham's Moriah and Israel's Jordan are the same crisis under different names. There is an Isaac to be sacrificed, a Jordan to be crossed, in the history of every redeemed soul. Abraham yielded his Isaac. Israel crossed the Jordan. What of you and me? This is faith's major crisis."[6]

The nation of Israel had many, many hurdles to cross in order to experience the blessings of the land God had given to them. Today, God's redeemed also must pass over many hurdles in order to experience the blessings in our spiritual lives. As was stated in the previous quotes, theirs and ours are matters of faith. The people of Israel faced actual battles and warfare; we face battles and warfare of a much different kind. Many Christians, and I dare say that we may also fall into this category one day, in other countries face the reality of physical violence against them. But for most of us living in The United States, we haven't had to cross that Jordan River just yet. Our battles remain that of our soul and spirit. Paul speaks of these battles in Romans 6 and 7, with the victory coming in chapter 8 as we learn to rely on God's Spirit and not our flesh. But for God's people of Joshua's day, their battles were physical battles against fierce enemies. As their leader, Joshua needed for God to provide complete assurance that His presence would go before them. He had promised that in Joshua 1 by saying that everywhere their feet would take them, that He would give them that land. He promised him success as he would take the time to meditate and dwell in His Word. He promised Joshua and the people great and grand successes in each of their battles, just so long as they would do just what the Lord commanded them to do. Hours before the actual battle, the Lord made an appearance to Joshua. Joshua's response was as natural as one could expect, "Are you for us, or for our adversaries?" The Lord's answer, I'm sure, caught Joshua off guard, "No; but I am the commander of the army of the Lord. Now I have come." To which "Joshua fell on his face to the earth and worshiped and said to him, 'What does my lord say to his servant?'" This was Jesus Christ, God's Commander! If it wasn't the Lord, He would've told Joshua to get up from being prostrate in front of Him! "And the commander of the Lord's army said to Joshua, 'Take off your sandals from your feet, for the place where you are standing is holy.' And Joshua did so." The ground on which Joshua was standing had become holy because of the very presence of Jesus Christ. Essentially, Joshua asked the Lord if He was friend or foe. The Lord's response goes to the very fabric of the foundation of our Christian faith. His answer summed up the entirety of all that had happened to the people of Israel and all that was going to happen from that day forward. The Lord responded to Joshua's "friend or foe" question with a momentous statement to which we all must come to terms, "No; but I am the commander of the army of the Lord. Now I have come." Once again, the Lord uses two of the greatest words ever uttered by our God, "…I am…." I am in the ever present. I am the commander of the Lord's army who is about ready to go to battle for you. Then, as only the Lord could say, "Now I have come." The Lord is pouring strength into His leader before this great battle. The Lord's answer penetrated Joshua's heart and soul, and he fell to his face in submission and worship. The Lord is verifying His promises that were made in chapter one regarding His protective and powerful presence. "Now I have come." The presence of the God of the universe is the unseen factor in every faith battle we'll ever face. The Lord's presence makes the testing of our faith possible to get through it successfully. Every trial is an opportunity to perfect our trust in God. Each trial is an opportunity to have our progress and effectiveness multiplied. Each trial is an opportunity to have God increase our faith and wisdom. Each trial is an opportunity for God to intensify our devotion as He cuts closer to the core of who we are. Each trial takes away the unusable in us to make room for the unusual through Him. Scripture proves this over and over. "Lord, if you had been here, my brother would not have died," cried Martha and Mary. "Lord, please come and heal my daughter. The Lord went with him." The presence of the Lord is THE game changer. It matters not what hurdles or obstacles lie in our way, the very truth of "now I have come" makes all the difference in the world. When Jesus was preparing His disciples about His leaving this life, He paints on the canvas of their fearful hearts, "And if I go and prepare a place for you, I will come again and will take you to myself, that where I am you may be also." (John 14:3) The morning my 94-year-old mother went to heaven, I had my only sister facetime me. As mom laid on her deathbed, I picked up my Bible and began reading John 14. I told her that the Lord has prepared a place for her and now He was calling her to be with Him! As I was reading and talking with my mom, my sister said, "Kevin, that's it. She's gone. She's in the very presence of Jesus her Lord and Savior." What a beautiful and blessed hope we have in Jesus that where He will be is where we'll take up residence! "Now I have come" fills in so many of the blanks for the Christ-follower. This, that or the other may not go right for us, but "Now I have come" changes everything. God's greatness is most realized in and through our weakest points. God is teaching Joshua and His people that He uses our weaknesses to display His glory when we realize we must depend on Him. This is the place God wants to lead us all. In spiritual terms, who we see determines revelation, which dictates how we see, which results in observation, so that, when we're tested, it causes the decision of what we'll do, leading to the commission of our life. God brought Joshua from "just a tribal leader," to one of the two faithful spies, to the successor of the greatest leader the world has ever known – Moses. This momentous event would be the defining moment in Joshua's life. The revelation of the Lord that day led Joshua to observe Who this Person was, leading to Joshua's decision to fall face down in worship, asking what the Lord wanted to tell him, ending up seeing Joshua remove his sandals with the highest regard and honor for the holiness of that moment. "And Joshua did so." The revelation of the Lord and Joshua's decision to worship saw the conclusion of Joshua's commission and commitment.

> **"Now Jericho was shut up inside and outside because of the people of Israel. None went out, and none came it. And the Lord said to Joshua, 'See, I have given Jericho into your hand, with its king and mighty men of valor. You shall march around the city, all the men of war going around the city once. You shall do this for six days. Seven priests shall bear seven trumpets or rams' horns before the ark. On the seventh day you shall march around the city seven times, and the priests all blow their trumpets. And when they make a long blast with the ram's horn, when you hear the sound of the trumpet, then all the people shall shout with a great shout, and the WALL OF THE CITY WILL FALL DOWN FLAT, and the people shall go up, everyone straight before him." Joshua 6:1-5**

Natural reasoning and warfare must be put aside when it comes to our God. There is nothing as more useless and silly to our natural wisdom and thought as to walking harmlessly around a fortified city for six straight days, followed by a longer walk of seven times on the seventh day, then blowing trumpets and shouting, but that was

God's strategic battle plan to conquer Jericho. This chapter speaks to us of the triumph of faith and obedience. Faith must come to the point of discerning God's will through His Word. When that is obtained, faith's action is that of complete and total obedience to that will and Word. As this is done, faith sees the end from the beginning and realizes that God's will and Word will come to fruition exactly as He said. He told Joshua what to do and they obeyed His instruction implicitly. God said in Joshua 6:5 that "the wall of the city will fall down flat." We read in 6:20, "So the people shouted, and the trumpets were blown. As soon as the people heard the sound of the trumpet, the people shouted a great shout, and the wall fell down flat, so that the people went up into the city, every man straight before him, and they captured the city," thus fulfilling the Word of the Lord EXACTLY AS HE HAD TOLD THEM!

When it comes to fighting battles, the Lord's way of doing things doesn't exactly fall in line with how we'd do it. The unconventional means of winning this battle proved to the people that victory over the mighty city of Jericho had nothing to do with their fighting prowess and everything to do with God's formidable power! The stripping away of every possible means of victory is the Lord's way of proving Himself to us and a doubting world. Years later, this would become very evident in the life of Gideon. The nation of Israel had left the God of their fathers once again. The cycle found in Judges was found on the bottom side of that cycle as we see the nation leaving their God and loving idols and non-existent gods. The Lord delivered Israel into the hand of Midian as they would come with hordes of people overwhelming their defenses, eating their crops and taking away their livestock. So, as the cycle repeated itself, God's people lifted their voices, crying out for the Lord to come to their aid. This time, the man for the task at hand was Gideon. As Gideon was threshing wheat in a winepress (in order to hide from the enemy) an angel came and said, "The Lord is with you, O mighty man of valor." First, Gideon was in hiding for fear of the enemy! Second, Gideon told the angel about his family's social standing, "Please, Lord, how can I save Israel? Behold, my clan is the weakest in Manasseh, and I am the least in my father's house." Gideon said that his family was the least in all the tribe and that he was the least in his family. In our terms, we'd say something like, "My family is puny and I'm the runt of my puny family. You must be kidding, right? You want me to do what? You really have the wrong man for the job. Be on your way." As the story proceeds, Gideon seeks several pieces of evidence to prove that the Lord had chosen him. The Lord kept coming back to him that he was the person of God's choosing. We read verifying words such as, "But I will be with you," and "But the Spirit of the Lord clothed Gideon." We read verifying actions such as the accepting his initial sacrifice and answering Gideon's prayers regarding the wet and dry fleece. Gideon was God's man for this specific task. Author and pastor, **Alan Redpath,** said, "When God has an impossible task to accomplish, he takes an impossible man, crushes him, and accomplishes the impossible task."[7] Gideon was living proof of that.

The day came to battle the Midianites. We pick up the narrative of Gideon in Judges 7, **"Then Jerubbaal (that is, Gideon) and all the people who were with him rose early and encamped beside the spring of Harod. And the camp of Midian was north of them, by the hill of Moreh, in the valley. The Lord said to Gideon, 'The people with you are too many for me to give the Midianites into their hand, lest Israel boast over me, saying, 'My own hand has saved me.' Now therefore proclaim in the ears of the people, saying, 'Whoever is fearful and trembling, let him return home and hurry away from Mount Gilead.' Then 22,000 of the people returned, and 10,000 remained. And the Lord said to Gideon, 'The people are still too many. Take them down to the water, and I will test them for you there, and anyone of whom I say to you, 'this one shall go with you,' shall go with you, and anyone of whom I say to you, 'This one shall** not go with you,' shall not go.' So he brought the people down to the water. And the Lord said to Gideon, 'Everyone who laps the water with his tongue, as a dog laps, you shall set by himself. Likewise, everyone who kneels down to drink.' And the number of those who lapped, putting their hands to their mouths, was 300 men, but all the rest of the people knelt down to drink water. And the Lord said to Gideon, 'With the 300 men who lapped I will save you and give the Midianites into your hand and let all the others go every man to his home.'" (Judges 7:1-8)

The name of "the spring of Harod" means "trembling," with an obvious allusion to the fear and timidity of the 22,000 men who were asked to return to their families. The trimming down of the forces that God was going to use to defeat this particular enemy began. According to Judges 8:10, the Midianite force numbered some 135,000, while Gideon's forces numbered a meager 32,000. But with God, that presented a problem. **The purpose wasn't only to defeat this enemy of God, but it was to turn the hearts of the nation of Israel back to Himself.** The Lord graciously asked those who were afraid to leave the ranks, lest they cause doubt and fear to become the overall atmosphere and attitude of Gideon's army. Deuteronomy 20:8 states, "And the officers shall speak further to the people, and say, 'Is there any man who is fearful and fainthearted? Let him go back to his house, lest he make the heart of his fellows melt like his own.'" Gideon sent them on their way. The word "returned" or "depart early" is used only in this verse. Other texts speak of "in the morning." Many biblical scholars say that this injunction was given in order that they might not incur shame when they left. God's great care is seen even for these who were frightened at the appearance of such a great number of warriors! But wait, there's more men that must be eliminated from Gideon's fighters! God wanted to make certain that His people and the watching world knew that the victory was completely the result of His formidable power and not the fighting prowess of this army, no matter how "small" it was.

The United States of America has an awesome military force. Our might can be seen all over the world. I'm thankful for all our men and women in uniform who defend our country and way of life. "Peace through strength" is a fantastic way to view our military might and power. There isn't a single thing wrong with having a great and grand military, ready to fight against all our enemies. Thank God for it and for those who volunteer to serve. Our economy has also gained greatly in the past few years. Again, we can be extremely thankful for God's rich blessings on our country financially. I've travelled abroad and each time I come home I knelt and kiss the ground. I love my country, and I thank the Lord every day for His awesome provisions He has given to me and my family. However, if we put our trust in riches or our military might or any other object, idea or person, then we'll begin to decrease. There is a futility of relying on anything else besides our God. Listen to God's clear and present warning found in Isaiah 31:1, 2, "Destruction is certain for those who look to Egypt for help, trusting their cavalry and chariots instead of looking to the Lord, the Holy One of Israel....For these Egyptians are mere humans, not God!" We read in Isaiah 30:15, "The Sovereign Lord, the Holy One of Israel, says, 'Only in returning to me and waiting for me will you be saved. In quietness and confidence is your strength.'" As we wait on God, leaving all the results and consequences with Him, we'll learn to trust and rely on His promises, living out His principles, experiencing His protection and prosperity from His hand.

Now, a fresh trial of faith was introduced to Gideon. Isaiah 1:25 gives us the meaning of this new test, "I will turn my hand against you and smelt away your dross as with lye and remove all your alloy." This idea is repeated in 48:10, "Behold, I have refined you, but not as silver; I have tried you in the furnace of affliction." The phrase "I have tried you" could mean "I have chosen." God was continuing to purge away the useless fighters that would have a defect in their approach to warfare. Those who knelt and brought the water up to their mouths were those who could keep a keen watch on all that was going on around them, thus preventing an ambush, leading to their deaths. Josephus, the Jewish historian, says that Gideon led them down to the spring in the fiercest heat of the noonday, and that he judged those to be the bravest who flung themselves down and drank, and those to be the cowards who lapped the water hastily and tumultuously. Whatever the case, the Lord saw the difference of character indicated by the two actions and chose His instruments accordingly. Here's the great commentator, Matthew Henry's take on this section of Scripture, **"God provides that the praise of victory may be wholly to himself, by appointing only three hundred men to be employed. Activity and prudence go with dependence upon God for help in our lawful undertakings. When the Lord sees that men would overlook him, and through unbelief, would shrink from perilous services, or that through pride they would vaunt themselves against him, he will set them aside, and do his work by other instruments. Pretenses will be found by many, for deserting the cause and escaping the cross. But though a religious society may thus be made fewer in numbers, yet it will gain as to purity, and may expect an increased blessing from the Lord. God chooses to employ such as are not only well affected, but zealously affected in a good thing. They grudged not at the liberty of the others who were dismissed. In doing the duties required by God, we must not regard the forwardness or backwardness of others, nor what they do, but what God looks for at our hands. He is a rare person who can endure that others should excel him in gifts or blessings, or in liberty; so that we may say, it is by the special grace of God that we regard what God says to us, and not look to men what they do."[8]** Through this very act of reducing the size of Gideon's army, God was proving Himself once again to His people, that He was all they needed to accomplish His purposes for them! **The quicker we come to terms with the principle of retreating from our own strengths and relying on our God's, the quicker we'll see Him work in our lives. Our difficulty comes in the fact that we want the Lord to change our circumstances instead of allowing Him to become the Director of those circumstances.** I've heard it said that the difference between Christians in America and Christians in lands of great persecution is this: Christians in America pray for deliverance from trials, while Christians in other lands pray for strength through the trials. Philippians 4:13 says it all, "For I can do everything through Christ, who gives me strength."[9] The *Berean Literal Bible* gives us this truth in these words, "I have strength for all things in the One strengthening me." The *Contemporary English Version* brings another viewpoint, "Christ, give me the strength to face anything."[10] Similar verses that stress this vital truth is Ephesians 3:16, "That he would grant you, according to the riches of his glory, to be strengthened with might by his Spirit in the inner man;" Ephesians 6:10, "Finally, my brethren, be strong in the Lord, and in the power of his might;" Colossians 1:11, "Being strengthened with all power according to his glorious might so that you may have full endurance and patience with joy." Speaking on Phil. 4:13, Ellicott states, **"I can do all things – properly, I have strength in all things, rather to bear than to do…It represents the ultimate and ideal consciousness of the Christian. The first thing needful is to throw off mere self-sufficiency, to know our weakness and sin, and accept the salvation of God's free grace in Christ; the next, to find the 'strength made perfect in weakness,' and in that to be strong."**[11] One of the, if not the greatest, truth for every single Christian is to learn this vital and valuable lesson: the key in retreating from our own strength is resting in the strength who resides within our hearts. Within the context of chapter 4, Paul is addressing the powerful concept of contentment. He said that he's happy with little or much, feast or famine, life's needs met, or life's needs found wanting. He summed it up with the marvelous truth of 4:13, "Whatever I have, wherever I am, I can see myself making it through anything that comes my way because of the One who makes me who I am!" Joshua learned this vital lesson before the battle of Jericho. Gideon learned this valuable lesson before the battle against the Midianites. The people of Judah learned this significant lesson when they left "the city of palms to go into the wilderness." Learning to move away from our own abilities and strengths in order to rely on the Lord is a giant step of faith. Proverbs 3:5 and 6 provide for us the order of seeing this principle come to reality, "Trust in the Lord with all your heart, and do not lean on your own understanding. In all your ways acknowledge him, and he will make straight your paths." Proverbs 3:1-12 gives us principles by which to conduct ourselves in advancing a full retreat of all that is us. Notice them with me:

- **Devoted Obedience – "My son, do not forget my teaching, but let your heart keep my commandments." (3:1)** The blessed life begins with obedience to the Word of God as is instructed. Our obedience to the principles and precepts of God is our foremost responsibility.

- **Devoted Obligation – "Let not steadfast love and faithfulness forsake you; bind them around your neck; write them on the tablet of your heart." (3:3)** Along with our obedience, faithfulness and consistency are keys in maintaining a focused and centered heart on the Lord.

- **Devoted Ownership – "Trust in the Lord with all your heart..." (3:5)** The Christian life isn't a life to be lived one day and forgotten about the next. The Lord isn't looking for part-time Christians to accomplish His will. While in Bible college, I had a roommate tell the rest of us in the

219

room that he was going to be a Christian when he got out of school, just not 100 percent of the time. All throughout Scripture, God demonstrated over and over how this will not and cannot work.

Leaving the way of living life found in most of today's population is an important step in making Jesus the Lord of one's life. A long time ago, I heard a great definition of humility. It says, "Humility isn't thinking poorly of yourself; it's not thinking of yourself at all." In God's economy or way of looking at life, the way up is down and the way to be blessed is found in giving yourself in service to others. The only way to accomplish this much needed reality in our Christian experiences is found in turning from our own wisdom and doing things, realizing that the Lord's way and wisdom is far greater.

With all that said, we come to the great truths found in John 15. In His teaching, Christ presents Himself as the vine, we're the branches and the Father is the vine dresser or husbandman. The whole focus is that of bearing fruit in order to glorify our God. As Christians, we're commanded to bear fruit in and through our lives. We're to move from fruit, to more fruit and on to much fruit. If no fruit is present in our lives, then the Lord will deal with that as only He can. John 15:5 is the truth that falls in line with the idea from retreating from our own strengths. The words, which are in red letters, telling us that Jesus Christ is speaking, says, "I am the vine; you are the branches. Whoever abides in me and I in him, he it is that bears much fruit, for apart from me, you can do nothing." Eugene Peterson, in his paraphrase *The Message,* writes, "I am the Vine, you are the branches. When you're joined with me and I with you, the relation intimate and organic, the harvest is sure to be abundant. Separated, you can't produce a thing."[12] **"Separated, you can't produce a thing."** It doesn't matter what version or paraphrase you turn to, the last part of verse 5 all repeat the exact same principle: for apart from Me you can do or accomplish nothing! The words bring out the fullness of the meaning found in the first part of the verse regarding the fruitfulness of the person who abides in Christ. The "abiding in Christ" will always precede the abundance of fruit for and to the glory of God. For it is with bearing much fruit that the Father is most glorified as we're told in John 15:8. What we have in verse 5 is the statement of two premises: the first is "I am the Vine, and you are the branches," and the second is, "Severed from me a branch can effect nothing," having NO independent fruitfulness or stability. **ALL ITS POWERS ARE DERIVED FROM THE SUPERNATURAL FORCE THAT IS GOD AND DEPENDS ON CHRIST BEING THE VINE WHO SECURES THE BRANCHES TO HIMSELF.** These words are meant for Christ's true disciples, who must learn to have constant contact with the Vine, thus securing His strength and sustenance on a moment-by-moment basis. The only reason any children of God have any fruit to show for their lives is because of their constant abiding in the Vine, for apart from Him the idea of bearing spiritual fruit is impossible. Matthew Henry on this subject says, **"It is the great concern of all Christ's disciples, constantly to keep up dependence upon Christ, and communion with Him. True Christians find by experience, that any interruption in the exercise of their faith, causes holy affections to decline, their corruptions to revive, and their comforts to droop. Those who abide not in Christ, though they may flourish for a while in outward profession yet come to nothing. The fire is the fittest place for withered branches; they are good for nothing else. Let us seek to live more simply on the fullness of Christ, and to grow more fruitful in every word and work, so may our joy in Him and in His salvation be full."**[13] For the Christian, we bear two types of fruit: inner and outer. The inner fruit is allowing God to nurture in us His attitude. The outer fruit is allowing God to navigate His actions through us. God must produce robust fruit in our lives. This and this alone must become our duty and destiny. The difficult part comes into play as we set ourselves to **abide in Christ's presence, attach ourselves to Christ's purpose and allow Christ to prune away everything that doesn't represent Him.** All of this is accomplished by doing this one thing – retreat from our own strengths and rely on Christ's strength. To put this principle in the simplest of terms so this becomes the reality in each of our lives is found in John 15:4-14:

- **Rely on His Power – vv. 4, 5**

- **Receive His Principles – vv. 7-10**

- **Relinquish our Preferences to His Priorities – vv. 12-14**

Oswald Chambers wrote, **"The golden rule for understanding in spiritual matters is not intellect, but obedience."**[14] No life-changing realities will come from people who cannot see beyond a box lunch. The disciples didn't see the potential in Christ's statement, "You give them something to eat." They only thought of their own resources, not noticing the Christ standing before them ready to produce awesome fruit in the lives of so many that day in the feeding of over 5,000!

Zerubbabel, governor of Jerusalem, was tasked with what appeared to be an impossible mission. God had spoken to his heart about rebuilding the temple. It's one thing to build this beautiful structure the first time under normal circumstances, but to bring this house of God back to its original condition was another story entirely. He understood the task that lay before him and his people. The job of completing this improbable mission would've been difficult in and of itself, but then opposition arose from all sides. So he needed some encouraging words. God's supply will always be sufficient. God simply told him this timeless truth, "This is the word of the Lord to Zerubbabel: Not by might, nor by power, but by my Spirit, says the Lord of hosts. Who are you, O great mountain? Before Zerubbabel you shall become a plain. And he shall bring forward the top stone amid shouts of 'Grace, grace to it!'" (Zechariah 4:6,7) The mountains that are our impossible tasks will become flat plains before us as we rely on God's Spirit and strength, while we retreat from our own strengths, wisdom and abilities. He had no answer to finding a way to get this command of God done. However, God gave him exactly what he needed to accomplish what was asked of him. In our daily lives, the most difficult tasks can be successfully finished if we would realize that we must leave the comfort "of the city of palms" and venture out into the wilderness, being led by God's presence and strengthened by His power.

Our human example of living the Christian life, the faithful and great Apostle Paul, understood this biblical principle totally. Paul was a Christ-hater and took delight in destroying Christians. He then met the Lord and the rest, as they say, was history. He experienced tremendous spiritual highs but went through terrible suffering lows. He shared many of his life's experiences with us throughout biblical text, but the one that tells us how he learned to retreat from his strengths is found in II Corinthians 12:7-10: **"So to keep me from becoming conceited because of the surpassing greatness of the revelations, a thorn was given me in the flesh, a messenger of Satan to harass me, to keep me from becoming conceited. Three times I pleaded with the Lord about this, that it should leave me. But he said to me, 'My grace is sufficient for you, for my power is made perfect in weakness.' Therefore, I will boast all the more gladly of my weaknesses, so that the power of Christ may rest upon me. For the sake of Christ, then, I am content with weaknesses, insults, hardships, persecutions, and calamities. For when I am weak, then I am strong."** The word Paul uses here for "thorn" might be translated "stake." It's used of stakes that are pushed into the ground to form a circle around a grave. This "stake" was often used as a means of torture in the punishment that we would call impaling. The Greek words for "impaling" and "crucifying" were oftentimes interchangeable. This idea expresses the biblical truth that we are to put ourselves to death daily. Jesus said this is the only way to become fully devoted disciples of His. "I die daily" was the testimony Paul wanted to leave with us. This "death" isn't a physical death as we know it. Spiritual death is the fatal blow that we must deliver ourselves upon ourselves, putting Jesus Christ first in our life and denying anything that would be harm to the name and cause of our Savior and Lord. Whatever this "thorn" might have been, it most assuredly was to give the readers the sense of some acute form of suffering, even excruciating in its character. Some ancient biblical scholars suggest that the thorn Paul was experiencing was the guilty conscience of putting Christians to death before his conversion. Others speak of this ailment or thorn as having extremely poor eyesight. Whatever it was, Paul didn't want to have it any longer. He sought the Lord in earnest prayer three times to have the Lord deal with it completely by removing it. There may be some parallel in the Lord praying three times in the garden before His death and Paul's approach to his specific issue. But the Lord's answer wasn't what Paul expected: "My grace is sufficient for you, for my power is made perfect in weakness." Once again, let me quote Peterson in *The Message,* "My grace is enough; it's all you need. My strength comes into its own in your weakness. Once I heard that, I was glad to let it happen. I quit focusing on the handicap and began appreciating the gift."[15] Paul literally said, "Most gladly will I rather glory in my infirmities." In the context of this chapter, he was saying, "I will gladly retreat my own strengths and abilities, leave the city of palms and enter the wilderness, because that's where I'll find the power and presence of the Lord!" He not only finds comfort in the Lord's response, but actual delight in his belief, that now the conscious fact of his weakness will be with him the rest of his earthly life, that it will be completely in balance that the might and power and strength of Christ will be in him and all around him always. In the phrase, "so that the power of Christ may rest upon me," the word "rest" is like the word found in John 1:14, to dwell as in a tent or tabernacle, and implies the idea that the power and strength of Christ was to him as the Shechinah cloud of glory surrounding him and protecting him at all times! Again, I turn it over to Matthew Henry at this point to gain some powerful insights for our lives today, **"The apostle gives an account of the method God took to keep him humble, and to prevent his being lifted up above measure, on account of the visions and revelations he had. We are not told what this thorn in the flesh was, whether some great trouble, or some great temptation. But God often brings this good out of evil; that the reproaches of our enemies help to hide pride from us. If God loves us, he will keep us from being exalted above measure; and spiritual burdens are ordered to cure spiritual pride. This thorn in the flesh is said to be a messenger of Satan which he sent for evil; but God designed it and overruled it for good. Prayer is a salve for every sore, a remedy for every malady; and when we are afflicted with thorns in the flesh, we should give ourselves to prayer. If an answer be not given to the first prayer, nor to the second, we are to continue praying. Troubles are sent to teach us to pray; and are continued, to teach us to continue instant in prayer. Though God accepts the prayer of faith, yet he does not always give what is asked for: as he sometimes grants in wrath, so he sometimes denies in love. When God does not take away our troubles and temptations, yet, if he gives grace enough for us, we have no reason to complain. Grace signifies the good-will of God towards us, and that is enough to enlighten and enliven us, sufficient to strengthen and comfort in all afflictions and distresses. His strength is made perfect in our weakness. Thus, his grace is manifest and magnified. When we are weak** in ourselves, then we are strong in the grace of our Lord Jesus Christ; when we feel that we are weak in ourselves, then we go to Christ, receive strength from him and enjoy most the supplies of Divine strength and grace."[16] Paul learned through personal trials and troubles that he was able to bear this "thorn, messenger of Satan," with satisfaction when he knew that bearing it was for the sake of Christ. **His greatest weakness wasn't only compatible with the highest strength known to man, it was the very source and condition of its power and energy**. While we aren't certain of the nature of Paul's "thorn in the flesh," we do know that it was indeed a great source of pain and suffering. God, in His infinite wisdom and inexhaustible sovereignty, did not remove the thorn when asked to do so. Instead, God chose to give him the resilient power needed to endure. In digging deeper in these verses, we see a man come to the end of his own logic and reasoning, accepting the absolute perfect wisdom and will of Someone who knew what was needed for this particular man to capture and win the prize – "the crown of righteousness." (II Timothy 4:8)

The truth of the matter is that we humans like to take credit for what happens to us. We enjoy the benefits of "one upping" the next person in telling how God did this or God did that in our lives. We also love to make ourselves the hero in the story line and having the strength to overcome any obstacle without any help from anyone else, and that includes God Almighty. How in the world do we come up with these fallacies? After a while, we begin to believe our own headlines, puffing our chests out in pride and letting everyone who will listen know just how great we really are!

Nothing could be further from the truth. The Lord knows this about us. He isn't taken back for one moment, stepping aside and saying, "Oh, excuse me, I didn't know who I was speaking with. Go right ahead and tell me what you think should happen." Deuteronomy 8 is very clear and sets the record straight. This chapter is full of the Lord reminding His people, Israel and us, about remembering Him through every circumstance in our lives. **"Be careful to obey all the commands I am giving you today. Then you will live and multiply, and you will enter and occupy the land the Lord swore to give your ancestors. Remember how the Lord your God led you through the wilderness for forty years, humbling you and testing you to prove your character, and to find out whether or not you would really obey his commands. Yes, he humbled you by letting you go hungry, and then feeding you with manna, a food previously unknown to you and your ancestors. He did it to teach you that people need more than bread for their life; real life comes by feeding on every word of the Lord." (Deut. 8:1-3)** Obedience, remembering and testing are pieces of the puzzle that makes perfect sense when they are understood within the context of "how the Lord led you." It's so easy to take the credit for the blessings in our lives and then to cast doubt on God's grace when the burdens come our way. Later, in verse 6, the Lord gives us what obeying Him looks like, "So obey the commands of the Lord your God by walking in his ways and fearing him." Live out His Word in a practical way in our daily life by walking in His ways, but then learn to grasp our standing with Him in a positional way by fearing or revering Him. The Lord continues to write about how He is bringing His people into a "good land of flowing streams and pools of water," alive with all kinds of vegetation for food and sustenance, along with all the necessary natural resources needed to build a successful family and nation. God then warns, "But that is the time to be careful! Beware that in your plenty you do not forget the Lord your God and disobey his commands, regulations, and laws. For when you have become full and prosperous and have built fine houses to live in, and when your flocks and herds have become very large and your silver and gold have multiplied along with everything else, then that is the time to be careful...." (Deut. 8:11-14) Man's natural inclination is to forget the means to the blessing and only focus on the blessing.

In this case, the means to the blessing is the Lord God Almighty. It's the story of the church of Laodicea in Revelation 3. We get to the point in our lives we're rich and see ourselves as having no need for the things of God. The warning continues, **"...He did this to humble you and test you for your own good. He did it so you would never think that it was your own strength and energy that made you wealthy. Always remember that it is the Lord your God who gives you power to become rich, and he does it to fulfill the covenant he made with your ancestors."** **(Deut. 8:16-18)** The blessings that God has in store for His people (and us) was and is God's free and generous gift. If they were ever to come to the place in their hearts and lives that they thought or imagined that the prosperity they had was a direct result of their efforts and enterprise, then all those blessings could be removed in a moment of time. And notice, this wasn't accomplished on any merit of their own, but as the result of His promises made to Abraham, Isaac and Jacob, their ancestors! God isn't finished with this chapter of warnings: **"But I assure you of this: If you ever forget the Lord your God and follow other gods, worshiping and bowing down to them, you will certainly be destroyed. Just as the Lord has destroyed other nations in your path, you also will be destroyed for not obeying the Lord your God." (Deut. 8:19, 20)** In everything we must always give thanks and praise. In everything we must remember our Benefactor – the God of gods and Lord and lords – Jehovah God!

The words of this chapter are full of caution and concern. We assume so much upon ourselves that our attention is often directed away from the Almighty. At the beginning of this chapter, we saw a nation of people leaving the comfortable confines of "the city of palms" and walking out into a wilderness situation. The picture of this trip presented to us is one that most of us have not and will not intentionally do but will have to be driven there by some unfor-giving or unwanted issue. One of the greatest Christians who ever

228

lived begged for his wilderness trip to end. It did not. Instead, we learn the secret of Divine Providence and power; God's infinite wisdom and inexhaustible power become our caretakers. The vital and valuable lessons that we learn are those the disciples learned that day the crowd of 5,000 plus were all fed and satisfied. We are to give others food to eat. The biggest obstacle we see in doing so is we have such limited resources, not noticing the Son of God standing right beside us ready to provide the resources for us to fulfill and obey His command. Oh, when will we ever completely learn? When we forget the former dealings of God with us, we brush Him aside as if He were in our way to obtaining credit and glory. Pride is natural in all of us. This damning trait MUST be dealt with, sometimes in the harshest of ways, but dealt with it MUST! The testing will come in order to humble us or keep us from gaining conceit beyond our own good. None of us live a single moment without giving evidence of our inept weaknesses, incompetent folly and incapable depravity. We turn to the Spirit of God, working His Scriptures into the fabric of our souls, with the blessed results of His sovereign rule over our lives. Therefore, in order to have a flourishing soul, we must learn to wage war on ourselves, retreating from our own strengths, relying on the strength of the only One who has the resources and power to the outcome of any situation!

"'Let's go across to see those pagans,' Jonathan said to his armor bearer. 'Perhaps the Lord will help us, for nothing can hinder the Lord. He can win a battle whether he has many warriors or only a few.'" I Samuel 14:6

"David shouted in reply, 'You come to me with sword, spear, and javelin, but I come to you in the name of the Lord Almighty – the God of the armies of Israel, who you have defied.'" I Samuel 17:45

"He said, 'Listen, King Jehoshaphat! Listen, all you people of Judah and Jerusalem! This is what the Lord says: 'Do not be afraid! Don't be discouraged by this mighty army, for the battle is not yours, but God's...you will not even need to fight. Take your positions; then stand still and watch the Lord's victory. He is with you, O people of Judah and Jerusalem. Do not be afraid or discouraged. Go out there tomorrow, for the Lord is with you!'" II Chronicles 20:15, 17

"After the Lord has used the king of Assyria to accomplish his purpose in Jerusalem, he will turn against the king of Assyria and punish him – for he is proud and arrogant. He boasts, 'By my own power and wisdom I have won these wars. By my own strength I have captured many lands, destroyed their kings, and carried off their treasures. By my greatness I have robbed their nests of riches and gathered up kingdoms as a farmer gathers eggs. No one can even flap a wing against me or utter a peep of protest.' Can the ax boast greater power than the person who uses it? Is the saw greater than the person who saws? Can a whip strike unless a hand is moving it? Can a cane walk by itself?" Isaiah 10:12-15

"But this precious treasure – this light and power that now shine within us – is held in perishable containers, that is, in our weak bodies. So everyone can see that our glorious power is from God and is not our own." II Corinthians 4:7

12

REALIZATION
& SUMMATION

The book of John contains more of Christ's doctrinal teachings than the other gospel accounts regarding the life of Christ. The only exception to this would be the Sermon on the Mount in Matthew 5 - 7. These doctrinal teachings hold many of the vital and prime characteristics of our Lord Jesus Christ. In John's passages of Scripture, we have presented to us Jesus' personal testimony regarding His majestic person and meaningful purpose of His coming to earth. John 10 provides for us the amazing truth that Jesus Christ is The Good Shepherd and how that relationship prospers and protects us, His children. One of those meaningful purposes of the Lord's coming to us is found in John 10:10: **"The thief comes only to steal and kill and destroy. I came that they may have life and have it abundantly."** These words are presented this way in *The New Living Translation*: **"The thief's purpose is to steal and kill and destroy. My purpose is to give life in all its fullness."**[1] Peterson presents it this way in his paraphrase, *The Message*: **"A thief is only there to steal and kill and destroy. I came so they can have real and eternal life, more and better life than they ever dreamed of."**[2] We read this verse in *The*

Amplified Bible this way: **"The thief comes only in order to steal and kill and destroy. I came that they may have and enjoy life, and have it in abundance (to the full, till it overflows.)"**[3] One of the meaningful purposes for Christ's coming to earth His first time was to provide for us "abundant living." If I may, please allow me to put these words into this thought for us: "The Lord Jesus Christ came to produce in each and every person a flourishing soul." This earthly adventure we all call "life" is meant to be lived in a beautiful way, experiencing a bountiful life that overflows with the goodness of God. The flourishing soul lives under the guidance and guardianship of the Good Shepherd, realizing a daily reality of a life lived, avoiding the thief's ability of stealing Christ's joy from us. The angel announced to the shepherds long ago that "Good news of great joy for everyone" was coming into the world in the Person of the Messiah, the Lord of heaven! The thief's purpose is to destroy that heavenly message by killing any idea in humans that they have an empty place in their souls that must be filled with something that will bring complete and lasting satisfaction.

The flourishing soul or its opposite is seen on every page of Scripture. For those who receive the righteous seed, which is found only in Christ, the journey we call "life" will take a drastic turn for the better. Experiencing the fact of resplendent sonship can only bring us to the place of rejoicing in such a salvation. Our focus will be removed from us and placed on our Savior, resulting in us loving Him more and more through the years, obeying His loving commands, and worshiping him in reverential awe! As we root ourselves in the Lord and gain a remarkable stature, we will come to the realization in our lives that we recognize the absolute need of retreating from our own strengths and abilities, relying on our faith in God. So, when troubles and trials make an unwelcome entrance into our lives, and come they will, we can learn to be resilient and supple because we have learned to lean on the Sovereign arm of our loving heavenly Father. We'll find during the storms of life that our God will lead us to places of such awesome refreshment that we would only discover because of having gone through such traumatic tragedies. The Holy Spirit opens up a wonderful window of truth in Romans 5:20 and 21 that perfectly describes what's available to our ravaged souls to transform them into flourishing souls, all because of the treasure known as God's wonderful kindness, **"God's law was given so that all people could see how sinful they were. But as people sinned more and more, God's wonderful kindness became more abundant. So just as sin ruled over all people and brought them to death, now God's wonderful kindness rules instead, giving us right standing with God and resulting in eternal life through Jesus Christ our Lord."**

In the times in which we find ourselves, so many of the goalposts of life have been moved. Our righteous foundations have been shaken or in some cases shattered. What we once believed to be a rock-solid conviction, we now look at with questioning eyes, wondering if what we ever believed was truth in the first place. Life seems so much about "self" and the procurement for everything surrounding "self." Oswald Chambers said in his sermon, "The Vanishing Gospel," these words: **"Self-realization is anti-Christian. All this is vigorous paganism; it is not Christianity. Jesus Christ's attitude is always that of anti-self-realization. His purpose is not the development of man at all; His purpose is to make man exactly like Himself, and the characteristic of the Son of God is not self-realization, but self-expenditure."**[4] The rise of "self-help" books hasn't helped the cause of Christ. In fact, the bringing in of so much "fluffy psychological pap" has hurt the maturation process of the Christian toward a flourishing soul. The depth of truths presented in most churches could be placed on a thin piece of paper, which in turn can and is easily torn into a million pieces. With this kind of approach to Christ's person and purpose, it's no wonder that so many Christians are experiencing a surface kind-of Christian life and experience, with no possibility of obtaining the status of a flourishing soul. Allow the truths of Hebrews 6:17-19 to wash over your heart and soul, perfecting God's very best in order to produce a flourishing soul in your inner being, **"God also bound himself with an oath, so that those who received the promise could be perfectly sure that he would never change his mind. So God has given us both his promise and his oath. These two things are unchangeable because it is impossible for God to lie. Therefore, we who have fled to him for refuge can take new courage, for we can hold on to his promise with confidence. This confidence is like a strong and trustworthy anchor for our souls. It leads us through the curtain of heaven into God's inner sanctuary."** The refuge for our ravaged souls is the Lord Jesus Christ, who is the only Person who has the power to create in each of us a flourishing soul. This is His promise. He is our eternal confidence.

In my many readings, I came across a news article about a teen in the Netherlands who had been sexually assaulted as a child and raped as a teen. In an Instagram post, she wrote, "Love is letting go, in this case. Maybe this comes as a surprise to some, given my posts about hospitalization, but my plan has been there for a long time and is not impulsive. After years of battling and fighting, I am drained. I have quit eating and drinking for a while now, and after many discussions and evaluations, it was decided to let me go because my suffering is unbearable...This is my decision and it is final. I breathe, but I no longer live." She finally succumbed to her wishes and died. After reading her story, I could only think of one thing: What if she had met Christ? What if after meeting Him, her fears and anxiety and stress would have been replaced with hope and faith and love? Her soul was far from flourishing; it was forlorn, frustrated and floundering horribly. If only...

I also read about a pastor who has left his wife and church and has renounced his faith. The article begins, "He's written best-selling books on Evangelical community for decades. but in the past two weeks, _____ has renounced his Christian faith, announced he is divorcing his wife of 21 years and apologized to the LGTBQ community for past words and actions." The article continues to quote this former pastor that his "faith in Jesus has undergone a massive shift. The popular phrase for this is 'deconstruction,' the biblical phrase is 'falling away.' By all the measurements that I have for defining a Christian, I am not a Christian. Many people tell me that there is a different way to practice faith and I want to remain open to this, but I'm not there now." This man pastored a mega-church from 2004-2015, wrote many books on relationships and Christianity; and yet, his soul was found outside the realm of flourishing. Many people have responded to this man in one form or another. One letter was from a pastor and friend, pleading with him to look at these impactful decisions and make them right. But he said one thing in his letter that caught my attention. He explained to him that he seriously doubted that he had had a true conversion and redemptive point in his life. What if he had truly come to redemption and the saving of his soul? What if he realized that he could experience a truly flourishing soul and live in the reality of John 10:10? What if he had truly experienced the truths of Hebrews 6? If only he journeyed through being rooted and grounded in the truths of God, experiencing resplendent sonship, rejoicing in his Savior. If only...

When my wife and I were teenagers, we decided to share Christ with some of our closest friends. She and I wrote down the names of our three first friends. We prayed over them, asking the Lord to give us opportunities to share the Gospel with them so they could be saved and know Christ. We then went to work. Together, we visited those on her list and then the ones on mine. Ironically, she had the name of a former boyfriend from junior high days, who happened to have a sister that was my age and in my class in high school. We went to their home, knocked on their door, only to be told that they weren't at home. We went there the next week - on the same night - with the same result. The very next week we faithfully made our way to their home on the same night. The sister was home that night, but she was busy, and she told us that her brother was gone, but he was actually hiding behind the front door after having looked out the window and saw that it was us. Frustrated, we prayed harder. Then, on a different night, after visiting one of my friends, we "just so happened to drop by their house." The guy on her list answered the door and looked completely shocked and surprised! He invited us in. His sister was also home and their parents were away for the evening. We sat around their dining room table, sharing the love of Christ with both of them. After I was finished talking with them, I asked them if they wanted to receive Christ and they both bowed their heads and trusted Christ as their personal Savior! Cindy and I went away rejoicing and extremely excited about their salvation.

As teens, we didn't really know what to do next. We let our "fresh fruit" hang out on the vine and didn't do any follow-up with them. Days turned into weeks and weeks turned into months. Cindy and I were married, and we left this boy and girl on their own to figure out what to do next.

After being in the ministry for some time, we heard that this friend of Cindy's had surrendered to the Lord for ministry work. I'm still trying to remember how we found out about it; but sure enough, it was true! Years went by. We changed ministries a few times in the mean while, but then, out of the clear blue, I received a message from this, now man. He was doing a sermon series about telling others about Jesus Christ, how they came to know Him, and he wanted to have us come and be in the final service, with him introducing me as the one who led him to the Lord. At that service, he had me come and sit on the platform while he read a letter to me explaining what happened that night. For the first time in our lives, Cindy and I learned what happened after we had left their home. This pastor, as a teen, went to his room that night and laid on his bed looking up at the ceiling. This is what he told the Lord, "God, I don't know what just happened tonight. If you're real and if this salvation that Kevin and Cindy told me about is real, then I'm in. I'm tired of living the life that I've been living. I'll be a voice for you just like they were to me tonight." He went on and told everyone his testimony. Because of his lifestyle that left his soul empty, he was ready to kill himself. He had it all planned out and he was going to do it that weekend when his family was gone. Then, a knock was heard at the front door. We were the last people he thought he would see that night! It wasn't the night that we had been coming for the past month. He couldn't believe it that we were at the front door. He couldn't hide anymore.

This young man was one of the top athletes in our high school. He went to his coach and told him that he wasn't going to play ball that season because he had something more important to do with his time. He went to the principal and asked if he could start a Bible study at lunchtime in the library. He was told he could. The Bible study grew from 5 to 18 to 30 and soon well over 100! He told his congregation that dozens of kids came to Christ in the next two years in that Bible study. Now remember, all of this information was all new to Cindy and me. We had no idea or clue that any of this had taken place! God used a couple of teenagers to share the Good News of the Gospel with a few of their friends and God did the rest! This pastor is now pastoring a large church in Northern Michigan, with a few thousand in attendance. Think about it, if only...we hadn't gone...he hadn't accepted Christ...hundreds of other people would still be living with ravaged souls instead of flourishing ones.

These three stories illustrate perfectly the results of having a flourishing soul or not. The young girl's soul in the Netherlands was left unattended and exposed to her own fears and anxieties, leaving her vulnerable and hurting. She never knew the Savior that could provide her with the abundant life that would satisfy her longings as a flourishing soul. The pastor who turned his back on all that was dear to him once "knew" the Lord and all that He could provide him has ended up a ravaged soul when he could've been living as a flourishing one. Our friends that trusted Christ have known what it means to live an abundant life just as Christ had promised in John 10:10. Remarkable. Three different individuals with three distinct results.

In our world today, there are way too many people who do not deal honestly with the condition of their souls. Worldly ideas and philosophies have replaced Biblical soundness in so many hearts and lives. As for many Christians, Christian catch phrases are repeated over and over again with a smugness of self-realization and self-awareness, but they realize little or no evidence of life-change or soul flourishing. For me there are three factors that keep me from giving up on the journey to life-change and possessing a flourishing soul: **The Word of God or Holy Scripture, The Holy Spirit , and some awesome people I know that have impacted my life for Christ**. God's Spirit has taken His Word to mold and make me after His image. So many mentors and teachers (any person in my life that has left an impression on me I consider a teacher and mentor) have poured their lives into my life, making a huge difference in who I am today. Biblical speaking, Moses had an intimate relationship with God, so much so that Scripture tells us that "God spoke with him face-to-face, as a man speaks to his friend." (Exodus 33:11) Paul spoke of this kind of life when he said, "I can really know Christ and experience the mighty power that raised him from the dead." (Philippians 3:10) Peter went through much soul searching and soul floundering before experiencing such fullness of life and soul flourishing! He came to this conclusion in I Peter 4:19, "So if you are suffering according to God's will, keep on doing what is right, and trust yourself to the God who made you, for he will never fail you." These men went through deep times of trials but came through their Red Sea experiences as men of spiritual depth, living the abundant life of a flourishing soul.

I close with this quote from Dr. Larry Crabb's book, "Inside Out."

> "If something is from God, it will inevitably promote the character of Christ in those who embrace it. Confusion should lead not to bitterness and discouragement, but to faith. God is still at work, requiring nothing from us we cannot do, moving through the wreckage of our life to achieve His good purposes. Our faith is often weak, but the kind of faith that develops to support us through times of overwhelming confusion is strong and resilient."[5]

> "The righteous flourish like the palm tree and grow like a cedar in Lebanon. They are planted in the house of the Lord; they flourish in the courts of our God. They still bear fruit in old age; they are ever full of sap and green, to declare that the Lord is upright; he is my rock, and there is no unrighteousness in him." Psalm 92:12-15

The distance between the life you're living at this moment, and a life enjoyed by experiencing a flourishing soul is closer than you think. So, go right ahead, leave the city of palms and venture out into the wilderness, looking to retreat from your own strengths and relying on His! The choice is now up to you. Your Red Sea lies straight ahead. Go for it!

NOTES

Chapter 1: A Righteous Seed

1. Eugene Peterson, *The Message: The New Testament, Psalms & Proverbs;* Navpress Publishing Group, 1993, 1994, 1995; pg. 193

2. Ibid; pg. 193

3. King James Version of the Bible; Oxford University Press, Inc; 1945; pg. 1204

4. *New Living Translation;* Tyndale House Publishers, Inc; 1996; pg. 864

5. *New International Version;* Zondervan; 2011; pg. 1032

6. Eugene Peterson, *The Message: The New Testament, Psalms & Proverbs;* Navpress Publishing Group, 1993, 1994, 1995; pg. 318

7. Charles Dickens; *A Christmas Carol;* Chapman and Hill; 1843

8. Ibid.

Chapter 2: A Remarkable Stature

1. William Wilson; *Wilson's Old Testament Word Studies;* Macdonald Publishing, Co; pg. 170

2. *The Amplified Bible;* Mass Market Edition; Zondervan; 1987; pg. 1142

3. Harry Ironside; *Ironside's Notes on Selected Books;* II Peter 3; Notes are public domain.

4. C. S. Lewis; "Letters to Malcolm; Chiefly on Prayer; Mariner Books; 2002

5. Chuck Swindoll; Goodreads.com; 24 Great Quotes from Chuck Swindoll

6. C. H. Spurgeon; "Metropolitan Tabernacle Pulpit Pilgrim Publications"; 2011; Biblesoft, Inc; pg. 46, 539, 540

7. D. Martin Lloyd-Jones; *Expository Sermons on II Peter;* Banner of Truth; pg. 251

Chapter 3: Rooted in God's Sanctuary

1. George F. Handel; Quotes.net; stands4 LLC; 2019

2. D. L. Moody Quotes; "Inspiring Quotations by Dwight L. Moody"; "10 Keys to Dwight L. Moody's Effectiveness"; Lyle Dorsett; *A Passion for Souls: The Life of D. L. Moody;* 1997; printed in the United States of America

3. John Calvin; Christianquote.com

Chapter 4: Reveling in Our Salvation

1. *New Living Translation;* Tyndale House Publishers, Inc; 1996; pg. 904

2. A. T. Robertson; *Word Pictures of the New Testament; Vol. 1;* Baker Books; 1982

3. D. A. Carson; "For The Love of God: A Daily Companion for Discovering the Riches of God's Word; Vol. 1"; February 24; Crossway Books; 1998; pg. 55

Chapter 5: His Ravishing Spouse

1. J. Sidlow Baxter; *Explore The Book;* The Song of Solomon; Lesson Number 66; Zondervan Publishing House; 1960; pg. 175

2. Ibid.

3. *The Amplified Bible;* Mass Market Edition; Zondervan Publishing House; 1987; pg. 1139

Chapter 6: Reward Accomplished in Secret

1. *Merriam-Webster Dictionary;* The World Publishing Company; 1970; pg. 462

2. Matthew Henry; *Matthew Henry Commentary on the Whole Bible;* Zonderan Publishing House; 1980; pg. 1227

3. A. W. Tozer; *The Pursuit of God;* Wingspread Publishers; 1982; pg. 44

Chapter 7: Resplendent Son-ship

1. H. D. Spence; Joseph S. Excell; *Pulpit Commentary; Vol. 2;* Lesson on I Kings; Delmarva Publications; 2015

2. Ibid.

3. Ibid.

4. Ibid.

5. *The Amplified Bible;* Mass Market Edition; Zondervan Publishing House; 1987; pg. 1112

6. *New Living Translation;* Tyndale House Publishers, Inc. 1996; pg. 920

7. *The Contemporary English Version;* American Bible Society; 2000; pg. 1036

8. *International Standard Version;* ISV Foundation; 2011; Pg. 1014

9. Francis of Assisi; *The Writings of St. Francis of Assisi;* Paschal Robinson; "Order of Friars Minor; Rule of 1221"; 1905

10. Ibid.

11. Chrysostom; *Expositor's Bible Commentary;* Lessons in Titus; Zondervan Publishing House; 1992

12. Ibid.

13. Sir Winston Churchill: "National Churchill Museum"; Westminster College; Fulton, MO

14. Oswald Chambers; "Men of Integrity"; Friday, May 30, devotional; May/June; 2003

Chapter 8: Resilient & Supple

1. Franklin Graham; Sermonquotes.com

2. Edmund Clowney; Christianquotes.com

3. Warren Weirsbe; *The Weirsbe Bible Commentary: Old Testament;* David C. Cook Publishers; Book of Ruth; pg. 478

4. John of Kronstadt; *A Treasury of Russian Spirituality;* G. P. Fedotov; Sheed and Ward, Ltd; 1999; pg. 391

5. Jeremy Taylor; "The Rule and Exercises of Holy Living"; Christianquotes.com

6. Woodrow Kroll; Christianquotes.com

7. Andrew Murray; *Collected Works on Prayer: 7 Books in 1"* Whitaker House.Com

8. Alan Redpath; *Men of Action;* Spring, 1996; As used by Churck Swindoll in "What It Means to be Broken"

9. C. H. Spurgeon; Christianquotes.com

10. Haruki Murakami; "What I talk about When I Talk about Running"; Goodreads.com

11. Epicurus; "Essential Life Skills"; Z. Hereford

12. *New Living Translation;* Tyndale House Publishers, Inc; 1996; pg. 932

13. R. C. Trench; Creative Media, Partners, LLC; 2015; James 1 - "Patience"; these notes are public domain

14. *The Amplified Bible;* Mass Market Edition; Zondervan Publishing House; 1987; pg. 1129

15. Eugene Peterson; *The Message: The New Testament, Psalms & Proverbs;* Navpress; 1993, 1994, 1995; pg. 482

16. Ryan Stephenson; "In The Eye of the Storm"; First Company Management; Franklin, TN

17. C. H. Spurgeon; "C. H. Spurgeon Quote of the Day"; June 7, 2019

Chapter 9: Refreshed Sojourners

1. Edward Mote; "My Hope Is Built on Nothing Less"; public domain; 1834

2. Matthew Henry; *Matthew Henry Commentary on the Whole Bible;* Zondervan Publishing House; 1961; pgs. 85, 86

3. Walter Torre, MA; ED; Bibleorigins.net; April 14, 2010

Chapter 10: Rejoicing in Our Savior

1. Chrysostom; Christianquotes.com

2. Matthew Henry; *Matthew Henry Commentary on the Whole Bible;* Zondervan Publishing House; 1980; Pg. 1867

3. Ibid. pg. 1166

4. *New Living Translation;* Tyndale House Publishing; 1996; pg. 904

5. Eugene Peterson; *The Message; The New Testament, Psalms and Proverbs;* Navpress; 1993, 1994, 1995; pg. 420

6. *The Amplified Bible;* Mass Market Edition; Zondervan Publishing House; 1987; pg. 1090

Chapter 11: Retreating from Our Outside Strengths

1. Billy Graham; "No Excuse For Rejecting God's Truth"; Aug. 21, 1963; Los Angeles, CA

2. Charles Stanley; "Life Principle 2: A Life of Obedience"; In Touch Ministries; Atlanta, GA

3. *New Living Translation;* Tyndale House Publishers, Inc; 1996; pg. 462

4. Louis Gigleo; "When Life Is Tough"; Rightnowmedia.com

5. Matthew Henry; *Matthew Henry Commentary on the Whole Bible;* Zondervan Publishing House; 1980; pgs. 215, 216

6. J. Sidlow Baxter; *Explore The Book;* Zondervan Publishing House; 1960; Book of Joshua; Lesson 3; pgs. 257, 258

7. Alan Redpath; Crossquotes; Wordpress.com

8. Matthew Henry; *Matthew Henry Commentary on the Whole Bible;* Zondervan Publishing House; 1980; pg. 252

9. *Berean Literal Bible;* Bible Hub; 2016

10. *Contemporary English Version;* American Bible Society; 2000; pg. 918

11. Charles Ellicot; *Ellicott's Commentary on the Whole Bible; Vol. 8";* Wipf and Stock Publishers; 2015

12. Eugene Peterson; *The Message; The New Testament, Psalms & Proverbs;* Navpress. 1993, 1994, 1995; pg. 224

13. Matthew Henry; *Matthew Henry Commentary on the Whole Bible;* Zondervan Publishing House; 1980; pg. 1594

14. Oswald Chambers; "Men of Integrity"'; Friday, May 30; Devotional; May/June; 2003

15. Eugene Peterson; *The Message; The New Testament, Psalms & Proverbs;* Navpress; 1993, 1994, 1995; pg. 388

16. Matthew Henry; *Matthew Henry Commentary on the Whole Bible;* Zondervan Publishing House; 1980; pg. 1837

Chapter 12: Realization & Summation

1. *New Living Translation;* Tyndale House Publishing; 1996; pg. 814

2. Eugene Peterson; *The Message; The New Testament, Psalms & Proverbs;* Navpress; 1993, 1994, 1995; pg. 213

3. *The Amplified Bible;* Mass Market Edition; Zondervan Publishing House; 1987; pg. 967

4. Oswald Chambers; "The Vanishing Gospel"; quoted in "Berean Call"; Feb. 2004; pgs 3, 4

5. Dr. Larry Crabb; *Inside Out;* Navpress; A Ministry of The Navigators; 1989; pg. 221

ABOUT THE AUTHOR

Kevin lives in Middletown, DE with his wife, Cindy. They have served the Lord in various capacities in Michigan, Massachusetts, North Carolina and Delaware for over 39 years. They have three grown children and five grandchildren. Kevin's life's passage from God's Word is Psalm 63: "O God, you are my God, earnestly I seek you; my soul thirsts for you, my body longs for you, in a dry and weary land where there is no water. I have seen you in the sanctuary and beheld your power and your glory. Because your love is better than life, my lips will glorify you. I will praise you as long as I live, and in your name I will life up my hands..."

CPSIA information can be obtained
at www.ICGtesting.com
Printed in the USA
LVHW080203051121
702469LV00004B/11